Kinder-
garten

Elzbieta Ettinger was born and educated in Poland and went to live in
America in the late 1960's. She is professor of Literature and Rhetoric
at the Masachussetts Institute of Technology in Boston. She is the
author of ROSA LUXEMBURG: A LIFE published by Pandora in
Paperback in 1988. She is currently working on her second novel
QUICKSAND, a sequel to KINDERGARTEN which is set in
Poland during the 1950's.

D1376235

Kinder-garten

Elżbieta Ettinger

PANDORA

LONDON SYDNEY WELLINGTON

First published in Great Britain by Constable & Co Ltd in 1970.
First published in Great Britain by Pandora Press, an imprint of Unwin
Hyman Ltd., in 1988.

All rights reserved. No part of this publication may be reproduced, stored in
a retrieval system, or transmitted in any form or by any means, electronic,
mechanical, photocopying, recording or otherwise, without the prior permission of Unwin Hyman Limited.

This book is sold subject to the condition that it shall not, by way of trade or
otherwise, be lent, resold, hired out or otherwise circulated, without the
publishers' prior consent in any form of binding or cover other than that in
which it is published, and without a similar condition including this
condition being imposed on the purchaser.

Pandora Press
Unwin Hyman Limited
15–17 Broadwick Street, London W1V 1FP

Allen and Unwin Australia Pty Ltd
8 Napier Stret, North Sydney, NSW 2060, Australia

Allen and Unwin New Zealand Pty Ltd with the Port Nicholson Press
60 Cambridge Terrace, Wellington, New Zealand

Copyright © Elżbieta Ettinger 1970

Ettinger, Elżbieta
    Kindergarten.
I. Title
813'.54[F]
ISBN 0-86358-311-3

Printed in Finland by Werner Söderstrom Oy

To

Regina Stahl

The author, while writing this book, was a Scholar
at the Radcliffe Institute in Cambridge, Massachusetts.
She gratefully acknowledges the support
of the Institute.

*The characters
portrayed in this book
are fictitious and any resemblance
to real persons, living or dead,
is entirely coincidental.*

Kinder-
garten

Elli, 1962

Choking, stiff, bathed in sweat, Elli jumped out of bed and, stumbling, groped her way toward the opposite end of the room. Sleepwalking, she waved both her hands to brush away the imaginary gas from over the crib. She could smell its sweetish taste. Her cold, twitching fingers touched the baby's warm lips. She felt them move. The baby's rhythmic breathing finally reached her. She crawled back to bed.

Lili, Emmi, David, the Old Man . . . Lili handing her the envelope, her shining auburn hair streaming in the summer air . . . Maria's stony eyes . . . the departing train . . . Emmi spasmodically clinging to her hand . . . Aunt Paula mounting the truck . . . Danny's black eyes burning with rage . . . the young girl with long plaits cutting off the cord . . . the Old Man tapping the silver cigarette case . . . Emmi dressing a doll . . . Lili frantically writing . . . Adam . . . you'll stay with me or I'll make you stay . . . the young girl rehearsing prayers . . . the gray-haired woman coming out of the attic . . . five shots . . . silence . . . a telephone ringing . . . Heil Hitler . . . Michael . . . look everybody straight in the eye . . . don't turn back . . . never turn back . . . never . . . never . . . a small voice, *Yidn hot rakhmones* . . . the half-wit madly dancing under the wall, oi, oi, moira, moira . . . David . . . he has stuffed the star into my mouth . . . you are what is written in these documents, that is the only truth, no other truth ever existed . . . my name is Isaak, let's divide it, you'll be hungry too . . . Abel . . . I need your help . . . farewell Abel . . . farewell friends . . . I'll save you, sleep, my love, sleep . . . you will never forget . . . I will not, Grandfather, I promise . . .

I am tired, they never let me alone, the same pantomime over and over, they gone and I still here . . . I try to forget, I try so hard, not to see their eyes anymore, not to hear their voices, not to smell their sweat, not to feel their anguish. I want to forget, forget, forget, their naked fear, our naked fear, but they keep coming back, they stare at me, they wait, they do not want to be forgotten, they know I promised, they will never let me forget, never.

1

IN OCTOBER David came from work, his face a bloody pulp. Danny and Elli put him to bed. The grandfather was already asleep. During the night David became delirious. He tossed in the bed, tore the compress from his face, and packed it in his mouth, moaning, "No, I won't, I won't, kill me, kill me . . ." After midnight the moaning grew softer and softer; he cried himself to sleep.

He slept for an hour perhaps — or a little longer — then opened his eyes and asked for a drink of water. He drank the water Elli brought him, clutched at the blanket, struggling to rise. His head dropped back heavily on the pillow. His eyes closed, he stammered with effort through swollen, bruised lips, "He said I must be hungry . . . he said . . . men with a hungry look are dangerous . . . I should put on weight . . . he said . . . hast du Hunger . . . he asked . . . I said yes . . . he asked me my name . . . David, I said . . . he tore off my armband . . . eat your star, David . . . he stuffed it into my mouth . . . I didn't . . . he helped me . . ."

He lay silent. Tears ran slowly from the corners of his eyes. Then he fell asleep again. In the small hours of the day he awoke. He took Elli's hand in his and said, "Wouldn't you read something to me, Elli? Something very pleasant, perhaps a poem, a long poem . . . if I fall asleep, don't stop reading, please . . ."

Her little room was very cold; the window, steamed gray. With trembling hands she rummaged among her books, unable to think of any poem, of anything at all. Finally she found a poem of Słowacki's, torn from a book. Meanwhile, the dark turned to dusk. She peeped into her grandfather's room and saw he was in bed, reading some papers. She greeted him wordlessly with a wave of her hand and opened the door to David's room.

The razor with which the young man had cut his throat lay on the floor, the edge pointed toward his torn, muddy shoe. He died late that night.

The clock struck seven, when the gate banged with a dull noise, and the yelling started. Danny quickly removed the boards of the "tomb." Aunt Paula and Aunt Adela were already waiting to crawl in. Elli ran for her grandfather and found him completely dressed, sitting in his armchair. She told him that the roundup had begun and she and Danny must go downstairs. "They'll certainly let us go," she said. "Our working passes are still good." Danny was employed as a roadworker in a forced-labor battalion in which Big Daniel and David had also worked; Elli mended German uniforms in one of the shops.

"I will stay here," the Old Man said. "You go."

"But you can't stay here," groaned Elli. "You know they will search the house."

"I said that I will stay here."

Somebody battered at the door. Danny let little Abram in. Breathlessly he whimpered that everybody must report in the yard; they were shouting that they will shoot on the spot every Schweinehund found indoors.

The daily quota for the deliveries to the trains waiting in the Umschlagplatz, a dispatch point inside the ghetto, had recently been increased. People who had exchanged fortunes for working passes were by now gone too. The German workshops had lost their status as sanctuaries. Aunt Wilhelmina had been taken from one of them not long ago. The Jewish policemen, their own families already deported and they themselves now fearing the inevitable, grew more brutal and were frantic to meet the quotas. They still believed obedience could earn them a reprieve.

The tomb was not really good anymore. Now, a decision had to be made for the two women getting ready to crawl into it. "Danny," said Elli and stopped. Paula was his mother. Elli would not have known what to say if it had been her own.

Danny told the women to wait. He went to the Old Man. "I said that I will stay here," Elli heard. His voice was hard and obstinate. She ran in after Danny. Her eyes were glazed with hysteria when she grabbed the Old Man's hand. "Grandfather," she shouted, "downstairs we can try to get you out! Here they'll shoot you!"

Beyond her hysteria lay mortal terror, and she knew he easily recognized it. She stood looking at him empty-eyed, something inside her dying.

"You all go," the Old Man said softly. "The aunts too. Remember your promise, Elli." He kissed her forehead; she kissed his hand, twice, as she had since the world was made.

Downstairs the two aunts were immediately pushed toward a truck loaded with older people and children. Aunt Paula did not hear the command to mount the truck and stood for a moment helplessly looking around, shrunk smaller than ever. One of the neighbors, lined up against the wall, shouted to the German taking aim at her that she was only deaf not disobedient. When she disappeared into the truck which pulled away instantly her face had still the look of an unjustly punished child.

Danny was sobbing as the officer checked first his pass, then Elli's. Without so much as looking into the papers, he ordered them to the left. It meant the Umschlagplatz. Only three people were standing at the right: the brother of a Jewish policeman, a girl, and a young man Elli did not know. Umschlagplatz was not necessarily the end. Danny and she would manage to escape. The truck moved on without the house being searched. The Old Man was saved.

The people crammed in the truck were talking in small voices telling each other their schemes for getting out. One had a friend in the service battalion; another an uncle shipping out corpses who knew just which German could be bribed. One woman took off her shoe, smashed the heel, and fished out a big diamond; another kept repeating they would release her the moment they learned she had a grandson in the German army.

The grip of terror, choking them when the truck's tail gate had been slammed, eased. They were like a herd of animals in a trap, pressed against each other for support; each begged the other to deny the undeniable and looked into the other's face, timidly, furtively, to see if his own alarm was mirrored there.

The truck braked violently, then halted. This was the Umschlagplatz. Obedience, the only hope of rescue, shut their mouths, set their legs in motion. One by one they jumped out of the truck. One by one they lined up as ordered. The line was long and deadly straight. They were counted and then directed toward a train standing on the far track. It was still early. The place was deserted except for the officers directing the operation. Usually crowded with people waiting to be loaded, the vast yard had of late become a sort of stock exchange; some transactions even led to liberty. When the trains were not filled to capacity, people were kept waiting for a day or two; everyone based his hopes on this waiting period. This was the time business was done; miracles could happen within minutes to say nothing of whole days. But today the stage was quiet and empty. The group which had arrived just ahead of them had completed the cargo of the sealed train now standing on the rails.

The Jewish policeman who opened their truck was Danny's friend. He could not help them, he whispered, anticipating a request; yesterday they had found his mother hidden in a barracks here, had taken her away, and beaten him senseless. He was shaking with fear. Danny whispered to Elli that they still had a chance to jump out of the train. She nodded. The line was quickly dwindling, the people disappearing into the darkness of the train. The officer kept counting, marking each group of ten on his pad. Ahead of them now was only a woman, holding the hand of a twelve-year-old girl. Fifty-nine and sixty.

Danny was the next. He put his right foot on the doorstep. His torn shoe hitched into it; he fell down. The officer pushed him forward with his gun. Elli saw Danny's furious eyes, saw him slowly rise from the ground, and fiercely slap the officer's face. Then he lay before her feet, a small hole in his right temple.

The officer ordered the corpse removed. She saw two Jewish policemen running toward the train and at the same moment felt a firm grip on her left arm. A plainclothesman signaled to the officer and, still holding her firmly, walked her all the way through the Umschlagplatz. She heard the officer counting sixty-one, sixty-two, sixty-three, and then she heard nothing.

At the gate, the man squeezed a piece of paper into her hand, winked toward the guards, and they let her pass.

She walked slowly through the deserted ghetto streets. Trucks, loaded with people and driving toward the dispatch point, passed her several times. Perhaps five or six. A patrol stopped her; she showed the crumpled piece of paper; they let her go.

She knew that she should feel something about Danny, about the other people, but, in fact, she felt nothing. At some point it started to rain. She kept walking. She roamed the streets, once crowded and noisy, now completely silent. This silence was worse than the noise once so appalling. It was almost dark when she stopped in front of their house. She opened the gate, crossed the yard, and, dead with fatigue, started to climb the stairs. She was shivering with cold. Suddenly she realized how late it was, how desperate the Old Man must be about them. Collecting her thoughts, trying to make up something about Danny for the Old Man, she rushed up the remaining two flights.

The entrance door was ajar, as Danny, who went out last, must have left it. The door to the Old Man's room was wide open. She saw him hanging, his feet, in slippers, perhaps twenty inches above the table. The cord was fastened to an iron hook from which a former tenant had removed the heavy old-fashioned lamp. The Old Man's footstool lay between the table and his bed.

She could not reach the cord without a ladder. She brought one from the basement and put it on the table. Then she got a big knife from the kitchen. She climbed the ladder and very slowly, embracing the man's waist with one hand, started to cut the cord. The body became heavier against her; she held it up, staggering under its weight. The cord was half-severed when the knife slipped from her hand. She climbed down to pick it up. When she was halfway back on the ladder, wet and shaking, the cord split and the body fell heavily on the bed.

The Old Man breathed. His open eyes were veiled, his mouth covered with grayish foam. She took a clean handkerchief from his drawer and delicately wiped away the foam and the tears leaking slowly from the corners of his eyes. At some unknown time he stopped breathing. In the dim light of the breaking day she saw a white sheet of paper fastened to the pillow with his silver cigarette case. She read his clear handwriting: "I took my life myself. Do not blame anybody. God bless you all. Herman Weil."

She destroyed the note, took the cigarette case, and left.

It was full winter when her mother's desperate message finally reached Elli in the basement where she was living with Benjamin and Abel. Abel had found her in the street, half-starved. The two young men had nursed her back to life. For several days she had lain on a blanket spread against the wall and let herself be fed by them. When she was strong enough to get up, she took care of the men's modest household, rarely saying a word, paying no attention to the people who were constantly coming and quietly talking with the two men. Some disappeared after a few hours. Others installed themselves for good.

Abel asked her once or twice about leaving for the Aryan side. She told him that she did not want to go. She had decided to stay in the ghetto. Then one day Abel came and told her that she must go at once; it was her mother's firm order. Everything was ready for her departure. He had found a Polish girl working in a ghetto factory who had agreed to lend Elli her entry permit, and he had brought the document with him. Her Uncle Michael, he said, would wait for her tomorrow, not far from the factory workers' exit. Michael would take her to Doctor Darski, and then she would quit Warsaw for good.

Elli stared wide-eyed at Abel, so senseless did all he said seem to her. She did not want to go, she said, she was quite happy here. And she was so tired. "Tomorrow at noon you will leave," commanded Abel. "No. I will stay." She looked straight into his eyes.

Then, at night, she again heard, "I will go, Grandfather" . . .
"And you will not forget" . . . "Never . . . I promise."

Next morning she got up and dressed, and took the permit
from Abel. He told her where to deliver it. "I can't walk you to
the gate. I must stay here. But I will see you again."

She waited near the control point for the group of Polish workers and joined them. The guard glanced at the permit automatically, then at her, and with the others she passed outside.

2

SHE HAD BEEN WALKING for ten or fifteen minutes when she saw Uncle Michael, his back turned as if he were looking in the opposite direction. Somehow he must have seen her, for without a word or a gesture he started off. She followed him at a distance of perhaps forty feet. After a twenty-minute walk they left behind the deserted streets surrounding the ghetto and passed through a more crowded area. She could follow him easily, for his massive body was visible at a considerable distance. At the corner of Marszałkowska and Złota streets, where the crowd became quite dense, he increased his pace. So did she. At one point she lost him and nervously tried to make her way through the crowd, mindful not to run, not to draw attention to herself. She saw him again, far away. She had breathed a small sigh of relief when she heard, "Amcha?"

"What?"

"Amcha?"

"I don't understand."

"You do. Don't pretend."

Out of the corner of her eye she saw a shabbily dressed man, small, hunched, unshaven. She was never very good at telling a Jew from a non-Jew, but this man left her with no doubt. "I *do not* pretend." She kept walking, very slowly now.

He trotted close behind her, whispering fiercely in her ear, "You are Jewish."

"I am not."

"You have run from the ghetto. You have a Jewish accent."

"You are crazy. Leave me alone."

"You go with me. The SS post is not far from here."

"I will not go with you. I do not know you."

"Come with me. Or I'll call a policeman."

"Go ahead. You can call ten policemen."

"How much money have you?"

"I have no money."

"A thousand will do."

"I have not one zloty on me."

"You gave the money to the guards, eh? To run away, eh? But you still have some left. Come on, give it to me."

"I guess you Jews have more money than we do. Blackmail is a profitable job nowadays, isn't it? Now, you better go away."

"Give me your watch."

"I'll give you nothing."

"You are Jewish and you sure have the Jewish chutzpah. I can smell a Jew right away. There in that gateway my pals are waiting, Polish policemen. I must bring them something." There was a pleading tone in his voice.

"Not from me."

"You were following a man. He disappeared. He left you."

"I followed no one."

"I saw him."

"OK. Go and find him."

"Show me your documents."

"Let us go to these policemen." She stopped and looked straight into his eyes. "I'll show them my documents."

"They are fake."

"It's none of your business. I'm not going to show them to you."

"They'll arrest you."

"It's none of your business." She turned toward the gateway he had indicated.

"Don't go." He grasped her hand.

"Don't you dare to touch me, you stinky kike. Take your dirty hands off me."

He quickly removed his hand. She entered the gateway. There was no one there. No longer looking at him, she turned away and started back toward Marszałkowska Street. Opening the door of a small café, she cautiously glanced backward, but he was not in sight. She sipped a cup of coffee slowly, smoked a cigarette, stared through the window, and left after half an hour. Before she went on, she once more made sure he was not following her, but he had disappeared. The "stinky kike" must have convinced him that he had made a mistake. Nothing else would have, she thought, as she shrugged her shoulders. Within twenty minutes she reached Złota Street where Doctor Darski lived. She walked up and down in front of the house, but no suspicious-looking person came by. She rang the bell to the ground-floor apartment. The maid answered the door and ushered her into the living room. The doctor was busy in his office, she said, and Mrs. Darska was in church.

During one of his last visits in the ghetto, the doctor told them that since he had gotten her out of jail on the grounds of her illegitimate birth, his wife had spent most of her time in church. She had talked herself into becoming a fanatic Christian. The only thing she requested when still in prison was not food, not clothes, but a rosary. He had told them she kept murmuring prayers from the moment she opened her eyes in the morning, pausing only to kiss the huge cross hanging around her neck; still she took the precaution of covering her face with thick crepe even in church. The doctor, himself an atheist, had laughed together with the Old Man over the obsessively Catholic atmosphere in which he had to live with his perfectly Jewish wife.

After half an hour or so Doctor Darski opened the door and, smiling, shook Elli's hand. "It's good you made it. Michael is already here. He told me a smaltzovnik was following both of you, and you stopped to take care of him. You did the right thing; all they have to do to check up on a man is to open his trousers. We were a little worried; you have no experience in dealing with blackmail. But you are a smart girl, you got rid of him, didn't you?"

Uneasily, she nodded.

"Now, I'll bring Michael here. He wants to talk to you."

Michael seemed nervous and embarrassed. He was the first to break the silence. "I had to leave you, Elli," he said. "I could not have helped you anyway, and if he got me, I would have been lost. I told the doctor about it in a somewhat different way. I thought it would sound better."

Certainly it would, thought Elli angrily. It would sound better than telling him you got so scared that you just left me in the middle of the street, with no documents, no money, nothing. You might have considered, though, that I have no idea how to cope with blackmailers, no idea that they could be Jews, right here in the middle of the city, that it's not yet two hours since I left the ghetto, while you live on the Aryan side all the time. But she nodded, and said, "It's all right, Uncle."

Later, Irena Darska came back from church, thanked Christ and all the saints for saving Elli, and they had dinner. With Irena murmuring her prayers, the doctor had a chance to talk, and he did his best to lighten the rather heavy atmosphere. Elli assisted Irena by putting Krysia to bed; the little girl, half-asleep, kneeling before a huge crucifix with a red lamp burning at its base recited long litanies, constantly corrected by her mother. She crossed herself with her small hands, her head dropping drowsily. Elli smiled at the thick curly hair of the small kneeling figure, the spitting image of her black-haired, black-eyed mother.

"You'd better stop smiling and start praying," Irena whispered in her ear. "You cannot outsmile them, believe me, but Jesus Christ and the Blessed Virgin might help you, as they helped me. I will pray every day, my child, that you obtain the grace of the only true faith, that you unite your heart with Him, who suffered and was crucified for all of us."

Later in bed when she thought about Irena, Elli still could not decide whether this woman pretended, was confused, afflicted, or insane.

Next day Uncle Michael started to work on her education. He said they would leave at night for Lublin; the remaining day he assured her she needed badly. He hung a small silver cross on her neck and handed her a prayer book. She must learn by heart, he said, "Our Father," "The Hail Mary," "The Apostles' Creed," the "Rosary of the Blessed Virgin Mary," and the seven cardinal sins — for a start; later, she would have to learn more. He would examine her before the departure in the essentials of the catechism. Then, his gray-blue eyes fixed on hers, he began, "You must always keep your head high, not drooped as yesterday. Under no circumstances ever turn back; someone might recognize you and call you by your former name. You are not you; you are somebody else, though we do not know who, since your documents are not yet ready. Someone might just in passing whisper to you a friendly 'Amcha,' which in Hebrew means one of our people. Do not respond. He might be simply probing if the fish will swallow the hook. We do not have any friends here, Elli; we are surrounded by enemies."

He rose from his place and started to pace the room. He

stopped in front of her and said, stressing every word, "That is to become your gospel, the true one, from now on. Everybody is your enemy; everybody wants to report on you. Watch out for Jews. They are most dangerous because they are lost and because they can smell another Jew."

He paused, and after a while went on, "Last week your mother took the Apfelbaums' boy, a five-year-old, to take him to a convent. At night in the station, the boy got thirsty. She went to get him something to drink. While she was gone a man approached the boy who spoke only Yiddish. The man did too. Before your mother got back, they shot the child behind the station building. Some women, unaware she was with the boy, told your mother what had happened. Obviously the poor child whom she had forbidden to open his mouth saw no harm in answering the man's friendly, 'Und vu iz deyn Mamasi?' "

Michael stopped and looked at Elli. "Do not trust anybody, ever. Keep repeating to yourself, 'This is my enemy,' no matter how friendly he seems. Confidence is a luxury we cannot afford; this you must remember every hour of the day and of the night. However, your eyes must be full of trust, and with those beautiful eyes of yours," he smiled stiffly, "you must look everyone straight in the eye — foe or friend, it does not matter — straight in everybody's eye. You must get rid of this air of a frightened animal. Your 'good looks' are good for nothing with that terrified expression. Do not ever admit to yourself that you might be followed. If you are, there is nothing you can do; if you are not, your fidgeting might attract somebody's attention. Many people get caught because their fear is conspicuous; they look sideways, turn back, blanch. They betray themselves. Or they trust; and others betray them." He stopped to light her cigarette.

She said, "Thank you, Uncle."

He put the match in the ashtray. "Your accent is wrong," he remarked. "The sing-song in your voice grew worse over there.

Here it stands for nothing but being Jewish. You must get rid of it. Talk slowly and think before you say a word. Furthermore, twice last night you said 'mayse.' You never used to mix in Jewish words. Also a habit acquired there. You better get rid of it."

She nervously fingered her hair, while he went on. "You must do something about your hair. The color is all right, but with these braids you look haggard and thin, typical of people long deprived of fresh air. Get yourself some rouge from Irena; she will find a hairdresser for you. Your hair must be cut and set. You also must be more at ease. You look tense and nervous. Every loud sound makes you jump. You must behave like a happy, self-assured young girl."

At this, Elli was sure she had made a bad mistake leaving Abel and Benjamin. She wanted to shut her ears, to run from this house, to go back to the ghetto where no one expected her to look happy and self-assured. "You see, Elli," Michael continued, "they are smarter now and no longer look only for black hair and hooked noses; they've learned that many of us are blond and blue-eyed. Instead they look for emaciated faces, melancholy fearful eyes, uncertain gestures. It's going to be more and more difficult now that so many people are hiding on the Aryan side."

He saw her squirming uneasily in her seat. "I know how you feel, Elli, but you must listen to me. You must know the truth. We have no money to rent a hiding place or pay enormous bribes; you cannot always get away with a small one. The Germans grow increasingly greedy and tough. Some Poles live off the Jews. We must have money for hiding those of our family who cannot pass as Poles. It cannot be wasted on those who can, like you or Lili. We can cope with the normal expenses of living as a Pole. Also, we have friends who offer temporary shelter as long as they believe we are Poles. They are decent people. They won't take a Jew into their house not because they don't like them, but because they are afraid. They have every reason to be. They are liable to a death penalty for hiding or helping Jews. Old Mrs. Darska's place in Lublin is no longer safe and none of you can come to Rejowiec. Daniel will tell you more about Miriam's incomprehensible behavior over there; anyway she told them we are Jews. The landlady, Mrs. Czemera, is what you might call a genuine Christian, a human being. That's why your mother and I can still stop there in spite of her husband — a dangerous drunkard. But none of you can go there. There still is Mr. Olszewski in Dubienka who knows the truth, our last resort in an emergency. But you will have to live with people who believe you are Aryan, people who are not after money. And that was what I was going to say."

He poured himself a glass of water, gulped it down, and went on, "We do not have money. We cannot bribe or ransom or trade; and this is one more reason to be on guard." He interrupted himself and asked, "Do you understand me, Elli?"

She nodded.

He made her sit on a sofa and sat close to her. He looked at her for a long moment. Then he said, "Do not believe a man who tells you you are pretty or nice or attractive. Do not get involved with any man, even if you like him. This is not a time for romance. The Poles drink a lot, more than ever, and have their reasons for that too. I don't blame them. But you must remember that when they are drunk nothing matters to them. No secret, no promise, no oath. They might mean no harm and still betray you; and this is the way it is. You will eventually have to learn to drink too," he forced a grin, "as your mother and I have; you can't get along without it. The Germans take care that there is enough vodka available; they know well what it does to people."

Again he lit her cigarette and said, "It is good that you smoke. Searching for a cigarette, lighting it, always gives you extra time to prepare an answer." He looked at her critically, "You must learn to smile, Elli. Your smile now is more like an unpleasant grimace. I noticed it last night at dinner. A healthy, hearty laugh is very important. Not that I suggest Polish girls are all smiles, or have reason to be. But they can afford the luxury of being themselves; you cannot. They also do not have to appear at ease or cheerful; you do. You must learn to observe people. A single move, a twist of the mouth, a blink of an eye, a seemingly meaningless word, might be a trap. Like a driver who must watch not only for himself but for other drivers too, you must watch not only your own words and behavior, but those of others as well."

He pondered for a moment. "Do not meddle in politics, Elli; there is considerable underground activity here, but you'll agree with me, I hope, one hump is enough in our situation. Besides there is one point about which some partisans agree with the Germans — that is the Jews. So save your patriotism for a more proper time."

She made a gesture as if she wanted to say something, but he was determined not to be interrupted.

"Remember," his face was grave, "if you are lost, you drag us down with you." He mopped his forehead and started to pace the room again.

"It might seem impossible to you now, this acting and pretending, watching every word and movement, controlling the expression of your face and the impression you make on people, day and night, night and day, with no rest. But you will train yourself to become somebody else, and then you will act and react in an automatic way with little or no effort. It will take time, but I know you will not let us down. You do not know our address yet in Lublin, and I am not going to give it to you. It is better for you and for us that, as long as it is possible, you do not know it."

"It's better you do not know . . ." Tossing in bed, sick with Michael's lesson, Elli heard clearly Lili's words when she asked her sister what the Germans are really after. That was just after the outbreak of the war — September, 1939.

✠   ✠   ✠

At the beginning nothing had really changed. Lili and she had gone to school, their father to his office. Elli had seen Polish soldiers in the street, some going by foot, some lying on horse-driven carts. They were dirty and exhausted. The passersby looked at them, dreadfully silent. The soldiers' weary eyes, their unshaven emaciated faces and torn uniforms resembled the retreating armies Elli had seen in the movies about the First World War. What she saw now seemed to her like another movie, a little scary but totally unreal. At school they were given gas masks and trained how to use them within fifteen minutes. The gym teacher took the class to a nearby park where the girls dug air-defense ditches. This again had more connection with Verdun than with reality. There were no soldiers to be attended to and Elli was neither cold nor hungry. Instead, however, things had begun to happen that she could not relate to what she had learned was a war.

First, in October, some streets had been closed to Jews. Listed in German and Polish on big white posters on boards, walls, and fences, they had included the main street which Elli had had to cross on her way to school. The German traffic officer and four gendarmes on the corners were picking out the transgressors. They paid no attention to the passing children. Every time Elli had to sneak past the Germans, she was wet with fear.

Then the Jews had been ordered to wear yellow six-pointed

stars, one on the chest, one on the back. The first day Elli went out with her mother and Lili — the yellow stars stitched on their coats — they had been caught in a roundup. A middle-aged German woman with a short haircut, narrow bloodless lips and watery eyes distributed pails and mops among the captives. They scrubbed floors for six hours. All but Lili. Lili stood at the window not even bothering to pretend she was working. Thereafter she refused to wear the yellow stars and mostly stayed at home. By then Elli's father stopped going to his office and never left home save after dark. Elli kept going to school. It was better to feel the cold sweat on her back twice a day crossing the prohibited street than to stay home. Home was not home anymore.

Soon, however, this hide-and-seek game stopped altogether. One morning a heavy blow in her back knocked Elli down in the street. In the course of a long diatribe she learned that the gutter was the place where she belonged, along with her filthy forefathers. She had lain awake all that night. When she got up next morning the war was "real" to her. After twenty-four hours she smiled with an air of superiority over the Elli she had been a day earlier, a mere kid with childish theories about wartime dignity and virtue. The contempt in the officer's eyes, the fury constricting his voice, and the loathing grimace distorting his face — that was The War.

At the end of October the family was given two hours' notice to vacate their apartment. The officer supervising the packing ordered them to leave behind everything but ten kilos of clothing for each. "Dürfen wir unseren Hund mitnehmen?" Lili asked him. "Jawohl, für Rassentiere haben wir Verständnis," answered the officer. Thanks to the new principles of warfare their beloved pug, Pickwick, was saved. They moved to a small two-bedroom apartment.

Shortly thereafter a German friend, Mr. Gründig, had paid

them a visit. He came to warn Elli's father against staying in Łódź. Łódź, he said, would soon be incorporated into the German Reich. He couldn't bear the thought, he whispered, that his friend should share the fate of the Jews who stayed there. "What do you mean, Egon?" Elli's father asked. "What fate?" "Oh, I don't know," said Gründig vaguely. "I can't come here anymore. One of my sons is in the Hitler Jugend and my daughter is a member of the Bund Deutscher Mädel. They are good kids, you know, but you never can tell. Take my advice, Emmanuel. Disappear." That night Elli's mother called the Old Man. It was agreed that one of the girls would go to Pabianice to see the Old Man. Ruth decided that Elli would go.

On the train Elli squeezed herself ever more tightly into her corner to make sure she was completely concealing the yellow star on her back. The one on her chest she covered with a book. She pretended to be deeply absorbed in her book but actually was concerned that she not be kicked off the train before it reached its destination. Elli was grim but not distressed and only a little bit afraid. She knew she must be careful and calm and she had not let the pangs of her heart bother her too much.

She remembered going slowly through the streets in Pabianice where even in darkness she could recognize every house and every tree. When Elli had last seen the Old Man, he had promised her he would take good care of himself in a spa, which meant he would reduce his card playing. Of course, she had not believed him. As long as she could remember, Aunt Paula, who with her family lived with the Old Man, had complained that cards were ruining his health, but no one would ever have dreamed of admonishing him.

She had loved to watch her grandfather, his attentive blue eyes flickering with amusement or irony, his long fingers tapping the silver cigarette case — impatiently when he disapproved, idly when the play grew dull. Before entering his card room, she had listened for his clear strong voice saying "full" or "pass" without a shade of difference. It was known in the family that the Old Man often invited future in-laws or business partners for a game of poker or bridge.

For years his house had been kind of a wonderland for her, later a sanctuary when she needed one. Sometimes, when she had stayed there overnight, she had seen the door of her bedroom open to let in all seven young Weils — the three girls in lovely long dresses and the four boys in tight-fitting, high-collared school uniforms, as she had learned to know them from the old family album. Sometimes they had been led by their mother in a dark wig with luminous black eyes shining in an ivory-colored face. At times, when she could not fall asleep, Elli would find her grandfather downstairs playing solitaire, never amazed at seeing her at any odd hour of the night, never asking questions or making remarks.

That day the kitchen was empty. Usually, at that hour Aurelia, the old servant who replaced Nanny many years ago, would have been busy fixing supper; Aunt Paula would have run in and taken Elli in her arms; Danny would have shrieked a Sioux welcome, their old childhood hail, and Stefa would have hushed him not to disturb the grandfather. Uncle Jacob had always had a surprise in his pocket; it had forever escaped his attention that the toddlers grew up.

Elli remembered that she bumped into Aurelia in the main hall leading to the dining room. Loud agitated voices were piercing through the closed door. Wordlessly, Aurelia pointed toward this door, her eyes red and swollen, her knotty hands fumbling mindlessly in the gray disheveled hair. She embraced Elli and made a sign of the cross on her forehead.

Elli put her coat on the wooden curved trunk ready to go

inside. Before she was able to knock at the door Aurelia grasped her hand and whispered into her ear, "Don't go there, my love, they are all nervous, angry; they are quarreling, mind you, at a time like this; don't go there, it's no good for you. Better stay with your old Aurelia."

Elli stopped before the door, listening. After a while she recognized in the uproar the voice of Uncle Michael; then that of his older son Daniel; the voice which interrupted him belonged to Michael's younger son David. The argument, Elli realized, concerned the factories. After the death of his wife the Old Man had left the management of the factories to Michael. Daniel and David had taken them over three years ago. Daniel, an excellent businessman, and David, a skilled engineer, had worked day and night to modernize and develop the business. When they had made it, David had married and fathered a girl, Noemi, now four weeks old. Daniel, the darling of the family, remained a bachelor. Elli had never been able to find out whether he was really in love with a married woman, or, as his father maintained, with his factories.

"No! I say no! And that is all there is to it." Those words were unquestionably pronounced by the Old Man. He put an end to a dispute. Elli remembered flushing as if the angry words had been meant for her. Aurelia kept mumbling behind her. Seeing Elli move forward, Aurelia crossed herself, repeating tearfully, "Oh, God have mercy, oh Holy Mary pray for us sinners . . ." Elli entered the room.

As usual, it was filled with smoke. The family was assembled around the big table, presided over by the Old Man. On his right sat Uncle Michael mopping his head; on his left, Big Daniel, nervously biting his full lips. Beside Michael sat Aunt Wilhelmina and Uncle Abram, then Aunt Paula and Uncle Jacob. Michael's wife, Aunt Adela, was missing. Beside Daniel sat David, then Felix, their Polish business partner, and Wilhelm Schwarz, a German industrialist. At the other end of the table, facing the Old Man, sat Doctor Kohn. The presence of the old family friends, Schwarz, Kohn, and Felix, was ominous.

Elli went to the Old Man, kissed his hand twice, hesitantly waved to her cousins, bowed to her uncles, aunts, and the three men at the end of the table, and remained standing, unsure of what to do. The Old Man interrupted the silence, "Bring her a chair, David. There is something more important we have to talk over: What's to be done to get out of here." As he spoke the last words his voice dropped into a low hushed tone. The Old Man certainly knew how to knock them cold. Then he sat back, a small malicious smile on his lips.

Doctor Kohn voiced the disbelief of all when he broke the silence, "I beg your pardon, Mr. Weil, did you say 'to get out of here'?"

"That's right." Elli remembered thinking that the Old Man's voice had been a little too loud.

"Would you mind, Mr. Weil, expressing your point more clearly?"

"I think, my dear friend, that I expressed myself clearly enough." The Old Man winked at Elli as if he wanted to say, "Old bore of a doctor, isn't he?" and went on visibly amused by the shock his words had caused. "Let's do something to get the whole family out of this stinking business." The almost beatific look on his face seemed rather strange amid these surprised, aghast, worried faces.

Aunt Wilhelmina's cheeks and neck had, by then, formed one big purple spot. "What do you mean, Father?" Her voice was badly pitched. "Do you mean I should abandon my houses, my factories, everything we scraped together working for years like slaves? Do you mean we should leave it and run somewhere like beggars?"

He gave her a rakish look. "You already are a beggar, my dear.

It's a pity you don't realize it yet. I see a total lack of communication here. Nobody seems to understand what I'm talking about. Too bad. Yes, you should abandon your houses and factories and run. Run as fast as you can and never, not for a moment, look back. You might turn into a pillar of salt if you did. You shouldn't, however, leave behind your jewelry and money. Those we will need."

"You know very well, Father" — this came out in a cracked hesitant voice — "that all I have are the few insignificant pieces of jewelry which belonged to our dearest mother, may she rest in peace. I will never part with them, not even if I starve. So help me God." There was surprising dignity and poise in her last words.

Then David rose. He went around the table and leaned over his father. Like Daniel, he was very handsome, tall, clean limbed. Uncle Michael listened to him attentively and nodded. David pushed the hair away from his forehead, cleared his throat, and turned to the Old Man. "We certainly will do whatever you say, Grandfather. What is, however, essential for all of us to know is whether you'll leave with us, sir?" He still had not been able to grasp that this old tree grown into the soil of this town would budge unless uprooted by force.

The Old Man looked at him, amused. "Why, of course, David, I'm going to leave with all of you." He turned to his oldest daughter. "When can I have the money, my dear? Within two, three weeks we can have the documents and leave the country." Stroking his beard, he said slowly, "If you think, Mina, you can get along the way you did up to now and survive this war, you'd better take my word for it that you cannot. You will not. There is not much choice. It's life or death."

"At your age, Father, one sees everything in dark colors." Aunt Mina put on a cheerful smile. "It's not all that bad. Just imagine, the other day I met two German officers in Abram's office and they appeared to be highly cultivated men. I talked with one of them for more than an hour about Bach and Beethoven. The other was educated at Oxford and spoke a perfect Oxford English. Both were distinguished, fine gentlemen. They admired my German. I am sure, Father, such men and a people who gave the world the greatest musicians, writers, scholars, are not capable of any of these atrocities that the terror-crazed Jews attribute to them."

Aghast, Elli realized that David was choking with laughter. He was holding his handkerchief to his mouth, his whole body shaking. She did not feel like laughing and scolded him. Then she heard her grandfather: "I am not going to lecture you on Hitler's policy, Mina. You should have heard something about it. If you didn't, you might improve your mind a little by reading the German press rather than talking to German officers. That, however, is your own business. Mine is to save my children and my children's children. I say," the Old Man rose, his voice now thick and angry, "I say that this war is going to last several years, not as some deceive themselves, several months or even weeks. And I say that the end of this war will see the end of European Jewry. I cannot tell you what means will be used to destroy us. What I can tell is that their range and quality will match the German efficiency, order, and cruelty." The Old Man opened his cigarette case, and the silence was so tense that everybody could hear it click.

"Father," said Mina. She was perfectly composed at that point. "Father, don't you realize that Jews, the poor simpletons, spread all kinds of absurd tales, because fear always was and still is the only human feeling they know? Since the beginning of time, every event, be it on a world scale or just in their stetl, has forced one question out of them: 'Iz epis git far Yidn?' Their sick minds work only one way, be it Napoleon or Disraeli, Piłsudski or Hitler; whether he is good for the Yidden or not, whether to run or to stay." She took a deep breath and continued with an ex cathedra air, "History proves that there is a better understanding between a German and a cultivated Jew than between a German and a Pole, or for that matter a Pole and a Jew. No one in his sound mind would question this. I am deeply convinced that, save for some restrictions natural in a time of war, nothing bad is going to happen to Jews in this country. Hence, I am determined to stay in my home together with my family."

She shot a sharp glance at her husband, commanding him, at least, to applaud. With downcast eyes, he patted her arm adorned with a costly little platinum watch set in diamonds.

The Old Man fixed his eyes on that watch, then moved to her diamond-studded necklace as if assessing, one by one, their value. Finally, he took from his vest an old-fashioned silver pocket watch dangling on a chain, thoughtfully glanced at it and said, "My time is precious. I have neither the desire nor the need to argue with all your silly nonsense. One would think a woman of your age and background should have more common sense. Your infantilism, to put it mildly, is horrifying. You are, of course, free to do whatever you wish; the same holds for your family. All I expect you to do is to deliver to me by noon tomorrow five thousand dollars."

Aunt Mina became hysterical. She cried in a high-pitched voice, "I know you don't give a damn about me and my family! You never did! None of you! All you care about is my money. And you have the nerve to make demands! Over my dead body! So help me God!" She began to sob spasmodically.

David lost his patience then. He jumped up, his black eyes flashing. He snatched a fruit knife from the table and gesticulating wildly, shouted, "You'd save your money over our dead bodies, Auntie dear! You envied Adam for having no family before God created Eve, didn't you?"

The Old Man half rose and motioned David to stop, but David

did not see him. "Do you remember how Aunt Ruth forced you to come here, saying that grandfather was very sick? Do you remember how furious you were when you found him sitting at this table? And yet, you refused . . ."

"Shut up, David, shut up!" The Old Man completely lost his composure. He looked like an enraged bull. "This is none of your business. Hold your tongue, you fool! Will you?" He banged fiercely on the table. Two apples fell from the fruit tray, rolled along the table, and noiselessly landed on the thick carpet. The ashtrays and glasses clattered.

"I beg your pardon, Grandfather." David trembled, his eyes wild. "I apologize, Aunt Mina." He sat down heavily and bent the fruit knife in his big hairy hands like a piece of foil. Bowed over the table, the disheveled black hair covering his face, he looked like a wounded bear.

"I do not give a damn for your apologies." Aunt Mina threw him a devastating look. "I know perfectly well what you mean. You would be happy to see me a beggar. But you will not." Then she glanced at her watch.

"Will I have this money by noon tomorrow, Mina?" asked the Old Man matter-of-factly.

"Father, I don't have the money, I don't have jewels, we have scarcely enough to support ourselves." This tumbled out hastily as if she were afraid somebody might interrupt her. Tears again flooded her cheeks. She was in a state of exhausted hysteria. Elli heard Daniel murmuring, "Scout's honor," and again her aunt, "Upon the memory of our dear mother, upon the well-being of my child, we have lost everything we had. All we have left are the walls. Houses, factories, machinery. What can you do with them? Can you eat them? Can you bite them? Can you take them along?" she wailed, swaying back and forth.

The Old Man again rose from his chair and violently pushed the heavy piece. His eyes narrowed into cold angry slits. He lifted his arm and, with his forefinger pointed at Aunt Mina, said in a dreadfully calm voice, "Get out of here. Get out of here at once and never come back again."

Tall, erect, he stood waiting. She got up heavily, taking her handbag, and slowly approached the door. Uncle Abram, his shoulders stooped, his head hanging, trotted behind her. At the door Aunt Mina stopped, turned to the Old Man, and said in a strained voice, "Father, I do not have the money. I swear." The door slammed behind them.

It seemed that the ominous silence would never end, that the Old Man would stand there forever. His eyes were fixed on that door but on his face strayed a disbelieving smile as if he were surprised at what had happened. Elli stared at the door too. She prayed for it to open and for her aunt to come back, promising herself never to misbehave again. But Aunt Mina did not return. Instead, Aunt Paula got up, approached the motionless man, and whispered, "Sit down, Father dear, please, do sit down." He sat down but did not take his eyes off the door. "I'll bring some fresh hot coffee now," said Aunt Paula a little louder. "I guess we all need it." Relieved to find an excuse, she quickly left the room.

Elli made a desperate effort to break the silence. She could not tear her eyes from the Old Man, who, chain-smoking, sipped his coffee. The engimatic smile still on his face, he seemed to be pondering deeply. Finally, with a mischievous sparkle in his eyes he said, "You all know what a Jewish duel is, don't you?" He looked around. "It's when one fights a duel with himself. That's what I've been doing for the last twenty minutes. I even came to an agreement with myself. The terms of this agreement are as follows: We will leave. All the men, except me, will set out for Russia. The rest, women and children and myself, will go to Warsaw." He paused for another sip of coffee. "For all I know the chances of survival in a big city, in a capital, might be better.

We will fade into the crowd, unknown, inconspicuous. **Another** advantage of our going there is that we won't be here." He chuckled. "I mean that we disappear, and our friends, Polish and German alike, won't have us hanging around their necks. In this way we will stay friends. Forever."

Mr. Schwarz could bear no more. He sprang to his feet, red and perspiring. "Mr. Weil," he said indignantly, "what's wrong . . . "

The Old Man interrupted him, "Please, be seated, Mr. Schwarz. Nothing's wrong. Everything is all right and I want it to stay that way. That's all. No offense, Mr. Schwarz. Will you have a drink, Mr. Schwarz? What about the rest?" Not waiting for an answer, he turned to Elli. "Please go and tell Aurelia to bring some cognac and glasses."

He filled the glasses himself. "One doesn't drink cognac like that," he remarked dryly as Elli gulped hers down. "You must learn how to do it properly, my dear, otherwise you'll never be a lady. One warms it up in his hands, smells it, tastes, and sips it." She blushed, in confusion.

"Well, I think we can call it a day. Thanks for coming, gentlemen," he bowed toward the other end of the table. "I'm sorry for this pitiful spectacle. I hope you didn't mind it too much. It's not worthwhile. Good night, everybody." He left the room.

Elli had stayed overnight. Cuddled in a rocking chair, she had tried to read but her eyes wandered idly over the letters. The big clock downstairs struck ten, half-past ten, eleven, twelve. Finally she got up, slipped into her robe, and went down. She knocked softly at the door of the Old Man's room and after a while heard his voice.

"Is that you, Elli? Do come in." Clad in a dark checked lounging jacket, he was sitting at his desk playing solitaire. His frock coat lined with fine sheepskin was carelessly tossed over a chair. "I heard you coming downstairs." He put a queen of spades over a knave, "You couldn't sleep, I know. It's been hard on you, just as on everybody else, I guess. And mind you, this is only the beginning . . ."

He looked hard at her. "You're thirteen . . ." "Fourteen," she corrected him. "And the end of your childhood, dear. Somehow, you must get used to this idea. It's terrible but it can't be helped." He stopped as if waiting for her to say something but she sat silent.

"It will never be the same, Elli. The end of this war will find you a grown-up girl with different problems and different experience. But you were happy, weren't you? You had a sunny childhood, loving, broad-minded parents — you have something to lean upon. In the days to come you'll find it very important."

He shifted his eyes to the picture of his wife hanging over his desk. Then he took Elli's hand in both his big warm hands and asked her, "What are you thinking about, Elli? Is there some way I can help you?" He did not wait for her reply and went on, "You probably think I'm the one who needs help. You're damn right. God! It's been a day!" He had shuddered all over, she remembered. "Your grandmother used to say, 'Jeder wird selig nach seiner Fasson.' Do you remember, Elli, how many times I've told you that? Man is like a guidepost, my dear. Always ready to guide somebody else, while he himself does not even budge. The more fool I."

He gathered the cards from the desk and started to pace the room. Suddenly he stopped in front of the desk. "It's not as simple as that," he said tartly. "She is my daughter. I love her. Just like the others." After a long pause he murmured, " '. . . those whom the gods would destroy they first drive mad . . .' "

He lighted a fresh cigarette and sat down heavily at his desk. He remained motionless a long time and then said loudly, "There

is probably no way out. Neither here, nor there . . . too late
. . . one should try . . . maybe some of them . . ." The cigarette burned out in the ashtray. He whispered listlessly, "What
did I do wrong . . . what did I do wrong . . ." Tears rolled
down his withered cheeks.

Elli had returned home next day around noon and briefly told
her mother that Grandfather had decided that all the men of
the family would go to Russia, that the rest would move to Warsaw, and that he wanted to see Ruth immediately. She went to
him the same day. When she came back she had a long talk
with her husband. Then they called the girls and their father
told them that he was going to Pabianice at once. There he
would join the others, and they would leave for Russia within
the next few days. "We'll have to cross the border illegally but
we are already well versed in keeping on the wrong side of the
law," he smiled, "so don't worry." He seemed cheerful, relieved
that the waiting, idleness, and sequestration was coming to an
end.

Elli remembered looking at this portly man with gray temples
and weary eyes and thinking: My father, my world, my everything; he is leaving us, he is going away, homeless, lonely. There
was not much time left. Ruth packed his small black patent
leather suitcase, made hot strong tea, and poured it into the
glasses from an old silver samovar. It was the only object Elli's
father had saved from his family's home, the only thing dear to
him; he had often repeated that he hated things and put no
value on them. How strange it all is, Elli had thought, how incomprehensible. He had to leave his home way back in the past;
now he has to do the same; and Grandfather would also have
to leave his home, and she hers.

At the table none of them uttered a word. Elli avoided her

father's eyes. She knew she would burst out crying if she saw
them again. Then Ruth said, "It's time, dearest." He rose and
took them in his bearlike arms, first his wife, then Lili, then Elli.
She felt the warmth of these big strong hands and for a moment
felt secure and safe as in the old times. Eyes brimmed with
tears, but none of them wept. He put on his overcoat and took
the suitcase from his wife's hand. Standing in the open door, he
turned back, again smiling, and said, "I will be back, I promise."
The door banged. He was gone. Elli ran to the window and
pressed her face to the dim pane. She remembered the towering
man marching straight ahead. As he rounded the corner into a
small back street, she had caught sight of the yellow star glaring
from his back. That was the last she saw of him.

Two weeks later they had again, all three, been caught in a
roundup and held for almost three days shoveling snow, peeling
potatoes, washing latrines. In biting frost and icy wind they
almost continually had been outside. The watery ersatz coffee
distributed twice a day could not warm them. Past midnight the
whole group had been herded into an empty unheated wooden
barracks, from which they were driven to work at four in the
morning. Elli's feet and hands froze and became swollen. The
potatoes slipped through her fingers, the knife dropped again
and again into the snow. If not for Lili's help, she would never
have finished peeling the assigned lot or cleaning the driveway.
The second night the officer who had admitted the people into
the barracks stopped Ruth. "So jung . . . so schön . . . schade
. . . oben ist es warm und gemütlich . . ." he hissed silently.

Back home, Ruth sat on a chair, staring blankly ahead. Then
she said, not looking at the girls, "Last week Doctor Weinstein
committed suicide with her two daughters . . . she turned on
the gas at night . . ." Lili jumped to her feet. "Mama," she

cried, "Mama, dearest, please don't talk like that. How can you?
You have Elli and me, we love you, we adore you, and nothing
else matters as long as we are together. We can stand a lot, Mama,
it's really not as bad as that." Slowly Ruth's stony eyes had turned
toward Lili. "You are right, Lili," she said. "You are perfectly
right, dearest. As long as we are together nothing else matters.
I have both my children, strong and healthy. I really have no
right to complain." That night Ruth had once again phoned the
Old Man.

The following morning Ruth had told her daughters that at
nightfall they would go to Pabianice. The rest of the day they
had spent making choices. All they could take were three small
suitcases. While their mother selected the warmest and least
bulky clothes, the girls went through family albums, papers,
books. It was not easy to make a choice. All the books had to be
left behind along with two big dolls they had saved from their
nursery. Elli sat on the floor surrounded by pictures, books, copybooks. Page by page she went through the albums, studied a last
time her grandparents, her parents, aunts and uncles, the funny
babies stretched on fluffy sheepskin, Lili and herself at different
ages. Then had come her copybooks with compositions in Polish,
German, history, she had once decided to keep for her children.
She had folded them together with her mother's school reports,
her father's diplomas, taken the armload into the kitchen,
opened the furnace, and one after another had set them on fire.
On the smoldering ashes she had put a parcel with the pictures
and a pack of letters from the Old Man, her parents, and Lili.
With dry, desperate eyes she had watched the flames slowly lick-
ing the papers.

But they could keep their dog. All day long Pickwick, sensing
a trap, had refused to eat and, squeezed into a corner, followed

Lili, his very best friend, with sad miserable eyes. Hesitatingly, Ruth had agreed that they take him along. When Lili dressed him in his warm coat and fixed his leash the animal was so tense that he could not walk by himself. Lili had to carry him all the way to the streetcar.

It had been decided that the family, accompanied by Felix and his brother-in-law Antoni, would leave as soon as the travel permits were ready. In the dining room behind closed doors, the Old Man had talked endlessly with Ruth and Felix. Occasionally Wilhelm Schwarz or Doctor Kohn had dropped in. Time pressed. The family store which was closed had become too much of a risk. The Germans might be tempted to loot it anytime. Not that anybody cared about the merchandise but all were afraid of the Old Man's reaction. He had said expressly that he would dispose of his property as he saw fit, but he would not allow any bandit to take it. Unperturbed, he had continued to read his books and to take his daily strolls. Every time he left home the household was in agony until he returned. Hardly a day passed without news about Jews being attacked and abused in the streets, and what they feared most was the Old Man's response to an insult. He ignored all their indirect hints and refused to let anybody accompany him. Every day around noon, regardless of the weather, he put on his overcoat, took his ebony cane, and went for a walk, a towering figure, one yellow star on his back, another on his chest.

And the day that all dreaded had finally come. It was a bright, crisp sunny December afternoon, when Felix's fourteen-year-old son Wiktor stormed into the kitchen and shouted incoherently, "Mister Weil . . . help him . . . he'll kill him . . . the officer . . . near the park . . ." Aurelia made the breathless, crying boy sit down, Ruth asked him to tell what was happening, Paula sobbed desperately. Lili, holding Wiktor's hand tried to calm him while Elli impatiently cried, "Speak! Speak! For goodness' sake, where is he?" The boy told them in a broken voice that he had been passing by the park with two friends when a truck arrived and a roundup started. Hiding across from the park, he had seen the Old Man coming. At the gate a soldier approached him and apparently ordered him to get into the truck which already was packed with people. The Old Man, the boy guessed, had refused and for a while talked to the officer, who had finally lost his patience and started to yell, pointing toward the truck. The Old Man had not moved. The officer pushed him and then — Wiktor rose and stood at attention as he said with pride and admiration, "Mister Weil slapped the officer in the face." He did not know what happened next, for he had run to tell them to save the Old Man.

"Only Wilhelm can help," Ruth said impassively. "I'll call him." She explained to Schwarz what had happened.

Half an hour later the Old Man came back and immediately retired to his room. The yellow star on his back was dangling by a single thread. He did not come to supper, but nobody expected him. When Schwarz came that night, desperate and perspiring, to tell them he had not been able to find the Old Man, they were all completely mystified. Convinced that, thanks to Schwarz's intervention, the Old Man had been released, they had not bothered to let him know. Schwarz could not understand what had happened either. He said that when he reached the park it was deserted. He had gone to the nearest police post, to no avail. For the following three hours he had run from one office to another. Most of them were already closed. It had been impossible to find out anything. He had inquired of all the sentries that he passed, phoned several German officers, but in vain. Later that night Schwarz called back to say that he had received a call from one of these officers. The man told him that he had just left the officers' club where his completely drunk friend kept talking about an old Jew whom he should have shot on the spot but let go instead. The drunk kept repeating two words, "judge, judgment." His caller had guessed that the old Jew Schwarz was looking for was a judge and asked if he was right. Schwarz had told him that he was.

Three days later, on New Year's Eve, the family had left Pabianice. The Old Man had never referred to the incident but did not leave the house until they went to the station. On the last day he had requested that Ruth call Mina and ask her to go with them to Warsaw. It was the first time that he mentioned his oldest daughter's name. Mina's phone had been answered by the maid. She reported that "Madame" with her husband and daughter had left by car at the beginning of December. "Madame" had not told her where they were going and had ordered her not to answer the phone. But a week before two Germans had moved into the apartment so she was no longer able to respect "Madame's" orders, she explained. A few hours later Schwarz returned from Warsaw. He had met Mina in front of the house where she lived with her family but she implored him not to give away her address.

The departure had been carefully prepared by Felix and Antoni. The night before they had transported the luggage on sledges to the station. It did not amount to very much; still it could have attracted undue attention. The Old Man had remarked dryly that the sledges reminded him of the Germans who, when they had come to Pabianice some fifty years before, had had their entire belongings loaded on such vehicles pulled by dogs. Now that they had made their fortunes here, he said, they had suddenly awakened to the new glory of their old Vaterland.

The family was ready for the road when the Old Man asked them to come to the dining room. He went himself to the kitchen and brought Aurelia in. For two days she had spoken to no one. She refused to accept the furniture and merchandise left in the store. She sat now between Ruth and Paula, crying silently. At the head of the table the Old Man got up. "It is not my habit to make speeches," he said. "I have never made a speech in my whole life, and this isn't going to be a speech either. It only looks so solemn" — a sour smile curved his lips. "Well, the moment is somewhat unusual, as everybody can see. In a short while I'm going to leave this house." He cleared his throat loudly, Elli remembered. "I'm going to leave friends who were part of my life, as this town and this house were. It is my decision to leave. Whether it is right or wrong, I do not know. We have become prisoners. All of us. But only up to a point. We still are free in spirit, we are responsible human beings. It's useful to keep this in mind." He looked toward the far end of the table where his grandchildren sat. "I hate to sound pompous but I must say that we are facing a monstrous catastrophe. One day, however, the wave of hate and madness will pass. That's the time when the parties start to count their casualties. The casualties are not the dead; they are done with and besides the dead are always right. The casualties are the survivors. That's why I talk to you now. I want you to understand that no living man can escape a judgment. Do not think, any of you, that survival is the main problem or the sole target. The main problem is to be able to live when that time is over."

Elli could not make much sense of what the Old Man was saying. Was it a farewell address? A justification of his decision? Or was it a confession of doubts he was no longer willing or able to hide? Or was it a warning? But whom could he possibly be warning? He had sounded pretentious and pathetic and not quite clear, really. It was unlike him to assume the pose of prophet. He reminded her at that moment of the times when she had thought he was like God. Save that that day he looked like a tired old man and his pose did not become him at all. Elli wondered if the others understood what he was after. She looked around. All faces were blank.

It was past six o'clock when at last Felix had come back to the small group waiting in front of the station entrance. The Old Man was standing next to David's wife, Rachel, looking at his great-granddaughter whom she held in her arms. Aunt Paula, leaning on Danny, was silently crying. Ruth was impatiently pacing the deserted street, Pickwick trotting behind her. Exposed to the cold north wind, covered with snow, they were chilled to the bone, but the heavy mantles of snow served to conceal the yellow stars. It was this which saved them when they had to pass through the waiting room and a group of Germans hunting Jews. The patrol picked up two elderly women with a child, commanded them to follow and left. With Felix and Antoni flanking the Old Man, and Wilhelm Schwarz in the rear, they reached the cattle car. One by one they scrambled through its high opening helped by the men. The car was almost completely filled with iron junk. Their luggage was piled in one corner. The girls arranged it into a comfortable sitting place for the Old Man and found two blankets to cover his back and legs. Elli prayed to God that the train would start moving before anything happened. Schwarz, impatient too and distressed, went to the stationmaster and returned with bad news. The train was being delayed because the Germans were searching it for smugglers and Jews.

Elli remembered that as the time passed she had grown restless and almost physically sick with apprehension. It had seemed to her that the carefully worked out plan was bound to fail and she envisioned them being dragged out, one after another, by those madly shouting soldiers brandishing their weapons. Then she had heard Lili whispering in her ear, "We will leave,

Elli, don't worry. Remember, last winter when we were going to Zakopane the train was also delayed and you thought we wouldn't go at all. But we finally did. Then it was because of bad weather, but just try to think about these morons in terms of a snowstorm. You cannot change the climate, can you? You just have to accept it. Cheer up, Schwesterchen, we will go."

Finally a voice had yelled, "Ist jemand drin?" She had seen a helmet, a gun, and then the opening had been bolted from outside. The clatter of the iron bolt was the most soothing sound she had heard for months. The next thing she heard was the Old Man's voice over the earsplitting noise of the rolling wheels, "Children, get out of your soaked coats or you'll catch cold. I hate people sneezing and blowing right in my face. And let's have something to eat, I'm starving." Nobody moved. He went on, "Don't worry, once we've started we'll keep rolling. Elli, will you pass me a cup of tea, please?" In a few minutes the atmosphere in the car had become that of a somewhat unusual but not unpleasant expedition. Lili took food out of the basket; Ruth, a pack of cards from her bag. The candle Felix fixed on a couple of bricks was met with cheerful applause. Elli thought of her father. What was he doing? They had always celebrated New Year's Eve at home together before the adults went to some big party. "Elli, I asked you to pass me a cup of tea." She put her coat on a rusty bar, poured some tea from a thermos bottle, and handed it clumsily to the Old Man. "Now, you drink it," she remembered him saying. Automatically she started to drink from the cup he put in her hand. It had been her father's lifelong maxim that all troubles dissolved in hot strong tea.

The Old Man examined his hand, then folded his cards and dispassionately announced, "Pass."

ELLI ROSTOW BEGAN HER DIARY THE NIGHT OF THEIR ARRIVAL IN
WARSAW:

Warsaw, January 1, 1940

*That was the most wonderful thing that could ever happen!
Daniel was waiting at the Central Station. We were completely
stunned. We thought he was in Russia; instead here he was,
smiling and waving with both his hands. He quickly explained
that they had been stopped by the Russians at the former Polish
border, so he decided to come back, phoned Pabianice, found out
from Aurelia that we were gone and since then had been waiting
at the station. He was talking, I was listening, and meantime
the train started to move, me inside with a heavy suitcase.
Daniel hopped in, threw the luggage out, and we jumped down
together. God, how happy I was to see him. I love him so much
— the Big Daniel — and feel so much safer with him near me.*

*He loaded us in two cabs and took us to his friend's house
on Prosta Street where we stayed overnight and where he told
us about their adventures. After they had been arrested and
held for two days in a Russian jail he had had enough of Russia
and decided to go back to Warsaw as did Uncle Michael who
is on his way there on his bike. David would also be back in
two or three days. They thought it would be less risky not to
make the way together. I am surprised that they disobeyed the
Old Man's orders. The Old Man did not seem to share our
enthusiasm. Aunt Adela and Miriam, Uncle Jacob and Stefa,
and my father have decided to stay. I'm happy of course that
Daniel and David will be together with us but I don't know
if they should have come back. David certainly missed Rachel
and Noemi, besides he is not on best terms with his mother
and sister. With Aunt Adela it started when he married Rachel;
Miriam, he used to call the princess of Chinese tea because she*

wet her bed when a grown girl, and she hated him for that. Daniel said Miriam was engaged to be married to a man (his name is Nathan) she met in Russia. He is a rabbi. Funny, I will have a cousin who is a rabbi. Never had one before.

This night all but the Old Man slept on the floor and we had lots of fun. Pickwick enjoyed it too. The baby (we call her Emmi) did not cry at all; I thought babies always cry at night. We had much luck because first thing in the morning Mama found an apartment advertised in a newspaper. It was the Old Man who said to try it this way, though everybody else thought it was a waste of time. Thousands of people come every day to Warsaw, all looking for a place to live, so who'd advertise? But he said that people seldom think of the simplest ways racking their brains instead over the most complicated ones, so why not try the simplest? And it worked. In the afternoon we moved into the new quarters. We had just enough money to pay the three months' rent and buy some lousy furniture from the landlady. She is a young and very attractive-looking woman, rather dramatic. Her hand on her breast, like Nero looking at Rome burning, she declaimed in a vibrant tearful voice, "I sacrifice my sacred hearth to alleviate the cruel fate of war victims! You have this shelter for nothing, so help me God! I swear on my child's well-being that nothing but compassion made me rise above personal considerations." The exorbitant rent for this appallingly neglected flat and the price for the junk she called furniture alone justified her calling us victims, and the reason she rented this apartment was that she moved to her sister's. Funnily enough she is the daughter of a well-known rabbi and the daughter-in-law of a famous cantor. She gabbled about the prominent persons she was connected with and the big favor she is doing us letting us live in her "nest." Still, we are lucky. The apartment is in a pleasant neighborhood on Koszykowa Street and has three rooms, a kitchen, and a bathroom. *The back room, windowless but pleasant, is for Mama, Lili, and me; the middle one for Rachel, Emmi, David, and Daniel; the front one, the biggest, with two windows and a balcony, for Grandfather, Aunt Paula, and Danny. We spent the rest of the day cleaning, dusting, arranging the furniture; at night everyone had a place to sleep, the adults in beds, we on the floor. It's going to be wonderful here. We are all together — and that's the most important thing.*

January 2, 1940

Right after breakfast the Old Man announced we have no money, and something must be done about it. Mama's friend offered to pay a handsome sum to anyone bringing her the jewelry that she had left in Łódź with Polish friends. At night Uncle Michael arrived and brought with him a permit to cross the border into the Reich. On the way back he was passing a small border town in the East called Dubienka and there he talked a German Bürgermeister into giving him this document. After long deliberations it was decided that it could be used by Mama for the trip to Łódź. The permit is made out to Michael Weil but is without a picture. Uncle said that it's unlikely they'd notice the first name, but I'm terribly worried. What if they do?

January 4, 1940

It's entirely different here. No yellow stars. Instead, we wear armbands — white, with a blue star of David in the middle.

✠ ✠ ✠

Elli and Michael traveled in two different compartments and reached Lublin at dawn. It was gray and chilly. With her hair cut and set, Elli felt terribly awkward, as if she had a wig or a big fancy hat on her head. It seemed to her that people were looking at her funny coiffure and rouged cheeks and that the purpose of the makeup was easily recognizable. Still she smiled at them in the compartment and also at the station until Michael nudged her in passing and, with his face expressionless, whispered, "Wipe that idiotic grin off your face." He looked equally angry when she stopped smiling.

Suddenly something about herself seemed terribly wrong to her. Her heart sank for one horrible moment until she realized that she was not supposed to be wearing her armband. She followed Michael into the station and stopped before a telephone booth. He was checking to see if he could bring her home. He talked briefly, then beckoned to her and handed her the receiver.

"Ma——" she started. Michael furiously grasped her hand and she finished, "——ria."

"Good morning, darling," she heard her mother's quiet voice. "I am happy you are here."

3

Elli's training started in earnest the next day. Two millers with whom they had made a good business deal came to dinner, and this, of course, called for a celebration. Elli soon discovered that every event was an excuse for drinking; even the lack of an event became an occasion for drinking. She did not get much to eat during this first day. Maria, as she now called her mother, was afraid her contracted stomach might get upset by too much food. At night, however, she had warm soup and some meat and drank her first shot of vodka. She liked it. It relieved her tension, relaxed her muscles. She grew warm inside, a feeling long forgotten, but welcomed. She felt light and sure of herself. After the second glass the forced smile disappeared from her face as laughing and talking too loudly she responded to the advances of the two robust millers. Being Aryan has its good side too, she thought. After the third glass Maria put her to bed. On the sixth day she made a bet with Daniel that she could drink a quarter bottle of vodka and remain sober. She won the bet.

Most of the time she spent with Daniel, who gradually introduced her into the new environment. He rarely left the room;

he answered the phone and waited on customers when Maria and Michael were away. The three of them lived in a sublet room stuffed with mill equipment, three beds, a huge table, and a big wardrobe. Over each bed hung a big holy picture. Their landlady, Mrs. Borek, lived with her daughter and son in the adjoining room. Behind a screen there was an oven, a basin, and a pail for common use.

Mrs. Borek was a gray, sickly-looking woman in her late forties, rough in manner but, as Daniel said, honest and kindhearted. Her twenty-year-old daughter worked in an office, her eighteen-year-old son in the Majdanek labor camp. His mother deplored this job; he would often come home dead drunk, volunteering information, which he never did when sober; he would occasionally fish out from his pocket a ring, a gold tooth, or a chain. However, what was most important, Daniel said, was that Mrs. Borek permitted them to run their business in her home, and allowed him to stay in the already crammed flat.

Daniel still looked much different from Maria and Michael, who both had the healthy complexion of people spending much time outdoors, and neither had his conspicuous features. Michael had grown a moustache which balanced his long nose; Maria, in her top boots and green leather coat with a scarf on her head, looked like a country gentleman's wife. It was the best of looks both for the Germans, who had some sympathy for the Polish gentry, and for the Poles, who respected them. Maria was like an animal, Daniel said smiling, which puts on protective color. Her manners, the way she talked and laughed and drank vodka and held her glass, fitted her new identity perfectly. Her voice became more harsh, her language less refined, her gestures brisk and sure. She could drink heavily with the millers, laugh and joke with them, cheerfully answer their courtesies and, when she seemed a little drunk, it was because she wanted to seem so. She was perfectly balanced. There was neither exaggeration nor slackness in her manner. She clearly did not underestimate the foe, real or potential. Whether talking to a miller, or to Mrs. Borek, whether alone with her family within the four walls of their room or out in the street, her behavior remained unchanged.

"Maria handles the German officials and the Polish customers with equal insight and awareness," Daniel was saying. "That's how the business was established and run."

It was a Sunday, the seventh day of Elli's stay in Lublin. They were alone in the apartment. Mrs. Borek with her family went to visit her sister in the country; Maria left for Warsaw; Michael rode his bike to Zamość. Elli was sitting on one bed; Daniel opposite her on another. She was staring at him smiling vaguely, remembering what had happened when they were left alone in this room for the first time.

It had been perhaps five in the morning, completely dark, as she heard the door closing softly behind Michael and tucked herself tighter in the blanket. Then she felt something huge and warm beside her. The member that touched her hip was hot and hard. Her mind suddenly clear, she moved aside. Daniel whispered hastily, in a strangled voice, "Don't, please, don't, I'll do you no harm, please, I'm starving. It'll take just a minute, I promise, please be good, Elli, it's agony, I can't stand it any longer . . ." She lay stiff, patiently waiting while he rubbed his member against her body. She felt uncomfortable and embarrassed. Big Daniel, the strong handsome Big Daniel, the prince charmant, begging *her* in that voice of a little helpless boy. What made this strong Samson-like man utter these imploring, wailing sounds?

Elli let Daniel come to her bed every time they were left alone. Invariably, it followed along the same pattern. He rubbed his member upon her stiff body, gasping and moaning, then she felt the wet, and he'd groan and kiss her hands. After all, it was only a few unpleasant minutes for her and to him it obviously meant a lot. If *this* makes him happy, why should she refuse? No harm done, no magic working. Nothing.

Daniel's thoughts, however, were elsewhere. "And the business, mind you, is only part of her job," he went on. "For more than six months she ran from one place to another to save what remained of our family. To take care of Miriam alone would be a full-time job. That incredible idiot! I told your mother in all earnestness, that I am more than willing to kill her with my own hands. Alive, she is a constant danger to all of us. When she left the ghetto, Doctor Darski hid her in an attic. Then Maria found a midwife here in Lublin and brought my beloved sister to her. Miss Weronika is a fine and good woman. Miriam had the baby in her home. Then one day she went to buy something in a nearby store and met a German who, she said, inspired her confidence. Why this bitch told him she was Jewish, I do not know, but she did. She brought him right to Miss Weronika's house to show him the baby, the living proof of her heroism. Because he did not believe, she said that she had fled pregnant from the ghetto. Miss Weronika bribed him with all her modest jewelry which we had to pay back, but of course Miriam had to leave at once. Maria shipped her off with the baby to Mrs. Czemera in Rejowiec. There, after a few days, what do you think my kid sister did? She told them she was Jewish. You see, Elli, she is so honest that she cannot stand deceiving people. She just must tell the truth. The surprised Mr. Czemera told her this was impossible, since she was the daughter of Michael Weil, who was not a Jew. 'Why, of course, he is,' she assured him. 'We all are.' She ruined our best hiding place, this whore. Maria went to Rejowiec and brought her back to Lublin. Now she is living here with Mrs. Czemera's sister, but any day I expect her to make her confession. Then I'll kill her, I swear."

Daniel got up, poured himself a glass of water, and gulped it down. "And one day, not long ago," he resumed, "we received a letter from our beloved cousin, Rita. She got our address from Irena Darska, this Christian apostle, damn her. Rita begged Maria to come and help them — Eryk Roth and herself. Maria went to Warsaw and ransomed them from the people who were holding her and Eryk. Before they left the ghetto, Eryk and his comrades robbed the Judenrat cashbox. The money lasted them only through the first months on the Aryan side. Maria found a hiding place for Eryk and furnished Rita with a baptismal certificate. Maria's old friend, Mr. Nowacki, found Rita a job at a doctor's house. Mrs. Nowacka gave the reference. One day the doctor's wife came upon Rita playing the piano, which she found somewhat unusual for a servant. Our dear cousin, before she took a powder, burglarized the house. The doctor reported it to the police; the Nowackis' house was searched. Somehow Mr. Nowacki convinced the police that his wife did not know Miss Jasinska — that's Rita's new name — very well. Maria took her to Rejowiec. It was dangerous after Miriam's stunt but there was no alternative. Then Czemera had one of his drunken fits, and Rita went back to Warsaw. She joined Eryk in his hiding place. Every week Maria pays off the people who are hiding them. And that is not all of it by any means."

Daniel grimaced unpleasantly and drained another glass of water. "Rachel lives with Emmi at some miller's near Hrubieszów. She has written twice already that she cannot stay there. Not that it is dangerous, mind you, but she just can't. She probably finds the country life boring. She wants to go back to Warsaw to find Mark, I guess. So at the present stage there is Miriam, who will explode any minute, and her baby; Rachel, who can't sit on her ass, and her child whom she'll leave, sure as hell, on our hands; Lili, at a miller's who was arrested a few days ago; you, to be wafted away; Rita and Eryk, to be supported, me, sitting here on pins and needles; and the business to be run. Quite an affair, isn't it?" He looked at her.

"You are ready for another glass of water, Daniel," smiled Elli.

"I am ready to tell you," said Daniel irritably, "that your mother — excuse me, Maria — is by far the most wonderful woman I have ever met." He stared out the window. "You know about Sioma, don't you?" he asked after a while.

"Uncle Michael told me that he died. That is all I know."

"He hanged himself. When he found me here, having followed my father from the station, he was all in pieces. He was my closest friend. David and he were the two people dearest to me. He fled from the ghetto in some small town, and God only knows where he was before he came here. He never told me. To look at him was enough to see he had gone through hell. We couldn't keep him here with all these people hanging around. He stayed four days, all the time in bed, a blanket over his head. Then Maria put him on a train and took him to Mr. Olszewski in Dubienka. It had to be Olszewski, who knows who we are, or no one. He agreed without a word to hide him. He kept him in a small shack across the orchard surrounding his house, and brought him food every night. This seclusion, though, must have been too big a strain on Sioma. He had been there over two months when one day some Germans turned up. He must have heard their voices and thought they were after him. When Olszewski came later that night to bring him food, the corpse was already cold. Olszewski cried here, at this table," Daniel banged with his fist on the table, "that he should have warned Sioma these harmless Wehrmacht men sometimes drop in for a drink. He should have." Daniel raised his voice, "Yes, that's what he said. He should have warned him but he did not," he yelled.

For a long while there was silence in the room. Then Daniel said more calmly, "Now, you must return the favor, and tell me about Danny."

Elli looked at him uneasily. "Is that necessary, Daniel? We have been together so briefly, and you keep telling me gruesome stories as if we were in the funeral business. You know he died, why go over it? Let's talk about something else. Tell me, how's Emmi? Did you see her? She must have changed a lot."

"She has," he grumbled. "Now, come on, tell me about Danny."

"Don't insist, Daniel," she pleaded. "I'll tell you some other time. I promise."

"You can't promise me anything," he said. "Tomorrow you'll go, and I do not know if I'll ever see you again. Look, Elli," his voice was gentle now, "it's not curiosity, you should know that. Danny was my own baby, my kid cousin, ten years my junior. I coached him in school, in football, in swimming. He wept on my shoulder when he first fell in love at the age of eleven. Then we were passing through that damned wall twice a day, working together, smuggling food . . . I grew more fond of him than ever before . . . not fond . . . I grew to respect him. The baby, the kid, proved to be stronger and more responsible than I. He would never let me deal with the guards; he knew they drove me mad. But for him they would have shot me the very first day I started to argue. He did the talking, the kid, at the border post, with our overseers, with the gendarmes. He wouldn't let me take more bread or potatoes than was allowed. Every night before crossing back into the ghetto he'd check my pockets; he knew that I might cheat and that cheaters got shot. He showed more reason and composure and maturity than I, or David, or many others. He realized earlier than I did how unequal were the chances — theirs and ours. He lectured me on the concept of the calculated risk. He would point out to me the Jewish informers working in our battalion. I do not know how he recognized them — they were so damn cautious. And he taught me how to work to save energy and have the work appear done. And I still had in mind that Danny, whom Aunt Paula tearfully begged to take one more piece of chicken, and of the little prince who ordered the dark meat removed from his plate. It was only three years ago, not thirty, or thirteen." Daniel's voice broke. He got up, took from the wardrobe a bottle of vodka and two shot glasses, filled them, and passed one to Elli.

Elli gulped it, rinsed it down with a cup of water, and pointed to her empty glass. Daniel filled it again. For a moment she looked at the transparent liquid in her glass, then slowly raised it to her mouth, leaned back, drained the glass, and started to talk. When she finished, there was an uneasy silence in the room, until she said, "I am ready for another drink, Daniel."

Daniel fixed two drinks. He put some bread and a piece of cheese on the table, but neither touched it. He looked at her with a strange expression on his face.

"Who was that man in the Umschlagplatz?" he asked. "Why did he get you out?"

She was slowly sipping her drink. "I do not know," she said. He tried to smile. "Maybe, you seduced him, Elli?"

"I do not think I am in a mood for jokes right now." she said grimly. "And if that's your reaction to Danny's . . ."

"Don't be silly," he interrupted her. "Did you expect me to cry? I wouldn't know whom to mourn first, Danny, or you, or me. He was very lucky. Not many of us can look forward to dying a soldier's death. He was killed in action. And we? They don't even hunt us down anymore; you can hunt for big game, but not for small-fry. We are exterminated like rats, and what I hate most is that kind of death. I envy Danny; I do hope to God there was enough time for him to realize he died victorious."

After a pause Daniel added, "Not in the process of delousing." He made several turns around the table and then sat next to Elli on the bed. "Don't you think," he said, "our life in the ghetto was far less humiliating than hiding in holes, eluding daylight, coming out in darkness, trembling at every knock at the door, knowing that constant fear, that endless waiting till they get you?" Receiving no answer, he went on, "It is too early for you to understand. There we were kept in a monstrous zoo. There was hunger, misery, sickness. But we were on our own. We did not have to hide, to pretend; we were ourselves. The danger was not immediate, not present every second, in every cell of your flesh. By putting us behind these walls, they humiliated themselves; by forcing us out into this omnipresent trap, they have humiliated us. And have also thrown a bone to the Poles who readily grabbed it."

She rose from the bed, angry. "Come on, Daniel, don't be absurd. They liquidated the ghetto to finish with us, not to drag the Poles into it. What you imply is not only unfair, it's perfectly crazy."

"That's what you think, baby. Before the Germans started 'Mein-Juden-Kampf' they knew they'd get assistance here without asking for it. And that is what has actually happened."

"Daniel, you are mad." Elli was desperate. "Why don't you think about Poles who have helped us? Felix, and Antoni, and Doctor Darski, and his mother in Lublin and Olszewski, and Mrs. Czemera. I am sure there are many like them, at least as many as those who would not help."

"Try to understand, Elli." His tone was that of an adult talking to a backward child. "The problem is not with those who will not help us. The problem is with those who help the Germans. Oh God, if we had only to fear the Germans . . . There certainly are many decent people, though less than you think. If the rest would just stay indifferent, see, that's what I mean. Indifferent. You probably realize the Germans can't very well tell a Jew from a Pole, unless it's a Jew in Hasidic robes. But the Poles can, even if the Jew makes every effort to obliterate the damnable stigma, to create a more welcome Slavic image of himself." He looked at her. "For whose sake did you cut your hair? For whose sake do women dye their hair and men, their eyebrows? Why did my father grow a moustache? It is not because of the Germans, Elli."

"Look here, Daniel," said Elli. Her anger was gone. She really wanted him to understand how wrong he was. "You are bitter and that's why you are being unfair. Why should you expect Poles to risk their lives to help us? I mean all Poles. You are blaming a nation for the prejudices of a handful of blockheads. This could happen everywhere . . ."

He interrupted her with passion. "I do not know what's happening everywhere. I know what's happening here. And that is what I am talking about. Why am I afraid to go out in daytime? Because of a 'handful' of blockheads? Why the wild chase after Polish documents for you? Because as a Jew you'd get shelter for a pile of money only, not for any other reason."

He stopped, sipped a little vodka, and said more calmly, "You asked me why I should expect Poles to risk their lives for us? You are right; I should not. But perhaps you can tell me why they are willing to risk it for money? For huge amounts of money. Mrs. Borek told me once her son takes bread to the prisoners in Majdanek. What she does not know and I do — because he himself told me — is that he trades it for gold."

"It is a matter of values, Daniel," said Elli. "You can't expect all people to have the same set of values. For one it is religion; for another, his ethics and conscience; for the third, money. One would help you because he considers it a duty; another, because he wants money."

"You mean everybody helps us, but for different reasons, is that so?" His eyes were dark with anger.

"No, Daniel, I don't . . . I know there are some who do not help at all. But I still can't see why you blame them . . ."

"Because I am so afraid of them, I guess," he said quietly.

"Exactly." Elli grew impatient. "That's why you're being unfair. Let me tell you that the first informer who stopped me when I left the ghetto was a Jew."

"Did I ever claim that Jews are better than Poles?" he said dryly. "I think they are worse. I'll go further and say that I don't give a damn for justifying them by the 'abnormal situation,' the 'instinct of self-preservation,' 'the pressures of danger,' and all that crap. We all live in an abnormal situation, which does not mean that we are all rascals. We all have a right to live, to fight for life, but not over the dead bodies of our own people. There are degenerates in every nation, I know that. I just did not realize there were so many among us."

He lit a cigarette, an obvious sign of his excitement because he smoked very rarely. "Jews making fortunes in the ghetto, Jews doing business with Germans, trading Jewish slaves, enjoying themselves in restaurants and clubs, serving in the police force side-by-side with Germans and Poles, working in the Judenrat, created to show that Jews themselves destroy Jews. I wonder," he was almost beyond speech, "if throughout Jewish history such an organized betrayal ever took place. And believe me," he turned to her, "nobody is to be blamed as much for it as we ourselves. They could not get the Poles to collaborate in any official way, but they got us."

"So there is no hope for us," said Elli mockingly. "Poles betray Jews; Jews betray Jews; the only honest and trustworthy people left are the Germans because they were kind enough to notify us in advance that they are going to destroy us and are merely pursuing their goal."

"You may laugh, but yes. I think that they are honest, if this word can be applied to monstrosity. I cannot think of a better one right now. It's not their fault that we, the whole world, did not believe they would do what they said they would. It is ours. It's not their fault they found willing collaborators in this country. It is ours. I do not know of any other statesman who informed the world ahead of time in detail, in writing, and in deed, what he was going to do. Perhaps my memory fails me, but what I remember from history is that leaders usually use all kinds of lies, traps, and shibboleths to delude those whom they intend to destroy. This one did not. Would you say that was dishonest? Did he declare his love for Jews and Poles? Did he conspire with Jews as Jews conspire with Germans? And I'll tell you more . . ."

"Shut up, Daniel," she cried. "Shut up, for heaven's sake! That will do. I do not want to hear any more. You are sick. You are obsessed by Jewish guilt, and soon you'll repeat after him 'Die Juden sind das Unglück der Welt.' You have no right to judge people by human standards in an inhuman time. All of them — Jews, Poles, whoever — could live out their lives, and never do anything wrong, if not for what had happened to them. Who is to blame for it? A few days before I left the ghetto I saw a woman devouring a chunk of meat. People said it was her dead baby. I do not know if that was true, but even if it were who'd blame her? Would she do it if not driven to the bottom of misery? Not human misery; the word *human* is not relevant there anymore. Who is responsible for what she has done? Who is responsible for that hell of vice and evil? Jews? Poles? The world? No one but the Germans. They kill us; okay, that's their goddamn right. But before they kill they amuse themselves immensely with little ingenious tricks that are worse than the most cruel death. We die a thousand deaths before the physical act takes place and what they really enjoy are the preliminaries not the final effect. To call them merely murderers would be flattering. They exist on human suffering. Leeches live on blood, jackals on carcasses, Germans on man's agony. And let me tell you, Daniel, I would not mind seeing every one of them eating the corpses of their children, living on the dust and ashes of their own making until the end of their natural lives." She gulped down the rest of vodka from her glass. "And do you know what I fear most? That I may not live long enough to enjoy the sweet taste of vengeance."

*

March 18, 1940

I finished reading Romain Rolland's Jean-Christophe. *Was struck with his remarks about Jewish women. Judith was the first intelligent woman Jean-Christophe met. The impression she made on him! Then, in Paris, anti-Semitism upset all his ideas about France; just like mine about Germany. "They hated all Jews, and called those whom they hated Jews." I did not realize there was anti-Semitism in France, save for the Dreyfus Affaire. After dinner we talked about this book, and I read aloud: "The Jews are quite erroneously reproached with not belonging to any nation and with forming from one end of Europe to the other a homogeneous people impervious to the influence of the different races with which they have pitched their tents. In reality there is no race which more easily takes on the impress of the country through which it passes; and if there are many characteristics in common between a French Jew and a German Jew, there are many more characteristics derived from their new country, of which with incredible rapidity they assimilate the habits of mind; more the habits than the mind, indeed. But habit, which is a second nature to all men, is in most of them all the nature that they have, and the result is that the majority of the autochthonous citizens of any country have very little right to reproach the Jews the lack of profound and reasonable national feeling of which they themselves possess nothing at all."*

The Old Man said that it's a very touchy point whether or not Jews belong. They do and they don't, like the man who had and didn't have a dog. When praised for the dog's qualities, he agreed the dog was his; when scorned for the dog's misbehavior, he denied ever having one. The Jews belong, the Old Man said, when they are accepted; they don't when they are not. Nor does assimilation help them very much once they are rejected, neither do their national or other feelings. Their patriotism is held against them as often as their separatism is, and at one time or another like a fish kept too long in the kitchen or an unwanted guest they start to stink; they are found to contaminate the very atmosphere they formerly were praised for improving.

March 21, 1940

The first day of spring. I went for a long walk with the Old Man. I like so much to walk with him but now he'd seldom let me go with him. People in the streets sometimes stop and stare at him — a distinguished man, tall as a steeple, impeccably dressed; they look at him with curiosity but not in an unfriendly way. On our way back home a boy, perhaps twelve or thirteen, called after him, "King David, King David." I wasn't even angry, rather amused. The Old Man said he wasn't sure King David would approve of this comparison. "He was a vain man," he smiled.

Next day Maria took Elli to a small village near Kraśnik to a miller whose name was Konstanty Chmiel.

4

Konstanty Chmiel owned one of the biggest flour mills in the district. The two-story, solid brick house, built shortly before the war, was spacious and well furnished, but the family life was concentrated in the huge kitchen, redolent with bread and cabbage. Mrs. Chmiel was a silent, pleasant woman, busy with the big household, a large hothouse, and a small girl whom the couple had recently adopted. Their own son was past twenty; a student of history at the Catholic University in Lublin before the war, he still lived there, occasionally visiting his parents. Mr. Chmiel was a middle-aged, middle-sized man, outspoken and authoritative. He had a cataract on his left eye and limped a little.

Elli met him briefly on the night they arrived. He helped Maria and her out of the coach which he had sent to the station, shook hands with Maria, and then cast a brief look at Elli with his good eye. "So, this is the girl," he said. "All right. Do come in. Welcome home." Maria embraced his wife with whom she was evidently on friendly terms, offered the little girl a chocolate bar, had hot tea and two vodkas with the miller, hastily talked business with him, and was driven back to the station to catch

the next train to Lublin. Maria told Elli that it was highly improbable she would be asked questions in this house; they had
never asked her any, and when she had requested Chmiel to give
shelter to her late friend's daughter he simply said to bring her.
In case she was asked her last name, Elli was instructed to say it
was Barska. She had not even a slip of paper to prove it.

Before the young maidservant took Elli to her room, Mrs.
Chmiel told her to come for breakfast at half-past seven. When
the maid left, Elli sat heavily down on her bed. She was trembling inside remembering Michael's instructions, convinced it was
hopeless for her to try to follow them. Maria's conduct (it was
now "Maria" even in her thoughts), the apparent ease she
showed in her relations with these people, the unquestionable
credulity and regard they had for her — all left Elli with a deep
sense of her own helplessness and inevitable failure. She looked
blankly at the huge gold-framed picture of the Blessed Virgin
Mary hanging on the opposite wall, then at the crucified Christ
right over her bed. The ruby-colored blood was dripping from
His nailed feet and hands, flowing down His chalk-white face
from under the crown of thorns. She still could hear Mrs. Chmiel
saying as she kissed Maria goodbye, "May the Blessed Virgin
Mary be with you," and Maria's "The Lord be with you." She
opened her book of prayers and looked at the small printed words
— her new religion. She sat, the book in her hand, unhappy,
downhearted, on the verge of tears. How could Maria have left
her alone, ignorant, helpless, among these people and these pictures? Why could she not have stayed in Lublin and waited there
for the documents? True, Mrs. Borek was already annoyed that
Daniel almost never left the house; she was made to understand
that he had to answer phone calls and wait on customers. Elli
had to stay home, it was said, because of a sprained ankle. But
how long could one stay home on account of a sprained ankle?
She had removed the bandage just before leaving for the station.

Well, she had to go, but how would she face these people? Would they really ask her no questions? What if they did? She knew, of course, that she had been born in Poznań, that her father was a POW and her mother had recently died, that she had no siblings, no family at all, and had seen Maria only once before her mother died. Maria had brought her here from Warsaw. She had never been in Maria's house and did not know where she lived.

All that, Maria said, might be necessary only in case Elli were confronted with some investigation by a third party. She made it clear that all kinds of things might happen which were beyond the control of Elli's hosts; a domestic might report her, a worker from the mill, or somebody met by chance in the house or in the village; finally, the house might be raided by Germans looking for runaways from the ghettos recently liquidated in the district or for partisans. Visualizing the dangers piled over her head, Elli felt more and more ill at ease. She heard, "Ihr Ausweis, bitte!" But then all became blank. For she had no reply, no identification card. What would she say? That she lost it? Forgot it? Where? At home? Where was her home? She fell on her knees and started to say the Prayer for the Dead.

The maid, who in the morning brought a pail of warm water for Elli to wash, found her kneeling, murmuring litanies in her sleep. She said loudly, "Praised be Jesus Christ." Elli, half-conscious, answered, "Amen."

The breakfast had already been served when she came down. There were only two settings on the table, one in front of Mr. Chmiel, who briefly returned her "good morning" and pointed her to the other one. His wife was busy at the huge kitchen stove. There was fat sausage, ham, and smoked bacon on the table, butter, a loaf of bread, and white rolls. In the middle stood a bottle of cherry-colored liquid. Elli timidly sat down but did not start to eat until Mr. Chmiel said, "Are you not hungry? I was told there is a food shortage in Warsaw. It is Warsaw you come from, isn't it? So don't miss your chance. Here you can eat to your heart's content. We have enough food, thank God."

She took a piece of bread and, buttering it, wondered why he had asked her if she had come from Warsaw? He had been told by Maria that she did. Did he have any suspicions? She should certainly have said, "Praised be Jesus Christ," when she entered the kitchen. Meanwhile, Mrs. Chmiel served a dish of hot sausages and fried potatoes and went back to the oven.

"I like to have a hearty meal in the morning," continued Mr. Chmiel. "You townsfolk are not used to it, I know." He looked at her with his one eye. "You look starved," he decided. "And you need lots of fresh air."

Her heart stopped. He knew. It was obvious. Only the runaways from ghettos looked starved and pale. But how had he discovered? When?

"Here, na zdrowie." He filled two shot glasses with the cherry-colored liquid and passed one to her.

Without a moment's hesitation she leaned back and drained the glass. Fire and flames burned her throat and stomach, and startled tears from her eyes.

"Not used to it, eh?" Mr. Chmiel smiled, obviously amused with her reaction. "It is my own concoction; ninety-six percent alcohol on sour cherries. This one is three years old. It's quite something, isn't it? You'll feel great, just wait a minute till it gets down. I've told you to eat. You can't drink on an empty stomach." And he put a couple of steaming sausages on her plate.

The fire in her died out. She wiped the tears away with the edge of the tablecloth and started to eat.

"Don't think I am a drunk," Mr. Chmiel turned to her. "You

might not yet be used to it, but you'll soon see that a glass or two in the morning makes a hell of a lot of difference during the day." After a while he added, "And that is all I drink during the day, unless I have to."

Elli smiled at him, "Why, I think it's a wonderful idea, Mr. Chmiel. To be honest I never had a drink in the morning, though we drink a lot in Warsaw, you know, it keeps one's spirits up." "You mean *you* drink a lot?" Mr. Chmiel was genuinely surprised. "A young girl like you? Too bad. That's what happens when there is no mother around." What was that? There is no mother around. Her mother was dead, how could she be "around"? Not only had she made a fool of herself bragging about her drinking, thereby confessing contrary to Michael's instructions she needed liquor to bear up, but she had invited Mr. Chmiel's comments in regard to her motherless state. She sat stiff, awaiting a blow. Mr. Chmiel refilled the glasses unmindful of his wife's soft reproach that Elli was too young to keep him company.

"Never mind," he said. "You see, she said she liked it. She'll not get more anyway, and if that's too much for her, let her go to bed after breakfast. She needs a rest, you can see it."

Elli gulped down the second glass. This time the flames just licked her insides. She wolfed down a second helping of sausages and potatoes, and burst out laughing when Mr. Chmiel, somewhat uneasy now, asked her if she was all right.

"Why, of course I am all right, Mr. Chmiel. I never felt better in my life. Don't you worry about me. I can take care of myself." And she fluttered her eyelashes at him.

A little startled, he smiled. "That's fine. Good girl! When I first saw you so pale and unhappy, I thought that's one of those poor war orphans, who'd like to bury herself in a hole, not to see, not to talk to anybody. But you know better than that. Good! War is nothing new for us. We Poles know how to face it.

Let them lick our asses, the dirty swines! They won't break us down! Not as long as we have such brave women as Maria and you, good alike in fair weather and foul." He rose from his seat, took his coat and cap from the hook, and left. Elli helped Mrs. Chmiel to clear the table, but when she offered to help with the dishes, the woman said, "No, Elli. I'll do it myself. You better go and have a rest. He is right; you badly need one. And if you don't feel like it, you don't have to drink at breakfast. My husband won't mind it. He enjoys company and certainly is glad to have you, because I don't drink. But don't do it again if it disagrees with you."

It did not disagree with her. She felt light and at ease until dark. All fears and doubts and suspicions accumulated during the long nights would now dissipate in the morning. But when the day was over they all came back to haunt her. At night she would examine her face for pallor, her eyes for the "sad melancholy" look. She would return to what Mr. Chmiel had said at breakfast and analyze each of his words. She would reconstruct scraps of overheard discussions between maidservants and farmhands. Finally, she would go over every word she herself had uttered during the day, test its meaning, phrasing, and spelling; and sometimes her sing-song tone would ring ominously in her ears and make her hair rise. As long as the alcohol worked she was competent and cheerful; when it evaporated, at dark, fear strangled her.

Why had she ever left her bed in the ghetto when hunger came? Had she stayed there her problems would have been at an end. It now struck her as strange that she had been the only one to be broken by hunger when everybody else in the family went on.

✠ ✠ ✠

First, she had just felt weak, drowsy, had kept sitting silently for hours staring at some distant point. Then she had stopped getting up in the morning. It had seemed to her that every movement, the slightest effort, would drain her of what strength was still left in her. She would lie in her bed, unwashed, unkempt, half-dreaming, struggling against the waves of consciousness. After some time, lying thoughtless had required no effort. At the beginning scraps of pale memories — a tree against a blue sky, her father disappearing at the corner, a new summer dress, Lili skiing, Lili dancing — all that had kept coming back to her over and over again. Then everything faded away. There was no problem any longer of losing strength, of killing thoughts. She ceased to exist. She was just lying still, feeling nothing, empty, relieved.

One day, Lili sat down on her bed and said that the Old Man was asking for her. She told him, she said, that Elli was not feeling well, but he insisted on her getting up and coming to him. "Elli, Elli, you must get up. Elli, listen to me, you must get up."

She had then opened her eyes but had not understood what it was Lili wanted her to do. Whatever it was, she wanted only to be left alone.

Lili put a wet towel over her neck, and holding up her chin, pressed a glass of water to her lips. The water rolled away from the corners of Elli's mouth.

They tried to revive her with brandy. In vain. "Elli, open your eyes. Look at me," Lili cried. "Elli, you must get up, now, Elli, immediately. Do you understand me? Listen to me, the Old Man, you hear me, he said you must get up." "Tell him I can't . . . I can't stand on my feet." "This is not true, Elli, I can't tell him that." "Lili, it's true, I swear." "Elli, you don't eat, you don't wash, you don't talk." Lili spoke rapidly, insistently, afraid that Elli would fall asleep again. "He is right; you must get up. If you'd just let me help to dress you, Elli, please, you'll see you'll be all right again, and tomorrow . . ." Elli couldn't grasp the meaning of Lili's words.

The next two days she had not so much as gone to the toilet. Lili fed her with water sweetened with saccharine, everything else Elli threw up. Once fragments of an argument between the grandfather and Lili reached her from the distance and faded back again.

Next she had remotely smelled something resembling wind and rain and seen Danny standing at her bedside. A small bunch of cornflowers was touching her cheek. She had looked at him, then at the flowers, and felt his hand gently on hers. She started to cry, listlessly, helplessly, and cried herself to sleep. The next morning she got up, washed, dressed and went back to her daily routine.

Then came the day when she had accompanied Daniel to reserve a place in the hospital for Miriam who expected her baby in August. Daniel had to pull her hand to make her turn toward a big white poster fastened to the entrance of the hospital. She had not even realized they were on the spot. She adjusted her glasses and read the poster. Once, then for the second time, then for the third. She looked for Daniel, but he had his back turned toward her. She looked again at the black letters, big and clear against the white background, and felt somebody pushing her. A small crowd had already gathered around them, silent, motionless, all eyes fixed on the poster. In its left corner the date was imprinted: DEN 22 JULI, 1942. It was signed: DER JUDENRAT IN WARSCHAU. In big headline letters it said that all Jews must report by July 22 at 11 A.M. at the assembly point at Stawki Street. Those employed in the Judenrat, in the Jewish police, and in the workshops were exempt. Below, in smaller print, the people were ordered to bring a change of clothing for the trip to labor camps in the East. Scribbled in ink was the amount of bread and marmalade waiting at the Umschlagplatz for those who would report without delay.

The crowd had increased, mute, dumbfounded. She still had before her eyes a louse making its way slowly through the thick gray beard of a man standing next to her. The louse reached the man's lips, but he did not budge, his eyes fixed on the white sheet. She felt Daniel's hand on hers. He steered her out of the crowd. All the way home they passed groups of people, silent, numb, reading the posters, still wet, dripping with glue.

After the noon meal, Elli had closed the door behind Aunt Paula and asked Lili to keep her busy. She was alone in the room with the Old Man. He was reading a book which he put aside when Elli moved her chair next to his. "What is it, Elli?" he asked. "You want to talk to me?"

"Grandfather," she had said then. "It's happened. They have started to liquidate the ghetto." She told him about the posters. "It's clear," he nodded. "That's how it began in other places. First they lure with bread to get rid of the weakest and most hungry; then they get to the rest and run the show to the end."

"What will we do? What will we do?" she had whispered to herself. Everything was finished. There was no way out. The illusionary lull cracked all to pieces. Somewhere at the bottom of her heart she had sometimes feared that this stagnation, this artificial truce, would end one day. Against reason she hoped for a miracle. She saw people around her rot, starve, disappear, but she believed *her* family would survive. Lili laughed at her saying that Elli had a secret arrangement with God concerning *her* family; and ridiculous as Elli knew it was, there was some truth in it. Because they still lived, on the surface of the quicksand indeed but not sucked in, her faith in God grew. Now, she saw He had just lulled her. He had cheated her. Heavy hands were dragging her deeper and deeper; every particle of her body was aching; a grinding machine was smashing her head.

And then she felt an acute, piercing pain in the back of her head, as from an electric shock; for a moment she saw nothing and knew nothing. Then something started to throb inside her head, to tremble, vibrate, quicker, wildly, until the whirl killed her fear.

When, calm and cool, she opened her eyes she had seen the Old Man's eyes fixed upon her and heard his voice. "What did you say, Elli?"

"Well, Grandfather, I said we must do something. First of all about you and Noemi, the aunts, and this happy paragon of motherhood, Miriam, and then about the rest of us." She had kept her voice even, dispassionate. "I mean, we must do something to get out of here."

"I'd rather stay with you," he glanced at her, "as long as you'll stay. You take care of me."

She jumped to her feet then, saluted him, two fingers at her forehead. "Your wish is an order, sir. I have some doubts, however, if this particular wish is executable. You know, Aunt Paula won't leave without you."

"Perhaps you better tell me your whole plan, Elli, and then we'll discuss it," the Old Man said quietly. "You seem to have it all set. When did you have time to work out the details? I thought it all surprised you. Or, perhaps you've your own intelligence network here?"

"Oh, sure, Grandfather," she grinned. "And it's as efficient as clockwork." Her eyes fixed on the table, she said, "Look, dear, I really have nothing set, but I'm going to call my mother as soon as I have your permission. I'm going to tell her what has happened and ask her to arrange, first of all, for the five of you to leave as soon as possible. Can I do it now, Grandfather?" She remembered how anxiously she waited for his reply.

He bent over her and kissed her forehead. "No, Elli, you cannot. It has all been arranged with your mother, though not exactly as you had planned it."

"What do you mean, Grandfather? What is arranged? By whom? When?"

"Sit down, Elli, let me explain everything." He waited for her to sit down. "You see, I also have my intelligence sources. And mine are more efficient, I daresay. I talked it over with your mother back in June. It was no surprise to her. This ghetto is not the first to be liquidated. You remember the blank Kennkarte the policeman found on her at the Central Station? That was when she first went in for some Aryan documents. She and Michael knew the situation. They see more people and places than we do, we're sort of cut off from the outer world. I told her then that I presumed that the Germans would start the successive 'resettlement' here in summer, to have it all cleared by winter. Winter's a hard time for them; they must cut all superfluous expenditures. Do you realize how much it takes to supply this quarter? Everything they spend here is pure waste. Besides," he continued monotonously, "they proclaimed a total solution to the Jewish problem. Maintaining ghettos is only a partial solution. Liquidating them is the answer. They must keep things going, their Führer must prove he is serious — to his people and to the whole world. You get what I mean, Elli?" She did not, but nodded anyway.

"I have asked your mother to make arrangements to get us out of here. Last week when I talked to her, she said that it's going to be very difficult. They have no cash, and without it not much can be done. She expected to borrow some money, and I believe by now she has it."

"Oh, Grandfather," how overwhelmed she had been, "I've known all my life that you are the wisest, best, and most adorable man in the world." How silly she was with that plan of hers, with that terrible "unexpected" news. He had again foreseen everything to save the whole family. God had not let her down.

"The only thing to do, Elli," she still could see his eyes fixed on her and hear the tone of his voice which filled her with anxiety, "is to fix a sort of timetable, and clear it with your mother. Will you do it for me?"

"Won't you talk to her, Grandfather?" That look of his made her feel uneasy.

"No." He was tapping the silver cigarette case. He then opened it, took out a cigarette, lit it, and inhaled deeply. When he spoke again, his voice was firm, eyes cold. "The first to go is Noemi. Then the men, Daniel, David, Danny, and Nathan. Then Miriam, Lili, Rachel, and you."

"And then?"

"That's all."

His face was white, blood-drained, his eyes stern, mouth tight as a weapon. She felt a surge of relentless fear overcoming her, her heart thumped, her stomach churned. She still did not believe it; she must have misunderstood him, missed something he said; there was no other explanation for that "that's all." She waited.

After an endless silence he had taken her cold hand in his big palms. "I know how you feel, Elli," he said. "I'd give the rest of my life to spare you this experience. But my life isn't worth a damn, and I can spare you nothing. You must be strong."

As in a silent film she had seen his lips moving as he mouthed words and sentences, but she did not hear a single word. *You must be strong, you must be strong, you must be strong,* pounded in her head. She wanted to interrupt him, to scream, "I'm not strong, please, stop it, stop it, I'm not strong, why should I be strong, please, don't say it again, I'm not, I'm not . . ." Then, she heard him again, and every word he said sunk deep inside her.

"Do you remember, Elli, when you were a small girl, I told you a story about the eternal wandering Jew? I know, it sounded then like a fairy tale, once upon a time . . . In your childish imagination you perhaps saw an old, hunchback Jew, in Hasidic robes, with a long beard, leaning upon a stick, a bundle in his hand, wandering through wilderness. Well, the wandering Jew exists. He is real. There is no end to his wanderings, nor is there an end to the wilderness. He still must be ready to pick up his stick and bundle and go. People chase him, throw stones at him, but he keeps going. In the past people would bait him with dogs. Now dogs are replaced by men; much more dangerous. Naturally, his chances are reduced. He must be young and strong to make his way, else they will destroy him. This is why I've made this choice. Moreover, there is a limit to human endurance, and naturally it is lower for older people. Those who have the slightest chance must not be dragged down by those who, beyond any reasonable doubt, have none. Do you follow me, Elli?"

Before she could scream her protest he had continued. "I want you to understand me; not just obey because I've the last word here. I want you to understand because my decision will stay with you for the rest of your life. It's not an easy decision. But there are no easy answers to difficult questions. I'm not suicidal, Elli. I enjoy living, I love life, every single day of it and I won't easily give up. Back in Pabianice, when the war broke out, I realized that it was my duty to live. For years, with all my children married and settled, I had considered my responsibilities completed. But war changed all that. I couldn't pick up my marbles and go home. You see, we never accumulated wealth in this family, we accumulated some experience and I thought that might be worth saving. I cannot save it. You can, and Lili, and Daniel, and David, and Danny, and Noemi. Perhaps it's just a crazy idea of an old conceited fellow; perhaps it's what's called the struggle for the continuation of the species. I don't know. But I'm vain enough to want to leave something behind me."

She shuddered as his voice now came back to her. "I sometimes wonder whether I'd like to live after this war is over." He was slowly stroking his beard. "It's funny—but I don't think I would. Not that I'd be too tired or too old. Rather, I'd be too bored. I can envisage now the endless deliberations about who is guilty, the measuring and weighing of the dimensions of complicity, tons of paper being printed, millions of words being said, only to conclude that the really guilty ones are the victims; for without them the problem of guilt would never arise. It's an outworn trick, disgusting, boring. You see, Elli," he had observed her closely, and her eyes flashing by turn with reproach, indignation, disagreement did not escape him for a single instant, "we stubbornly refuse to admit that wars do not make people any better; wars do not teach them any 'lessons.' If they do, they are in hatred not in love. Cruelty breeds cruelty as hatred breeds hatred not love, compassion, understanding. Still there is an unjustified expectation that *this* war will be the one that'll change the world. None will. Just or unjust, aggressive, defensive, small or big, it kills conscience in man."

The familiar mischievous twinkle sparkled in his eye and his voice lost its gripping quality, as he resumed. "I like an easy life, a pleasant life, and I can't see that life is going to be either in the future. Too much has already happened. It's not that I'm going to shorten my days," he looked reassuringly at her. "I just want to explain to you that I'm not particularly interested in rehashing the old stuff about crime and punishment, guilt and innocence, neither am I interested in pretending that the world can be better: let's just kill several million bad guys. No, no, I'm fed up." He twisted his face. "I've had it. But you might find it amusing, exciting to transform the world and you have the kind of holy revulsion necessary for a crusader. No, no, I don't mean that," he laughed, seeing her shock. "I was talking about those who want to reform the world. Though much against the will of the people usually. But since I always believed that one who doesn't want to reform it at twenty is a zero and one who still wants to do it at forty is a fool, you have my blessing to go on and improve the world. Will you, Elli?"

She had answered then, dully, "Yes, I will, Grandfather," just to make him stop. She wanted to scream in his face that he was no God and no Nazi to condemn people to death. She opened her mouth, but he wouldn't let her speak. "With Aunt Paula's deafness and Aunt Adela's conspicuous looks," he went on quietly, "it's a lost game. We cannot expect your mother to perform miracles, can we, Elli?"

A click, a throb, a whirl: the protective mechanism in her head worked again. "No, we cannot, Grandfather," she answered coldly.

"You will call your mother tomorrow." His voice had the familiar commanding quality. "You will tell her I want you all to leave within a month. Make it clear that a month is all I can give her. Ask her when Noemi can leave, and in what order she wants the rest of you to come. Be sure to follow my orders strictly."

"Grandfather." She remembered herself overcoming the nauseous feeling in her stomach, and her reluctance to talk to this man who caused it. "Grandfather, I'd like to go and see Eryk. He has good connections in the Judenrat. Perhaps he can get certificates of employment in the shops for you and the aunts. He got them for Aunt Wilhelmina and Rita. I'll go and ask him to get them for you." She was decided to go to Rita's fiancé, regardless of the Old Man's response.

"You are most welcome to go," he smiled. "I appreciate your concern. Moreover, Eryk might succeed in making clear to you what I vainly tried. He is better equipped to do it, I guess. Yes, Elli, do go to him."

She had gone the next day. The Judenrat, the Wailing Wall

of the ghetto, always black with flapping tailcoats, always ringing with lamentation, curses, threats, was entirely different that
day. Men and women, pulling hair from their heads, hitting
them against the walls, seized by fits of rage, hysteria, despair,
were a common thing here; nobody paid any attention to them.
No one but the poorest of the poor, the most ignorant of the
ignorant, came here for help. That day the place was crowded
with people different in looks and in behavior; they were silent,
solemn, expectant.

Eryk Roth was sitting behind a desk piled with papers, violently arguing with a balding man opposite him whom he
addressed as doctor. Eryk had a lean, intelligent, bespectacled
face, with shrewd eyes that swam with myopia. His wavy black
hair was thinning at the crown, making him look much older
than his twenty-two years. The clean-shaven face was tinged
with small black dots; it was not easy to keep it that smooth.
His mouth was big and full, with a small notch in the middle of
the lower lip. He was tall, slightly stooped. His nervous well-
groomed hands carried the burden of the conversation. "First,
second, third," — as usual he was checking off his remarks with
the right hand on the fingers of the left, as if no one could catch
up with him unless coached. His arguments — concerning the
recent deportation order — were neatly marshaled, and when he
pinned down his opponent with the final "fifth," the man got
up and, without a word, left.

Eryk had motioned her then to the vacant chair. "I vaguely
felt that you'd pay me a visit," he said, smiling. " 'Forty days,
and Ninevah shall be overthrown,' eh?" He was mildly examining her as his fingers played with a pencil and his long legs swung
to and fro. "Yes, indeed," she said. "Any more quotations?
What about 'a time to love'?"

"Did you come here to exchange views on the wisdom of our
ancestors?" he asked politely. "If that is the case, I'm profoundly

sorry, but I am very busy today. I'd be delighted, however, to continue this edifying conversation some other time. I regret to say that you have chosen the wrong time and the wrong place." He rose from the chair.

Her face began to burn, her lips to tremble, but she would rather have died than cry in front of him. "You know perfectly well why I have come here." She remembered the effort she made to get these words out.

"You think I do? You might be right. You are a smart girl." He sat down again and started to read a paper that he took from the pile. Dry stubbornness covered his face; his mouth was taut, his cheekbones moving. She was all tense, when she said in the offhand tone he imposed, "Don't you think something could be done before the 'city shall be overthrown'?"

From behind the paper he drawled, "Lots of things could be done." He adjusted his glasses and took another paper from the pile.

"For instance?"

He signed the paper, put it on a second pile, and started again to play with the pencil. "For instance, finding a hiding place on the Aryan side."

"For twelve people?"

"I didn't say that. You said it."

"So, what else?"

"Buy Aryan documents."

"For twelve people?"

"Again the same nonsense. No! Not for twelve! For one, for two, for three."

"What do you mean?"

"I mean it depends on your means."

"You know that we have no money."

"You expect me to give it to you?"

"And even if some of us get out, what about the rest?"

"You want me to tell you?"

"Go ahead."

"Before winter they'll be moved to labor camps in the East."

"You mean the ghetto will be liquidated?"

"I didn't say that."

"No! You even denied it to the man who was just here."

"Indeed."

"But you know the truth."

"You overestimate me."

"No, Eryk, I don't. But have it your way. Who'll be sent to these labor camps?"

"The unproductive element. People without Arbeitsamt Karte."

"Eryk, I need three such certificates."

"Only three? Fine. For whom?"

"For Grandfather, for Aunt Paula, and for Aunt Adela."

He burst out laughing. "Have you lost your mind? You think you can fool them in such an idiotic way? The basic mistake of you people here is that you underestimate them; you consider them fools. To fight your enemy you must give him due credit."

"Nobody is going to fight anybody. And we both know that certain people get along with these documents."

"Look here, Elli." His voice lost its sarcastic undertone, it was serious and friendly. "I really can't do a thing. You have no idea what's now going on here. And obviously I don't have the money to buy you one, or two, or ten certificates."

"But you have the right connections." She could not control her voice any longer; it became sharp with aggression. She knew that Eryk was a close friend of one of the Judenrat's high officials deported—as Eryk himself had been—from Germany to Poland.

Eryk took his glasses off and started to clean them with an impeccable white handkerchief, blinking his myopic eyes. Then he carefully refitted the spectacles, neatly folded the handkerchief, put it back in his pocket, and, watching her closely, said, "Listen, Elli. You said that there is 'a time to love.' This time is different. It is 'a time to kill.' You are too young to understand, but you must accept that in a time like this everybody is concerned only with himself. To put it plainly, everybody wants to save his own skin. You save yours. This is the best piece of advice you ever heard in your life. When we meet again . . ." Slamming the door, she heard, ". . . you will thank me for it."

After Eryk only one man remained—Professor Frude. She had had him in the back of her mind since she talked to the Old Man, but she felt her throat constrict at the very thought of facing him. Professor Frude was considered omnipotent in the ghetto. A former professor of law at Warsaw University, an active member of many Jewish organizations, he enjoyed a special status with the Germans, but nobody quite knew why. He held no official post, but was known to be leaving the ghetto and even traveling abroad. Some people suspected him of collaboration; others, of close ties with some officials in Berlin from the time he had studied and lectured in Germany. Still others maintained that he was related to a top German government man. The professor's friendship with her father dated back to the German university days. She had not seen him for many years, but vaguely remembered that what she liked most about him was his appearance, which strongly resembled her father's. Several times she heard people talking about him, always in the same terms: he was powerful, but had categorically refused to use his influence when asked for help.

He lived alone with an old maidservant, whom he had been allowed to bring to the ghetto, in the house on Chłodna Street reserved for the top officials of the Judenrat and the Jewish police force. She went there.

The maid admitted her to the professor's studio. The walls of the room were lined with shelves of books. Books were everywhere; on the desk, on a huge table standing in the middle of the room, on chairs, on the carpet, piled on the floor against the walls. Professor Frude was sitting in a rocking chair, his head propped high against a leather pillow. Lightly rocking, he was reading a book. Elli was standing in the door, unable to move, to utter a word. Finally, he noticed her, and asked in a kind, pleasant voice, "You want to talk to me?" She nodded. He motioned her to a chair next to his, and put the book aside. He had the good-natured, tired, slightly prominent deep brown eyes of an old, wise, compassionate Jew, eyes that inspired confidence and safety. From behind the horn-rimmed spectacles they looked at her with attention and understanding. She trembled all over seeing this face, seeing her father.

"Will you have a cigarette?" he asked gently.

She accepted with gratitude.

When she lit the cigarette, he asked, "What can I do for you?"

Scarcely audible, she told him who she was and presented her request: three certificates.

He kept looking at her, with that profound friendly understanding, and said softly, "I am sorry. I wish I could be of some assistance. But this is not my field. I can offer you no certificate, no advice." She left.

Later that afternoon, she remembered, she had found the Old Man sitting alone, playing solitaire. She told him that Emmi was all set. "What about the others?" he asked, not lifting his head from the cards spread on the table.

"I did not ask her."

"Why?"

"Grandfather, please, listen to me. Just listen to me, please."

"Yes," he said dryly.

"I do not want to leave. I want to stay here."

"Because Eryk refused to help?"

"No, Grandfather. I just think my place is here. I belong

here. I do not want to go. And I think that you should ask the others if they want to leave. I think it's their decision . . ." She had on the tip of her tongue "not yours," but courage failed her.

"That's what you think." His face reddened as he kept his blue watery eyes pinned on her. "I could simply tell you not to meddle, but I'll try to explain once more.

"I overestimated you. You didn't understand a damn thing I told you. You don't want to leave because the three of us must stay here. Right?" She nodded, not to argue. "I told you why we must stay, right?" Again, she nodded. He said, a little more calmly, "Do you think I know who'll lose? Whether the one who'll stay or the one who'll leave? No! I do not know. It's a gamble. I'm not going to condemn or save anybody if only because there's no way of knowing where's life and where's death.

"Even if my decision saves your life, Elli, I'm not sure you'll be grateful to me. Perhaps you've already observed that it's much easier to die than to live. I'm doing nobody a favor demanding that you leave the ghetto." He rubbed his forehead as if hesitating whether to go on.

"It's damn true," he spelled out with obvious reluctance, "that the only time Poles stop fighting each other is in order to beat a Jew. Do you know that this land was at one time considered a haven for Jews?" He was almost shouting. His eyes were bulging in his red, sweating face while he spat out the wrathful words. The yellowish skin on his temples seemed about to crack over the swollen veins. "That Jews from England, Spain, France found shelter here? But these countries at least abandoned medieval practices while here Jews continue to be destroyed with the zeal and fanaticism of the Crusaders." He lowered his head. "There are brief periods of peace, then they hear The Voice and the old Lied starts again. This wall has shut us out from the life of our fellow Poles; but it has also protected us from them."

The Old Man lit a cigarette, and went on hoarsely, "So, why do you think it's a special grace to live among them? Why do you refuse to see the truth? To stay here is to choose the path of least resistance. I don't expect any of my grandchildren to chose it. I don't expect them to surrender to the dangerous conviction that no one is in control of his own destiny; that our destiny is suffering. It is not! Do you hear me, it is not!" He banged on the table. "Wisdom does not come from suffering. There is no such law laid down either by God or by man." Then his anger subsided. "There are better ways than martyrdom to preserve one's identity. This ridiculous endurance is a slave's religion. Who will help men who accept damnation as part of their religion or fate? No one. People despise them and the gods do too."

He had moved over to the window, mopped his head, and, leaning heavily against the cracked wooden frame, turned to her. "Now, this Eryk of yours. Didn't he tell you he is not 'his brother's keeper'? Didn't he advise you against becoming one yourself? Regardless of how he refused, you shouldn't blame him. He is not a Cain; he simply shares the heritage. He is not an exception; he is the rule." His words came out evenly, monotonously. "You should know that the beginning of wisdom is to understand how little concerned with someone else's life other men are and how desperately preoccupied with their own. Once you accept this you'll save yourself many disappointments. You must learn to cope with your suffering alone. Suffering is the single property you own all by yourself; otherwise you'll always find partners."

He returned to the table and said calmly, "Do you see now why I am not doing you a favor? And why you have to go?"

"I will go, Grandfather."

"Don't forget what you've seen here. Never."

"I will not. Never. I promise."

She still could see herself standing then, facing this man who was forcing this promise — tantamount to treason — from her. She wanted to take it back the minute she uttered it but instead, during the next phone conversation with her mother, Elli told her in what order the Old Man wanted them to leave.

The days had passed, one after another. The news about the liquidation had spread quickly. People from the Aryan side came in flocks to buy what the residents had to sell. They were mostly workers in the factories located in the ghetto, streetcar drivers, policemen. The prices they offered depended on the decency and compassion of the buyer. For the Jews the only thing of value was ready cash. It could bribe a guard, buy a certificate, or, on the road, a drink of water. Things were useless; they could not be taken along, either to the train or to the Aryan side.

Three days after Ruth sent a message that two more people could leave the ghetto Rachel brought a young couple home. They were engaged to be married and the young man wanted to buy his fiancée some clothes. The woman tried on, one by one, dresses, coats, skirts piled on the table. When the choice was made, the man took out his wallet, and then the Old Man said, "You have there your pass, don't you?"

"Yes," said the man. "It's my permit to enter the ghetto. I work here in a factory, and she does too." He pointed toward the woman.

"If I offered you the clothes the young lady picked out and some more for you, would you let me have that pass?"

Elli couldn't help smiling at the remembrance of the man's gaping mouth.

"What would *you* do with it, sir? There is a photo in it," he finally blurted.

The Old Man smiled. "Right you are. I do not need it for myself. And, as a matter of fact, I would like to have your bride's pass too. Not for myself either."

The man looked at the four girls standing around the table, then at the four young men dumbly watching the whole scene.

"But you have here a whole bunch of people. How can they get out on one pass or two?"

"That's what we have to talk over," said the Old Man. "If you are willing to help."

The man looked at the woman; she looked at him. Then she drew him aside; they whispered for a few minutes, and the man said, "It's a big risk, you know that. I won't do it for a couple of rags. If you can give me cash or gold each time they use my pass or hers — we can talk about it."

The Old Man smiled again. "I do not have money or gold. But I do have a house, two factories, and land. You can have all that for your passes and sell it as soon as the war is over. You will be a rich man."

The man was clearly dazzled. "We won't keep the passes forever," continued the Old Man. "They will all leave within a month or so. We'll set a schedule and on the agreed day you will bring here one pass, which you'll get back on the Aryan side. Once in a while you can leave the ghetto without a pass; you surely have done it before and know the ways."

"Oh, that is simple," said the man. "I can take a pass from a night-shift worker, and so can she. Or I can tell my foreman that I left my pass at home, and for a little something he'll give me a oneway pass. I sure can manage that, but . . ." He did not quite know how to frame his words. ". . . but . . . I don't know . . ."

"What is it you do not know?" interrupted the Old Man impatiently. "Go ahead, tell me. I want you to have everything clear."

The man breathed deeply. "And what if one of these . . ." He looked around embarrassed. Again the Old Man smiled, but his fingers were tapping the cigarette case.

"You mean, if any of them survive? Yes? That's what you mean?"

The man looked relieved. "Yes, sir," he nodded.

"You are afraid they might take back what I promised you, aren't you?" The man nodded again. "Yes, sir, that's what I mean."

The Old Man got up from his armchair and approached the man. "Look here, young fellow," he said. "I am the sole owner of this property. I am in full possession of my faculties. I will sign over to you everything I mentioned. You will get a written document, signed by two witnesses, and nobody can ever contest my will. Besides, you can believe it or not, in this family a word is a word."

The man did not look quite convinced. Again he whispered with the woman and then said, "You see, sir, if you wanted the pass for one person, it would be different because . . ." The Old Man cut him short. "But I do not want it for one. I thought I made it clear. If you don't like the deal, you are free to go." And he pointed his finger toward the door.

The man was stunned. The Old Man obviously seemed too proud for a person sunk in misery. "I like the deal, sir," he said quickly, "but I am really not sure if they won't take it away from me." He paused and sighed, "Later."

"Listen to me, young man," the Old Man stressed every word. "I can give you proof in writing that the property is yours. But I cannot guarantee today that none of them will survive."

"Sure, I understand that," said the man. "You see yourself it's a big risk, sir, but I'll take it. I want to help. Will you give me this document today?"

Wordless, without giving him a second glance, the Old Man took a sheet of white paper from a drawer in the table and a fountain pen from his vest. Within ten minutes the document was ready. Daniel and David signed it.

The man read the paper slowly, helping himself with his forefinger, folded it carefully, wrapped it in a handkerchief, and fastened it with a safety pin inside his trousers.

"Do you want me to bring my pass first, or hers, and when?" he asked.

"First, let me have yours, day after tomorrow, when you finish work, after it's dark."

✠   ✠   ✠

It was dark when they left — Noemi, Daniel, Nathan, Miriam, Rachel, Lili.

It was dark in October, when David came home . . . God, if she could stay in darkness and never see daylight again. But no. Another day was creeping into the room.

Soon it became routine to help Mrs. Chmiel till three or four o'clock in the afternoon. From breakfast until then Elli was at her best. Mrs. Chmiel, confined to her kitchen and hothouse, gave a willing ear to the long stories Elli composed about her lonely childhood with the bedridden mother and a father interested only in military affairs. She would go into lengthy descriptions of the long white dress she had worn at her first Holy Communion, her late aunt's wedding in the church at which she was a bridesmaid, of the Christmas tree she had every year, and the sumptuous Easter breakfasts which lasted until night. She fabricated these stories from what she had read in books and had heard from classmates, but sometimes she felt uneasy to be using this kindhearted woman in order to train herself. At noon she would usually have a snack with Mrs. Chmiel and then work in the hothouse for the next three or four hours. She was glad to be left alone by then, her imaginative invention all gone. Back in her room she would rehearse litanies, prayers, psalms, and when the maid came to call her for supper, she would invariably have the prayer book in her hand. Then, it occurred to her that in this house in which, save for the Sunday Mass, nobody seemed to pay much attention to religious practices, her overzealousness might seem suspicious. She exchanged the prayer book for another one at the time she expected the maid to come. By suppertime she was always quite depressed, and her pitiful efforts to put on a mask of cheerfulness made her still more nervous and tense. Once or twice Mr. Chmiel said, laughing, that she badly needed a drink to cheer her up. But he adhered strongly to his principles. Vodka was never served at night.

One Sunday when they came home from Mass and Elli was slowly climbing the stairs to her room, she heard Mrs. Chmiel calling her. She stopped, uneasy, for it was not usual for Mrs. Chmiel to keep her busy on Sunday. She detested Sundays anyway, constantly afraid of some mishap in church. The first time she went with the Chmiels to Mass, she was acutely aware of the danger of being a newcomer in a small village church. All nerves, she was watching the people in front of her. She knelt when they knelt, rose when they rose, crossed herself, beat her breast, and repeated, "Mea culpa, mea culpa, mea maxima culpa." The Litany of the Blessed Virgin presented no difficulties. She joined in a loud and clear voice, "Holy Mary . . . Holy Virgin of virgins . . . Tower of Ivory . . . Morning Star . . ." She did not know the song that followed, so she moved her lips imitating the singing. She considered her first Mass rather a success; the second time she felt much more at ease, since her first appearance in church had drawn nobody's attention. Today's Mass had been her third performance.

"Yes, Mrs. Chmiel. What can I do for you?"

"Listen, dear. Do you know any people living here?"

"No. No one save you, Mr. Chmiel, and the servants."

"Is it possible that your parents had some friends living here?"

"No. I don't think so."

"You see, Elli, the first time we went to church together a certain Mrs. Pichcik, the wife of a small local farmer, wanted to know if you were our relative. I said you were not but your late mother was a friend of our friend. She asked me your name. When I told her it was Barska she said something was wrong with it. I did not even argue. Today again she came to me after Mass, and inquired if I had registered you. I said I don't know, that's my husband's affair. Then she questioned me if I were really certain your name was Barska, if I had seen your papers. That's why I wondered if you knew anyone here, because I'm sure now she must have confused you with somebody else. Don't you think so, Elli?"

"Yes, Mrs. Chmiel. I think you are right."

"No! No! She is wrong! All wrong!" Mr. Chmiel yelled, emerging from behind the door, his face purple. "Why do you talk to these rogues, to these churls? How many times have I told you not to! How many times?" He grabbed his wife's shoulder and shook it vigorously. "I told you how damn ignorant these boors are and how damn dangerous. It's nobody's business who lives under my roof! I am sole master here! It's nobody's business whether I registered my guest or what her name is! I've told you over and over again, when one of these people asks you a question just send him to me to get the answer. I keep repeating it, and you keep chatting with them. Oh God," he moaned, "why hast thou created a woman, that brainless creature?"

Mrs. Chmiel was not very impressed with her husband's outburst, but she was visibly upset about Elli. "Did I say anything wrong, Konstanty? Did I harm her?"

"Anything you ever may say to such as Mrs. Pichcik is wrong, for the only language this scum understands is a kick in the ass. And whether you harmed Elli or not, you'll have to wait and see."

September 25, 1940

It's true about the ghetto although it's still called "Seuchen-sperrgebiet." The date of the resettlement is unknown. Some people say it won't be earlier than next year; others, that the end of this month is the deadline. It's almost impossible to find a flat in this quarter which has been overcrowded as long as it has existed. The Poles must move out from there; Jews living here can exchange apartments with them. This barter is likely to absorb only a small fraction, mainly rich Jews, as the rents in this otherwise undesirable area at once jumped up fantastically. Several of our friends called today, all desperate. Don't know what we'll do.

September 28, 1940

Never in my life have I heard the word "Jew" mentioned as often as now. It makes me sick. It scares me. I don't feel as if I belonged to those people that I saw in Nalewki Street. They are entirely different from the Jews I have known all my life. I think and think and can't figure out what I have in common with these black men, with earlocks, in long robes and yarmulkes. I don't even understand the language they speak and I don't like, to put it mildly, the noise they make, the way they talk with their hands and bodies. I don't think I love Jews more than Poles, except, of course, my family.

Elli spent the rest of the day over her prayer book, though by then she knew it by heart. She murmured absentmindedly, "Hail Mary full of grace . . . the Lord is with Thee . . . blessed art Thou among women . . . and blessed is the fruit of Thy womb, Jesus. Holy Mary, Mother of God . . . pray for us sinners, now . . . and at the time of our death." In the back of her mind she knew that her excellent religious training was meaningless in the absence of any identification document. The prayer book could not replace it.

When she came down to supper, Mr. Chmiel and two unknown men were already sitting at the table. In the middle stood the familiar bottle of cherry-colored liquor, half-empty.

"Let me introduce you, Elli," said Mr. Chmiel. "This is Elli Barska; this is Mr. Pichcik, and this is Mr. Majchrzak."

The faces of the two men were red and sweating. The kitchen was overheated as usual, but this was not the only reason. They clearly lacked Mr. Chmiel's ability to keep a clear head. Their voices were loud and shrill as they invited her to join them. She saw Mr. Chmiel's eye nervously blinking as one of the men poured her a double vodka shouting, "You are late, miss, now you must catch up with us." Mrs. Chmiel, her face drawn, was just serving a steaming dish of bigos. In passing, she whispered in Elli's ear, "Don't listen to him, first eat something." But Elli could not eat. The piece of bread she put in her mouth stuck in her throat. Why didn't he let her know he had company? Why didn't he let her stay upstairs? "Na zdrowie," shouted the two men in unison; both had their eyes fixed on the glass she held in her hand. She drained it to the last drop. Afterwards she started to eat. She knew she could stand alcohol only with substantial food and was determined to be cool whatever was going to happen at this table.

Nothing really happened. There was much talking and shouting, singing, toasting, and drinking. The first bottle was replaced by a second one, then by a third. She was careful not to let one single glass pass, though after the second bottle was drained, the two men did not watch so closely whether she kept up with them. She was stone-cold sober when, around midnight, they both were lying under the table.

Three days later Maria came. Elli's name, it appeared, was Warska not Barska; the man who made out the document mispronounced it. With the new name she could not stay at the Chmiels'. Maria was taking her to a miller's where she had already taken Lili a few days ago. She hardly had time to tell Elli that much as Mrs. Chmiel didn't leave them alone for a single moment.

Mr. Chmiel, bidding them goodbye, smiled broadly at Maria. "Elli is always welcome in my house. She is a brave girl. One night we had an 'inspection,' didn't we, Elli? Because a bloody boor had some reservations about Elli. Fools! She gave them the lesson they deserved. When they came back to their senses, both of them agreed no one but a Polish girl could drink like that!"

5

THE FAMILY of Katarzyna Mirońska was well established and well known in Janów. Almost twenty years a widow and now in her sixties, she ruled with a firm hand her family, the two modern equipped flour mills, and a big farm. Each of her two sons ran a mill; her spinster daughter lived with her. Both sons had married into families of good standing and substantial fortune. Each had a personal estate and a comfortable house within walking distance of their mother's.

Janów, surrounded by unpenetrable, widespread woods, was notorious by that time as one of the most important centers of the Polish partisans. The local people were raided from time to time by the Germans and mercilessly punished when suspected of aiding the underground. Hostages were being taken and shot; houses and whole settlements set on fire. The Germans were reluctant to show up there, for death warrants issued by the Resistance hung over their heads. For that reason Maria considered Janów a rather safe place for the girls to stay.

Old Mrs. Mirońska decided that the girls should live in the house of her younger son Henryk. Her stern face brightened when she greeted Maria, though she hardly looked at Elli. She immediately called in a servant and ordered him to see Elli to her son's house. Maria was her guest, she said, and would spend the night in her house. Maria excused herself for a moment and caught up with Elli on the road. "You wouldn't even know how to behave toward Lili, dear," she said softly. "You wouldn't know if you had ever met her before. Well, you did. According to your documents you are sisters. I realize this may be risky, but I do not dare confuse either of you more than you already are. It might be too hard for you to pretend you are strangers and eventually do more harm than good. So you both have the same last name, the same sets of parents and grandparents. I also retained your original first names and dates of birth. I'll talk to you about it tomorrow before I leave. I just wanted you to know that you can greet Lili as your sister."

The meeting did not turn out exactly as one between two sisters separated for several months. First of all, Lili lacked the information that Elli was her sister, and greeted her with a polite "How do you do?" though they were alone in the room. There were also all the events that had taken place since that September day when Elli last saw her. Lili knew, Maria had told Elli, that the Old Man, David, Danny, and both aunts were gone. But she knew no details. This thought had tormented Elli from the moment Maria had told her she would meet Lili. Elli looked at her uneasily. She was paralyzed by a sense of guilty complicity in the unjustifiable, irrevocable things that had happened in Lili's absence. Now she was facing the only person whom she wanted to absolve her. She approached Lili and repeated softly what Maria had just told her. Lili's restraint was immediately gone. She hugged and kissed Elli, tears running down her face, whispering she had feared that she would never see her again. She looked at Elli with bright smiling eyes, happy. Elli remained silent, withdrawn.

September 9, 1941

It's easier now to bribe the sentries at the ghetto outlets. Mama suggested that, instead of her coming here, Lili and I meet her on the Aryan side. We chose the day of my birthday. We left through the gate at the bridge and met her in a hotel on Chmielna Street. It's silly that I don't even know what to write about this day. I was happy to see her but I felt so strange walking through these "Aryan" streets as if I were on a stage, a resentful audience staring at me, waiting for me to trip. I do not belong there anymore. I felt out of place among these people, moving freely, walking at ease, brightly dressed, laughing, talking. Mama, a small silver cross resting on her chest, took us to a restaurant for dinner, then to a café. Both places were crowded, shrill with talk and laughter. Choice food and drinks were being served by elegantly dressed waitresses. I looked at my calloused, burned feet in wooden shoes and the shining knee-high boots (the latest fashion) of the chattering women sitting at the tables. It all made me sick. I wanted home. The food choked me. This food I was dreaming about all night. The people frightened me. I felt something mounting in me I couldn't even name.

When we again passed the gate at Chłodna Street and I put on my armband, I felt relieved.

That night I awoke covered with cold sweat. I dreamed that we were sitting with Mama in a restaurant, each with a big yellow star plastered on our foreheads.

Next morning Maria came and took the girls for a walk. They passed the mills, the farm buildings, silently heading forward. In the middle of a field, gray, bare, covered with frozen snow, Maria stopped. "Here no one can hear us," she said. She opened her bag, and took out an envelope. "These are your documents. Each of you has a Kennkarte and a baptismal certificate. These certificates are all right, backed by entries in a birth register in the diocese. They are uncontestable, unless someone can prove the entries are false. It's highly improbable but not impossible. The stamps and signatures on your documents are forged, but it's a good piece of work. You have nothing to fear. Now, you both were born in Płock — this is the diocese where the priest was willing to put in the entries — but you have spent all your life in Krotoszyn. Krotoszyn is a small town near Poznań. It is now the Warthegau, Germany, and it is unlikely you'll meet anyone who knows much about this place. Your father was a professional army man, killed in the September campaign. Your mother died soon after. You met me by accident in Warsaw in the street. You had come there looking for an aunt, who had, however, been deported for forced labor to Germany. You had seen me once only before the war and recognized me as your mother's friend. I offered to take care of you. That is all you know about me. You do not know if I am married or not, if or where I work, where I live. If asked, you would say I refused to give you my address. You think that I may live with a German and that is why I refused. Or, perhaps, I do not want to be bothered by you. You have no family, no relatives, neither your mother nor father had siblings — this deported aunt was a distant relative — all your grandparents died before you were born. After the death of your mother, you worked as servants in different places to make a living; then you decided to go to Warsaw. The rest you already know." She stopped, took a box of cigarettes out of her bag, offered them to the girls, and, covering the matchbox against the strong wind with her palm, lighted her cigarette. They lit theirs from hers. "You must settle between yourselves," she continued in an even voice, "what your parents looked like, the house you lived in, et cetera, so that your stories are consistent.

"Now, here on this slip of paper," she handed it to Lili, "are listed the dates and places of your parents' birth, and the first and last names of your maternal and paternal grandparents. Please destroy this paper as soon as you memorize all this, the sooner the better. It's a lot of stuff and that was one of the reasons I wanted it to be identical for you both. There's less chance you'd mix these data up."

She stopped again, looked at Lili, then at Elli, pulled the girls close and embraced them. "I am not going to tell you how you should behave. I do not believe in such instructions. You must work it out for yourselves; you must feel, experience, and absorb it in order not to look or behave artificially, in order to make the experience yours. There is one thing though I must tell you." Her hand holding the cigarette trembled but her face remained calm. "The only way to make the Germans and the Poles believe you are Aryan, Catholic is to convince yourself that you really are; to inculcate that conviction so deeply in your hearts and minds that no human power, no inhuman means will ever tear the truth from you. The only truth from now on is that you are what is written in these documents. No other truth exists or did ever exist."

She tried to smile.

"Now I must find jobs for you; and as soon as that is set, I'll be back here to take you away. These people here are honest and decent. They are all practicing Christians. Old Mrs. Miroń-ska goes every day to the six o'clock Mass. You'll go to church with the young couple — Sundays only, I believe. I have never talked with them about Jews, so I do not know what their feelings are. I hope you'll be able to avoid discussing that question too. In case you have to, do not show any strong feelings on either side." She stopped. "I must go now. I am happy you are

together; you'll feel much better. I hope to God to see you soon."
She kissed them with her cold lips. Tears were running slowly
down her face.

That same afternoon Elli suggested to Lili they go for a walk.
Her burden was too great; she wanted to tell Lili everything, to
get rid of it. They walked along a muddy road as Lili chattered
about Henryk and his wife, Wanda. Wanda was six months
along with her first child. Lili said they were both very pleasant
and hospitable. Henryk was busy all day in the flour mill, Wanda
had a big household to care for and enjoyed Lili's company
and help. "If you feel like it, you can help her too, she'd . . ."
Elli interrupted her. "Listen, Lili, I want to tell you something."

"Do you really want to?" Lili looked at her, then dropped her
head.

"I think I do."

"Elli, I don't want to sound indifferent or anything, but perhaps you'd rather not talk about it?"

"About what?"

"I know you want to tell me what happened after I left."

"And you prefer not to hear it?"

"That's not true, Elli, you know it is not. I do not want to
make it any harder for you."

"Don't you understand that I can't live with it all by myself?"
Elli's voice was harsh and tense. "I told Daniel about Danny, but
I said no word to anyone about Grandfather and David. I
can't stand it any longer."

"What do you mean, Elli, you did not say a word? You
must have told Maria." Lili's face was tight with the effort of
getting words out.

"No, no, no!" cried Elli. "I didn't! I told her they both
were shot during a selection in our yard."

"This is not true?" It sounded like a plea for denial.

"No, it is not," Elli said in a quick hard voice.

"Elli, dear, do tell me everything. I want to know." Her voice had gone blank; she leaned forward to take Elli's hand, but Elli stepped back.

She told Lili about David, then about Danny. When she came to the point where she climbed the ladder to cut the cord the Old Man was hanging on, she choked with brief laughter. She went on talking, how the knife slipped from her hand, but the laughter became more and more shrill, hysterical, wild, until she could not talk anymore. In a tremendous blowup she saw Lili's terrified eyes, a huge bare tree, the gray heavy sky on her head, and she shook and bubbled, torrents of laughter disrupting the icy silence. She never finished her story.

Wanda was a cheerful, easygoing girl, preoccupied with her first pregnancy and with the big household. She had only two farmhands, so that the girls spent a lot of time helping her with the household chores and the big animal farm. From five o'clock in the morning she was busy in the cow barn, pigsty, and poultry house. She baked her bread in the huge oven in the kitchen and pickled mushrooms, cucumbers, and cabbage and stored them for the coming winter. Whenever there was a pigsticking she would make blood pudding and liverwurst, cook sausages, smoke hams. Pigs were earmarked and could be killed only by the authority's approval, Wanda explained to them, but a liter or two of vodka and a part of the pig took care of that. There was an abundance of food in the house, and should one of the girls allude to Wanda's hospitality, she would say there was enough food to feed ten more guests. She willingly accepted the girls' help, but when Elli's attempt to milk a cow ended in her being fiercely kicked by the angry animal and after Lili left the poultry house open, she asked them, smiling, to abstain from outdoor work. "You are town girls," she laughed. "You'll never learn how to deal with the animals. You better stay with your books and, if you want, clean the house and help with the dishes."

Every day in the afternoon the girls studied their lessons. With the door of their room locked, they learned by heart the first names of their parents, the dates and places of their birth, their mother's maiden name, the first and last names of their maternal and paternal grandparents, their prewar address in Krotoszyn, and so on. The most difficult were the names of the grandparents; most confusing were the maiden names of the grandmothers. They would repeat silently for hours, Aniela born Kowalska, Zofia born Malińska, Józef Przeorski, Jan Warski, only to pin the wrong wife to the wrong husband, or to couple the paternal grandfather with the maternal grandmother. They kept examining each other, but Elli's progress, in particular, was astonishingly slow. She was sometimes desperate about her futile efforts, and finally announced she had a block in her head and would never acquire the abracadabra of the names and dates and places. Besides, she said, even if she somehow got them fixed in her mind, she would certainly confuse them if investigated.

August 15, 1940

What I like most is when everybody is home and we sit after dinner, talking long into the night. If not for the war, we wouldn't be allowed to stay up so late or to take part in their conversations. The Old Man often goes back to the First World War and tells funny (or not so funny) stories of how they managed to live through the alternately invading German and Russian armies. The story about a man who smuggled tea across the border is great. He used to declare at customs that what he had in his bag was fodder for his horse. When, astonished, the customs officer told him that a horse would rather starve than eat this stuff, the man shrugged his shoulders. "Let him drop dead if that's what he wants; I try to do my best for him."

The Old Man says that what's most noble and most base in man shows off under extreme conditions; heroism and turpitude are equally common and equally flagrant. A man can share with you his last piece of bread but can also destroy you to get yours. That's why, not to make bad blood, the Old Man doesn't let Mama and Uncle Michael work here but in the distant Lublin district. None of us is allowed to talk to friends about their trips, documents, business.

At other times they'd remember old family stories, long-dead aunts, uncles, cousins. It's fantastic how they can remember dozens of names, maiden names, wedding dates. They even seem to know whether Great-grandaunt Deborah, born August 3, 1851, married for love or whether it was a marriage of prudence, and what happened to each of her nine children. They can trace offspring in all parts of the world along with their children and grandchildren who seem to multiply without end.

One night when Henryk was already home from work, a car braked screaming in the yard and three German officers rushed into the room without knocking. The girls had barely time to leave by the back door. They were not registered in Henryk's house; he had asked them to stay outdoors in case of such a visit and to come back only if it were unavoidable. They stood under a big tree without coats, shivering, the loud voices reaching them from the house. "Elli," said Lili, "tell me your father's name."

"Stanisław."

"Fine. Your mother's?"

"Anna."

"Good. Her maiden name?"

"Przeorska."

"Excellent. Her father's name?"

"Józef."

"Very good. Her mother's first name and maiden name?"

"Zofia born Malińska."

"Oh, Elli. No, darling. That is our father's mother."

"Anna born Przeorska."

"But Elli, dear, that is *our* mother."

"I don't know. I don't know any other names." Elli trembled all over. "Lili, what if they call us in? What if they came after us? Why are they shouting so loud?"

"Don't worry, Elli." Lili kissed her. "That's their usual way. And it's certainly not because of us. Besides, we have documents. Henryk would somehow handle the matter of registration. I am sure they are looking for the partisans. Try, dear, try to remember the name of our mother's mother."

"Eleonora Warska."

"But, Elli! For heaven's sake! That is your own name. You mustn't, dear . . . why don't you . . ."

At this moment they heard Henryk's voice, "Lili, Elli, please do come in." The way from the garden to the house was the longest trip Elli had ever made. "The girls were busy in the barn," Henryk explained to the Germans, "but there is no one else in my house."

"Isn't it a shame to keep the young ladies at night in a cold barn," said one of the officers mockingly in excellent Polish. "Look, they are shivering." He turned toward Elli. "What was the young lady doing there?"

"One of the cows is with calf and was not well all day long," said Lili quietly. "That's why we went there."

The officer smiled. "That seems to be more a veterinary's job than yours, miss. Wasn't it your boyfriend from the woods who was not well?"

Elli said quickly, "Oh, no."

The officer's eyes darkened. "I did not ask you. When I did, you did not answer me. So shut up." He turned again toward Lili. "Come on, miss, you better say it now. We'll find him anyway, and I promise you'll accompany him if you won't tell the truth."

Only now did Elli see that Wanda had disappeared from the room. One of the two officers must have noticed it too, for he shouted to the Polish-speaking officer to find out where she was. He turned to Henryk, who said his wife was far in her time and probably had to go to the bathroom.

"Let me see this bathroom," shrieked the officer furiously.

"But you wouldn't . . ." said Henryk embarrassed.

"Yes, I would, I sure as hell would," the officer yelled.

Henryk led the way to the bathroom. The officer banged at the door. There was no reply. He kicked the door open. There was nobody there. In the same moment Wanda appeared in the back door, and, asked by her husband where she had been, said quietly that she was not well and had gone to get some fresh air. "You know I can't stand cigar smoke, dear," she smiled at Henryk. The officer quickly translated her words to his comrades and then ordered Henryk to lead them to the barn.

"I made it," whispered Wanda as soon as they left. "There were three partisans in the stable, and they'll certainly search the stable too. We didn't tell you, we never tell anybody, it's better that you do not know." The girls' looks must have struck her, for she added, "Don't worry. The boys left and are far away now. Nothing can happen to them." She went to the kitchen, put more wood in the stove, and a big kettle over it. "We all need hot tea," she announced. "And perhaps something to cheer us up, too." She put smoked ham and bread on the table, poured vodka in three big glasses, and was just preparing tea, when they heard the car starting, and Henryk appeared in the door.

November 4, 1940

The cat is out of the bag! Aunt Wilhelmina came today, but she was not the same. Really miserable. Last night two Gestapo men came to her, requested her to take only her coat and follow them. A limousine waiting downstairs stopped first in front of her house in Łódź. During the whole way none of them uttered a word; in vain she implored them to reveal the purpose of the trip. Once inside her apartment they asked her, very politely, to show them the hidden vault. Which she did. All tools at hand, they removed the bricks, instructed by her decoded the lock, and took everything out. She said they refused to give her even Grandmother's ("may she rest in peace") jewelry but I'm sure that if she had to lick their boots she cadged something out. They drove her back to Warsaw and courteously clicked their heels at her door.

We'll move in a few days. Today we had our last lessons and bid farewell to our teachers. Again one chapter closed. It all happens so quickly. Miss Brzezińska implored us to continue to learn languages "there." Why did she say "there"? Why are people afraid to spell the word "ghetto"? What do they feel about it? How does it feel to live on the "Aryan" side with the ghetto that close?

November 8, 1940

Danny came home with a bad wound in his head. Aunt Paula fainted. He wouldn't say a word how it happened. I would like to move out of here.

November 10, 1940

We moved today.

November 12, 1940

Mama came to our new home, brought food and money. She'll be back tomorrow.

November 15, 1940

The ghetto was sealed off today. It was the last day Mama could come here. Heavy guards — German, Polish, Jewish policemen — are watching the ghetto outlets. Along the walls — on both sides — patrols. Day and night.

November 21, 1940

The Old Man went with Lili and me to wait for her. Through the loose bricks in the wall Mama whispered to me that she loves us, and then I saw her go. My world came to an end.

Shortly before Christmas the girls received a letter from Maria saying she had found jobs for them in Chełm, a town about two hundred miles east of Lublin. She also said she would try to come and take them away right after Christmas, so that they could start work at the beginning of January. And she wished them and their hosts a Merry Christmas.

Christmas was a very busy season in Janów. The preparations for the holidays kept everybody busy from early morning till late at night. Pigs were slaughtered; quarters of beef, trimmed; geese and turkeys, roasted; piles of sausages, cooked; dozens of cakes baked. This went on for days and days in all the three related households, though it was to the old Mrs. Mirońska's house that the whole family was invited. Lili once asked Wanda who was supposed to eat this stupendous amount of food, and Wanda smiled that the men, when drinking, could eat without end.

The sumptuous Christmas Eve dinner was attended only by the members of the family, Lili, Elli, and the priest as a guest of honor. Before dinner Elli showed Lili how to break the wafer, a lesson Irena Darska had taught her. Later the whole family drove to the Christmas midnight Mass. The night was frosty but clear and windless. The peasants gathered at the entrance of the church bowed respectfully when Mrs. Mirońska stepped out of her carriage, followed by her daughter and Mr. Gruszyński, an old family friend. Immediately after, Henryk's coach stopped with Wanda, Lili, and Elli, and Stanisław's, with his wife and their two boys. Mrs. Mirońska went straight into the church; her sons shook hands and exchanged greetings with friends.

The real festivities, the huge feasting and drinking, started the next day. By six o'clock there were about thirty guests sitting around the massive oak table in Mrs. Mirońska's house. Elli was sitting between Stanisław and a middle-aged man whom Stanisław had introduced to her as the head of the district, Mr. Bolesław Lis.

"Henryk told me he had two guests from Warsaw," he looked over Elli's head to Stanisław. "Is this one of them?"

"Yes," answered Stanisław. "I introduced her to you already, old boy, don't you remember?"

"Sure, I do. Let's drink to our friendship, young lady," and he poured the light green vodka in Elli's shot glass. Elli had already discovered that while she could stand Chmiel's spirits or straight white vodka, any other brand, especially homemade liquors with different kinds of herbs and fruit, definitely made her sick.

"I would rather have white vodka if you don't mind," she said politely, pointing toward a bottle standing near her place.

"Oh, come on," laughed Mr. Lis, "this is not poison." He lifted his glass.

"Please, I'd rather have the other one," repeated Elli.

"Not used to our rough stuff, eh?" roared her neighbor. "Delicate town girls can't stand a good strong drink." He looked at her with his small blue eyes. Elli gulped the green alcohol down but her mouth involuntarily twisted. The man immediately filled her glass with the same liquor which was still burning her throat.

"Leave her alone, Bolek," intervened Stanisław. "Of course she is not used to such strong drinks."

"She comes from Warsaw, doesn't she?" said Lis.

"I have already told you twice that she does," said Stanisław impatiently.

"When did you come here, miss?" Lis fumbled with his empty glass.

"She came two weeks ago," said Stanisław quickly.

"Why can't she reply herself? Afraid the testimony won't stick together?" Lis filled the glasses. "I just wondered why didn't Henryk register them?"

"Stop this nonsense, Bolek," Stanisław was angry. "He did not because they came just for a few days, and you know how busy Henryk is."

Lis looked at him. "Came for a few days and are still here, eh?"

Stanisław rose from his place. "Listen, you . . ."

"Don't get so nervous, Staś, sit down, sit down," said Lis. And then drawling each word. "But the young ladies are not that busy. They could have come and registered themselves — if their documents are in order. Are they?" He turned toward Elli.

"You want me to bring them right now?" asked Elli sharply.

"Don't be so touchy, miss," laughed Lis. "I meant no offense.

But with all those kikes roaming around, sneaking into the most incredible places, we have to be cautious, don't we?"

"Yes, we certainly do," said Elli, loudly.

January 28, 1940

Uncle Henry was killed in a battle near Kutno. He was drafted in the first days of September and ever since we tried to find him. Now his companion in arms sent us a letter saying that he himself buried Uncle Henry. I loved him so much; he was the youngest and most cheerful of all my uncles; he used to send us funny toys from abroad and always took us to the movies. It's hard to imagine I won't see him anymore; but he died a soldier's death.

July 30, 1941

The house committee organized a party for the young people from our house. The hostess played Chopin, an actress recited poems of Mickiewicz, Słowacki, Asnyk; then we danced. Lili didn't want to go. She said she wasn't well but I didn't believe her. At night, when I came back, she said a grave is not the proper place to dance upon. It is more proper to make love with Abel?

August 9, 1941

Danny came from work badly beaten. He has three fractured ribs; his whole body is bruised, his face smashed. Aunt Paula did not shed a tear; her face has become a stony mask.

"Would you believe, miss, Kazek, our organist, that man over there," Lis pointed toward an albino sitting next to Lili, "found one the other day right behind the main altar. The impertinence of the Yids has no limits! There is nothing sacred to them, not even a church. Hey, Kazek," he shouted toward the albino, "did you tell them how you discovered that stinker behind the altar?"

The albino's face was crimson. He blubbered, "Sure, Mr. Prefect, sure, with all respect." It was clear that he did not understand what Lis wanted from him.

"Are you talking about that Moishe Kazek found in the church?" interrupted a young man from the other end of the table. "Last week on my way back home from Zamość," he went on, "I was stopped by three Jews on the bridge. Of course, at first they did not tell me they were Jews, but when I started to talk with them, they confessed they had jumped out of a train, and for three days had been hiding under the bridge. You should have seen them! Half-naked, looked like wild animals, could scare you out of your wits. And would you guess what they asked me for?" Triumphantly, he looked around, positive no one would. After a prolonged minute of silence, he said, "Neither for food, nor for shelter, but for the way to the woods where our boys have their quarters. Ha, ha, ha," he roared. "I asked them what the hell did they want from our boys. To fight, they said. Ha, ha, ha, just imagine, these little Yids fighting side by side with our brave boys!"

There was general applause and merriment at the table. Only old Mrs. Mirońska sat solemn and motionless at the head of the table. Mr. Gruszyński was whispering something to her.

"Know what I told them?" continued the young man, obviously satisfied with the impression his story made at the table. "I told them, better get out of the way of our boys, they fight for *our* country." He stopped, waiting for the effect.

"And what? They got it? What did they do? What did you do?" they shouted one over the other.

"Nothing," said the man sternly. "Nothing. I went home."

Mr. Gruszyński rose from his place. "Why did you not hand them over to the Germans?" he asked quietly. "Like Kazek did."

The young man looked uneasy. Obviously he was not sure whether this was reproach or mockery. "Why should I?" he said. "I was cold and hungry and wanted to get home before dark. Besides, let them do their job themselves." He squirmed uneasily on his seat and then added, "And I am a Christian."

At that Mrs. Mirońska rose from her place. She looked majestic in her high-collared black dress, a big golden cross on her breast, her head in a crown of thick silver hair. "No," she said emphatically. "No. You are a heathen."

December 28, 1940

Our food rations consist of bread, marmalade, and sugar. A month's ration is hardly enough for a week. Now and then David brings some food from work, and we have already received two food parcels from Mama. People who have money can buy everything, real butter, ham, coffee, tea, sardines, the fanciest food. We buy potatoes and bread, and milk for the Old Man and Emmi. We are not exactly hungry but we often fancy with Rachel, Lili, and Danny what we'd like to eat. Anyway, I won't touch cabbage for the rest of my life once we are out of here, or carrot marmalade.

December 31, 1940

New Year's Eve. The last we spent in the train. Where will we spend the next? Will the war be over? The dinner was unusually rich, for there was one chicken in the last parcel, and, if not for David, it would have passed in a very pleasant atmosphere. Out of the blue he said that if he could only help it, he wouldn't bring up his child as a Jew. The Old Man said that that's far from being a very original idea, that people had tried and still try to hide from their children their true origin imagining they can protect them from suffering. "I don't believe myself," he said, "you can go on living in deceit. You may lie once, or twice, or a hundred times, but you can't lie all the time. Can you bring up a child with no background at all, or with a fake one? Perhaps, but you'll bring up a cripple. And he'll pass on this disaster to his children. When I was a young man, I heard my uncle saying that he was proud of being a Jew. I asked him what it was that he was so proud about? His poverty? His constant fear? His rootlessness? He replied that whether or not he was proud of being a Jew, he still would be one, so he prefers to be proud of it. It's as good a reason as any. I talked once to Lili's friend, whose parents had converted to Christianity. The girl was brought up in a convent. She was never told they were converts before they had to move into the ghetto. She detests Jews, she detests her parents, she detests herself. I suggested to her that she try to accept her present life as the cross Christ meant her to bear. She told me she did not believe in Christ any longer. Her ordeal is outrageous because it's senseless; the very reason she suffers is abominable to her. Of course, Hitlers do not happen all the time, but he had predecessors and will have successors. The only way for us not to live on all fours is to be proud, and if you think of it, we have some reasons to be proud."

I'm not sure at all we really have, I mean, more of them, or better ones, than other people have. David didn't seem to be convinced either, but he didn't argue.

Maria, Lili, and Elli spent the New Year's Eve in a train. On the first of January, 1943, they arrived in Chełm.

6

BEFORE THE WAR Chełm had been one of those towns which, deprived of a great city's attractions, still throbbed with life. With several divisions stationed near the Russian border the officers and their wives, possessing a knack for a gay social life, turned it into a desirable post for those to whom the capital's glamorous parades and receptions were denied. The second large group in the town had once been Jews — peddlers, craftsmen, small shopkeepers, for the most part desolate, God-fearing, orthodox in manner, speech, and looks.

Now the face of the town was entirely changed. The officers who survived the September campaign had gone to POW camps, into hiding, to join the Resistance. They left behind families struggling for daily bread, wives working in offices, selling home-made cakes, keeping small shops, cafés, restaurants. The Jews had disappeared too. The ghetto in Chełm had been duly liquidated. Now, a considerable group of Poles, mostly women with children driven from their homes in regions incorporated into the Third Reich, had settled here. There was also a big camp on the outskirts of the town where Russian prisoners of war and Jewish kriegswichtig laborers were incarcerated. The

German need for social life was assuaged by a brothel in the middle of town, supplied with frequently changing teams of girls from the occupied countries. Besides, there was a mushrooming of Amts, Verwaltungen, Behörde, Büros.

It was on the outskirts of the town just opposite the labor camp that Maria sublet a room for the girls, and it was with a Verwaltung that she had found a job for Elli and with a Büro that she had placed Lili. On arriving in Chełm she took them first to one of the new restaurants.

The restaurant was run by four war widows, the youngest of whom was in her early twenties; the oldest, in her forties. Maria had known them for more than a year. Because there were many flour mills in the town itself and in the district, she had frequently been here on business. Passing as a war widow herself, she developed a close friendship with the owners of the restaurant. The four women were initiated into the carefully guarded secret of Maria's real relationship to the girls. Maria cautioned the girls that this was the extreme to which they were allowed to go; in all other cases they must stick to their story. It was a precaution taken by many families, particularly those with a military background, that its members pass for strangers. The oldest of the women, Natalia, whose husband had been a colonel before the war and was now a high-ranking officer in the underground, never referred to him other than as Mr. Skotnicki, although their name was Janowski. To outsiders she was a widow. She had two sons, eighteen and twenty, about whom she never talked, though one or the other showed up from time to time. Both were in the underground. Natalia was a lively, handsome brunette with a special gift for talking business with the Germans who enjoyed the excellent kitchen and free drinks in the restaurant. Luckily, the German machine was so riddled with graft that a woman caught for forced labor or a man arrested without a night permit was an exchangeable commodity. Various officials were manipulated by Natalia in a small alcove behind the main room and the victims usually freed within a few days. More grave offenses, however, were beyond the repair of her charm and table. Her partners, the blond vivacious Iga whose husband was killed in battle, the dark-haired Mela, who sent parcels to hers in a POW camp in Germany, and the youngest, Hanka, who had lost her husband in September, a week after their wedding, revolved round Natalia like satellites, busy with maintaining the actual business from which she operated.

When the introductions were over and the breakfast finished, Natalia warmly invited the girls to come every day for a hot meal, with or without money. The accounts, she said, they would settle later with Maria.

Next, they went to install themselves in their new home. It was almost an hour's walk from the restaurant so they rode in a horse-drawn droshky, the only means of transportation that still existed in Chełm. Clippity-clop, the old worn mare dragged heavily over cobblestones thickly covered with muddy snow. They drove for a mile or two past a cemetery, through an open gray field, and stopped just opposite an iron gate with a barbed-wire fence extending from both sides.

"Here we are," said Maria. The girls took their suitcases while Maria paid the cabman. They followed her through a broken wooden gate to an ugly, decaying house. The creaking door was answered by a creature wrapped in something resembling a faded purple curtain; its fringe swept the floor raising small clouds of dust. From under a thick woolen shawl peered two owlish eyes and the wrinkled toothless face of a woman in her late fifties.

"Good afternoon, Mrs. Kowalik," said Maria. "I've brought the girls." The woman murmured something, led the way through a bare corridor, and left them in front of a door. The room was dark and cold, with two iron beds, a table, and a hanger.

"There is no stove here," said Maria, "but I have bought a

sawdust oven, and they'll bring it tomorrow. Wood and coal are expensive and hard to get. You'll have no difficulties in getting sawdust. You'll have to be very careful, however, never to leave it burning when you go out, for the whole shack could catch fire in no time. And never go to bed until you've extinguished it." They were all sitting on one bed. Elli blinked nervously at her watch. She knew Maria must catch the night train for Lublin; she dreaded the moment of parting. "Tomorrow morning you must go and register. In the registry office they'll ask you where you came from; you'll give the address of Mrs. Mirońska. Then you must each go to your office. Lili has a job in the administration of the flour mills which belong to Robert Posch, Herbert's younger brother. I have known Herbert Posch for a long time," she continued in an even flat voice. "He is a good and reliable friend. He is German, always was; but he has lived here for over forty years and people know him. He is very sympathetic to the Poles and very helpful. He has, of course, many friends among the Germans, and as far as I know is using them for a single purpose, to help people. Herbert actually gave recommendations for both of you, otherwise you wouldn't have the jobs. Elli, you have a job in Die Treuhandstelle für verlassenen Judenbesitz . . ."

"Für was?" Elli jumped up.

"Don't get upset, darling." Maria smiled at the question put in German. "In every district they have an office set up for the administration of Jewish estates, which they, out of courtesy, prefer to call 'abandoned.' It's just an office, like any other."

Elli shuddered. Her first impulse was to run from this dark room, from the barbed wire she could see through the window, from the "abandoned" Jewish estate. But where could she go? Behind this fence? Into the street?

"You will get in your office an employment card stating that you are indispensable there. This is to obtain the Arbeitsamt's permit to work. Without it they would enlist you for forced labor in Germany. Do not go to the employment office together, because when they have to fill a transport to Germany they take everybody who comes for a permit regardless of his employment card. Should this happen to one of you, the other must immediately inform Mister Posch. When you have the Arbeitsamt's stamp, you will be safe and can start work." She rubbed her forehead.

"I do not know when I shall come again; I would rather limit my visits here. In case I do not come, for say more than a month, I'll write you a brief note, just to let you know everything is all right." She looked at them. "Everything will be all right. I am sure it will. Cheer up, girls; I'll see you soon." Lili smiled faintly, Elli did not try. "I have a long way to the station. I must go. God bless you." She embraced them, and with her head held high, left.

The first people they met in the morning were a group of workers with the Star of David armbands, going through the gate. Four sentries impassively watched the black cavalcade, wrapped in rags, shuffling their feet. The men pressed against each other for support and warmth. The temperature was 21° below zero. The girls passed the cemetery gate and within half an hour came to the corner of Lubelska Street.

"It's still early," said Lili. "Let's go into the church." In the entrance they crossed themselves with the holy water, then knelt down in a far corner of the huge almost empty chapel. Two old women in black shawls were kneeling on the bench; one lay prostrate in front of the main altar. When she finished the Lord's Prayer and the Hail Mary, Elli said her own prayer composed of the family names. She looked at Lili. Lili's face was calm and she seemed to be meditating rather than praying. Her eyes were wide open, thoughtful.

"God, please, let them register us," prayed Elli. "Don't let them catch us in the Arbeitsamt, please."

In the registry office Lili took Elli's Kennkarte and went to the window. Elli, sitting on a bench in the corner of the hall, heard her saying, "Of course, she is here, she is my younger sister. Do you want to see her?" The clerk expressed no such desire and shortly after they left the building with the first precious stamp on their documents. Lili suggested that they go first to Posch's office to get her employment card and then to the Treu-händer's to get Elli's, and finally to the Arbeitsamt where Elli would wait outside until Lili came back. Within the hour they collected the cards and approached the notorious employment office. They parted in a back street; it was agreed that if Lili did not return in an hour's time, Elli would go to Mr. Posch. Lili was back in fifteen minutes, smiling. "Go ahead, dear," she said. "It's easy as pie."

Elli felt her heart in her throat as she climbed the stairs. Everything was always easier for Lili than for her. She repeated listlessly all the names, dates, places. She was flawless. She handed the employment card and the Kennkarte to the clerk behind the window.

He studied them for a while. "You have been here already, haven't you?" he asked.

She could not say a word. He was checking something in his files. "Oh, no," he said, "the first name was different." His head deep in the papers, he asked, "Your name, please?" Hearing no answer, he repeated, "Your name, miss?"

She looked at him. Her lips moved but no word came out.

"Don't you understand Polish, miss? What is your name?" The clerk was looking at her more surprised, than angry. "Look, miss, I have no time to waste on you. Would you please tell me your name."

Blank.

"Are you dumb, miss?"

She smiled idiotically. She could not tell her name. She had forgotten it.

"Why didn't you ask somebody to come with you?" He sounded sympathetic. "And what are you going to do in this office? Perhaps some mechanical work? Putting down numbers and things like that? Is that right?" She nodded. He filled in the form looking for the data in the documents she handed him. Then he put a stamp in her Kennkarte, returned the documents to her, and smiled encouragingly. "It must be hard on you. Good luck."

The first words she said to Lili when she saw her in the street were, "Warska. Eleonora Warska." Clear and without hesitation.

Lili looked at her in amazement.

Each morning they would leave home at six, pass the silent black group emerging from the iron gate, stop in the church for a few minutes, and then part to meet at home twelve hours later. After a week's struggle they discovered the mystery of the sawdust oven. They got used to bringing the water from the only working pump in a deserted yard behind their house, but when Elli slipped on the ice and badly injured her knee, Lili assumed this chore. Elli nursed the knee for a long time. She was terribly afraid of the dark yard.

Every day Elli passed a showcase in which a huge inscription in block letters, DIE JUDEN SIND DAS UNGLÜCK DER WELT!, was illustrated with pertinent pictures, changed every Monday. And every day at the entrance of the office she would pass her boss, Herr Rahm, holding a watch with a second hand. He was a handsome man, forty or forty-two, impeccably dressed, clean shaven, fragrant with strong lotions. On the stroke of seven he would greet the latecomers, pleasantly smiling, "Arbeit macht das Leben süss. That's what you would learn in a labor camp if you can't learn it here."

Elli, an untrained Bürokraft, was assigned to the accountant's division, which occupied one middle-sized room crammed with people, desks, papers, counting machines, and typewriters. She was received very warmly here, and after a few days was less tense. The accountant was Mr. Mikołaj Jemelianow-Baryński, of Russian extraction and with a strong Russian accent. He was a very tall, well-built man in his middle forties with grayish hair and gay eyes. He was said to have miraculously escaped the purge of the Polish intellectuals in Lwów. His first assistant was Mrs. Ola Kalińska, a refugee from Poznań and a former actress, a warmhearted person who recited the role of Ophelia or of Antigone while recording long rows of figures on endless sheets. She immediately took Elli under her wing and scrupulously tucked away the piles of paper on which Elli made her first steps in typing. Herr Rahm would not stand waste of paper any more than waste of time. He made a daily tour throughout the office's twelve rooms, each day at a different hour, but the alarm signal, put in motion by his secretary the moment he left for the inspection, functioned faultlessly. Mr. Baryński's second assistant was Mrs. Molska, whom the war had brought from Gdańsk. Her husband and only son were killed in the Westerplatte battle. She would invariably start the day by telling the same story about her boy who once got lost when he was five; she connected it somehow with his untimely death. There also was Waldek, a nice boy of sixteen, who did all kinds of errands and supplied them with the latest news from the front which differed widely from the official press reports. During the first day Elli's new friends learned everything about her; she was relieved to get rid of her story quickly. There was only one tense moment when Ola exclaimed excitedly, "Oh, you lived in Krotoszyn! Of course, I know this little pleasant town. It's near Poznań. I had very good friends there. You must tell me more about your life there."

Someone, who never heard about Krotoszyn and was not

interested in it, interrupted and somehow they never came back
to it.

It was dark when the girls left home in the morning and dark
when they came back. On a Sunday they decided to take a closer
look at the route they passed every day. The camp, surrounded
by watchtowers, seemed to have no end. It spread eastward and,
within sight, the rows of wooden barracks multiplied infinitely.
While they were leaving for church at half-past eight a huge
truck stopped before the gate. Prodded with the rifles of pro-
fusely swearing guards, a group of men trudged out. Their
emaciated bodies were barely covered with dirty rags; their feet,
bare and swollen; faces, unshaven and haggard. They moved
like automatons, mute, lifeless, the Russian prisoners of war,
at the nadir of existence. Before the truck pulled away, two
guards with shovels hopped in and threw out a lump of human
flesh.

The smell of burning, the girls now discovered, came from a
place opposite the cemetery. As they approached, the smell
became stronger. A man passing by volunteered the information
that since some Jews were supposed to be still hiding here, the
Germans set a house on fire from time to time. Decaying houses,
quilts ripped open, feathers covering the cobblestones, scattered
books, photographs, papers; greedy hands were still searching
the remnants of the ghetto for hidden treasures. The smell
of burning and filth did not bother them. One group of youngsters was busy tearing up the floor in a falling house; another
was hacking to pieces a huge wooden case. "Sunday," said Lili.

December 14, 1940

*David has built a long wooden case along the kitchen wall to
store coal and wood. For the past month he brought one board*

every day (he got special permission), and worked at nights on it.
When it was finished today, Danny said it looked like a tomb.

December 21, 1940

The tomb is quite useful. Now we have a place to do our
homework. It's warm only in the kitchen. We use the tomb also
for a stage; when Mark takes Rachel out to a show, she repeats it
later at night for us and she looks just marvelous on this stage;
we have a carbide lamp for a limelight. I think Mark's in love
with Rachel. Could it be that she is deceiving David?

December 23, 1940

The Old Man requested we find a teacher to continue German
and English. As if the other lessons, the house chores and the
battle against the bedbugs weren't enough. These damned in-
sects keep streaming in from the neighbors and every morning
we paint with lysol all doorframes, sashes, each crack. Anyway,
Lili found that language teacher. Nelly is a young girl from
Vienna, who graduated in English in London where her father
was a consul. Her brother — a Sorbonne graduate — offered to
teach us French for nothing. The people here are language crazy.

After Mass the girls went to the restaurant. They had dinner
and sat for a while with Iga and Hanka. Around seven they
went back home. Lili was having her daily struggle with the
oven and Elli was dusting the room when they heard a knock
at the door. They had not seen Mrs. Kowalik since the day they
moved in and she obviously was not looking for their company,
so it could hardly be she. But it was after the curfew and there
was no one else in the house. Lili said, "Please come in."

The door opened and in came a lanky, narrow-shouldered young man. Walking softly, he came toward Lili and whispered, "Keep silent. Otherwise she will hear and raise hell." He had very fair thin hair, meticulously parted in the middle and brushed aside, a short snubbed nose, narrow lips, and small blue eyes in a badly pockmarked face.

"Who are you?" asked Lili.

"I've told you to keep silent," he hissed.

Lili did not speak quietly. "Who are you? And what do you want?"

He giggled. "Don't be in such a hurry, chick," he made a further step toward her. "All in good time."

Lili managed to kindle the fire, washed her hands in the basin, and sat down on her bed. "Either you will answer my questions or I'll ask Mrs. Kowalik to take care of you," she said lighting a cigarette.

"You hit the point, kitten," he said. "The trouble is she *is* taking care of me."

Lili got up. "I don't give a damn whether she is or not. Please get out of here." She flung the door wide open and stood waiting. He tiptoed toward her, fiercely pushed her away, locked the door, and put the key into his pocket. "Now let's sit down and talk quietly. Or, you'll be sorry."

He knows, flashed through Elli's mind, dear God, he knows. Lili adjusted her hair in the mirror and went to the oven. She poured tea in two cups, passed one to Elli, took a biscuit, and, with her marvelous legs dangling, started to eat. When she finished the biscuit, she helped herself to another and poured more tea in her cup. Then she lighted a fresh cigarette, took a book, stretched herself out on the bed, and seemed to be deeply buried in reading. Elli sat motionless with the cup in her hand. For a while nothing but the rustle of the pages disrupted the silence. The man looked suddenly at his wristwatch and, visibly struck, quickly opened the door and disappeared. Lili put her book aside and said, "He will be back."

August 2, 1940

Sometimes I can't understand Lili. She behaves as if nothing really had happened, I mean, the war. Not that I expect her to suffer or anything, but she doesn't mind Aunt Paula and me doing all the cleaning and cooking nor does she seem to care about our everyday troubles. I'd say she is remote or abstracted if not for her dating Martin, looking in the mirror, and fussing about her looks. That's far from being abstracted, isn't it? When I say it wouldn't hurt her if she helped in the kitchen she answers that with the three of us it would be too crowded; as if everybody belonged there but her. I've told Mama that it's really unfair, but she says that Lili is different and I must leave her alone. Sure, she is different. For one thing she is beautiful, with that thick auburn hair and huge brown eyes, tall and slim. She keeps her head lifted high as if she were looking for something in the sky. She walks as if she were dancing, floating through life hardly touching the ground. Boys are crazy about her. But then, all she thinks about is fun. She never seems to be upset and keeps repeating not to worry because everything's going to be all right.

It's not enough that she doesn't give a rap about anything but she's also the one whom Mama takes to the fancy cafés; for Lili, of course, wouldn't dream of wearing an armband, and Mama does not wear it either. Mama says she's not good at playing two parts; once it was decided she was rein arisch she sticks to it. I wish I could be like that. I went with them once without my armband. People stared at me all the time. Lili said I was hysterical, but it wasn't true. I could swear I'd been recognized at least twice; by an older woman, and then by a young man.

Both looked at me with that smile that leaves no doubts. I didn't turn back, not to let on I was afraid, but all my pleasure was gone. What's most conspicuous about me are my hips. I never knew before that Semitic women are broader in the hips than Aryans. I was always unhappy, wanted so much to be slim like Lili. Now I know I was right.

August 3, 1940

I couldn't finish yesterday about Lili because Aunt Paula asked me to buy a battery for her hearing aid. She is so desperate every time Danny goes out that he mostly stays home. It was much easier for him in the winter because after dark his hair and nose were less likely to attract attention. He never says anything, but I myself have heard children calling "kike" after him. Once a German slapped his face in the middle of the street. A neighbor who saw it told us. When Danny is away, Aunt Paula shakes all over and cries silently until he comes back. At seventeen she still treats him like a child. He is furious because he cannot move without her interfering with him. I told her once she'd be happy if she could keep him under her bed; she cried, I was sorry, and nothing changed. Sometimes we would tease "Polly Hütchen" as we call her, about her eyes running with water, but we all know she has a heart of gold. She weeps when Mama leaves and when she comes back from every of her expeditions; she weeps when the Old Man goes for a walk and when he comes back and when she has news from her husband and daughter and when she has none.

I admire Lili very much, and I think I always did. Her joy of life, the happiness she radiates is what I envy her most. I try so hard not to be gloomy, but I guess I always was. Perhaps when I fall in love it'll change.

I was stunned the other day when I overheard her talking with

Danny. He said he'd rather die than live like a caged animal.
She said that as long as man is alive there's always some hope.
His life is hopeless, he complained, because his hair'll never grow
blond nor his nose straight. She can go out, see friends, enjoy
life, as he cannot. And then Lili said, "I don't enjoy this kind of
life, Danny. All I'm trying to do is to make the best of it since
I can't change it. But I'm weary too." I've never heard her talk-
ing like that. Nor does she seem to be weary.

August 5, 1940

Martin brought Remarque's All Quiet on the Western Front.
What importance does a single human life have? And what im-
portance has his experience? I found a passage in this book
which appealed to me very much: "We are not youth any longer.
We don't want to take the world by storm. We are fleeing. We
fly from ourselves. From our life. We are eighteen and we had
begun to love life and the world; and we had to shoot it to
pieces. The first bomb, the first explosion, burst into our hearts.
We are cut off from activity, from striving, from progress. We
believe in such things no longer, we believe in the war." I copied
it and put it in Mama's new wallet. Didn't say anything about
it to her; she'd have a nice surprise when she finds it there.

The next day Elli wasted more paper typing a single report
than she did during her whole training period. Ola asked her
if something was wrong, if she had some trouble, if she could
help. Elli answered that she just had a headache; and immediately Waldek brought her some pills and a glass of water. She
could not forget the pockmarked face.

She was in no hurry to get home ahead of Lili and so walked very slowly. To face this man alone would be more than she could bear. She was sure he would be back at night and wondered whether he would come alone or with the police. He had said that they would be sorry, and the furious look in his eyes left her with no doubt that he meant it. Perhaps he was a plainclothesman? But why did he say that Mrs. Kowalik was taking care of him? Why was he so upset when he saw that it was late? Immersed in her thoughts, she passed the church and walked along the cemetery fence. The way which usually seemed endless to her and which she dreaded she now trod without fear. She heard steps behind her and slowed down. To have somebody walking behind her upset her and she would always let the person pass. But the sound of steps quickly faded away; whoever it was crossed the street. She resumed her way. The lights of the camp's watchtowers were nearer and nearer. Suddenly she stumbled over something and fell down. She felt an acute pain in her knee — the same one she had hurt at the pump — and she got up with effort. The doctor had told her she must be very careful, for a lymph might develop and be difficult to heal. Although it was pitch dark, she realized that she was standing at the cemetery gate. She struck a match. Holding it against the wind in her folded palm, she bent down. His face in mud, a man was lying across the road. She turned him up and saw a face covered with dried blood and dirt. A single earlock was glued to his cheek; a bloody flap of skin was hanging where the other was torn off. She lifted the man's hand; it fell down like a log. A car passing slowly cast light upon the upturned head. She saw a boyish face, no more than fifteen or sixteen. One of the eyes hung out; the other, wide open, was glazed with horror. The Hasidic robe was torn on his chest, near the bare feet lay a skullcap. She gripped the boy's feet, dragged the body behind the gate, shut it, and went home.

Pock-face did not show up.

The following day she gratefully accepted Mr. Baryński's offer to walk her home. They made their way, as was their habit, mostly in silence. Baryński, a man of exceptional wit with a mine of exciting stories about places he had seen and people he had known before the war, rarely talked when they were alone. In front of the house he kissed her hand and left. Lili was not yet home. It took Elli half an hour to make the fire, then she fixed some food.

Lili came around seven; and after supper she said, "I didn't talk to you last night, dear, you seemed so exhausted. Now look, Elli, and please don't misunderstand me. The other night when this man came here you looked as if the sky had fallen on your head. You shouldn't . . ."

"I know I shouldn't, Lili," Elli interrupted her. "But I can't pretend as well as you, and I bet you were as scared as I was."

Lili shrugged her shoulders. "Sure, I was. But why should any idiot see it?"

"What do you mean any idiot? This man knows." Elli whispered the last words.

"Knows what?" Lili looked at her genuinely puzzled.

"You know what I mean, Lili." Elli was tired of this senseless conversation.

"Elli, my dear, my dear silly little sister, please do not ever think of it. You'll drive yourself mad. How could *this* ever cross your mind? Why? This is something you never, do you understand me, never dare to think about. Think whatever you want, that a man wants to seduce you, rape you, rob you, but everything else is out of question. Do you un——"

The door opened, and Pock-face squeezed in. He went straight to Lili. "I am very sorry about Sunday night," he said quickly. "I didn't mean to be rude. I just had one drink too many."

"It is all right, Mr. . . ." Lili looked at him, waiting.

"My name is Ignacy Kosiński." He bowed.

"Nice to meet you, Mr. Kosiński," said Lili. "I am Lili Warska, and this is my sister Elli."

"Can I sit down for a minute?" the man asked.

"By all means." Lili motioned him to the only chair but continued to stand herself.

"I know I should explain my intrusion," the man spoke hastily. "I live here in this house. On the second floor. I wouldn't like Mrs. Kowalik to find me here. She is now in the basement." He flung up high in the air a key he had in his hand and caught it again. "Never mind, I will say I didn't know she was there when I locked it. But I don't have much time. I must let her out before she'll notice. You surely understand that. Miss Lili, will you have dinner with me tomorrow?"

"Thank you very much, Mr. Kosiński," Lili smiled in a friendly fashion. "It's very nice of you and I'd certainly be delighted but till the end of the week I have to work overtime."

"What about next week?" He couldn't conceal his fury.

"I can't promise but I hope I'll have more time next week." The door slammed behind him.

"Oh, là, là," Lili brushed an unruly forelock out of her eyes. "I do not like that."

The following Sunday Lili introduced Jan Zamojski to Elli. They had dinner together in the restaurant. Jan was on very friendly terms with all four of the women. It filled Elli with apprehension. When she heard him ask Natalia about "Mr. Skotnicki," she knew she was right. *One hump is enough in our situation,* Uncle Michael had said. Was Jan only a shield against Pock-face or was Lili involved? Elli saw Jan twice during the next week, once he dropped in for tea, then disappeared and showed up after several days. Pock-face continued to pester Lili every night. Finally she gave in and had dinner with him. When she came back, she repeated, "I do not like that."

It was Saturday night and they discussed plans for Sunday when they heard a droshky stopping and a light knocking at their window. "Maria," cried Lili, and ran to the door. Maria came in, a big bundle in her arms. She put the bundle carefully on the bed and untied it.

"Emmi," whispered Elli.

"Yes, I brought her. We could not keep her in Lublin. I am cold and tired. Let's have some tea and I'll tell you everything."

It appeared that Emmi's mother turned up with her in Lublin and announced that she was going back to Warsaw. She was in contact with Mark. He had rented a hiding place together with his mother and invited her to join him. She would not think of taking the child with her, she said, trusting the family would take good care of Emmi. Maria, in presence of Rachel's father- and brother-in-law, told her that once she abandoned the child, she would never get her back. Rachel agreed and left.

March 11, 1941

Rachel had a cousin living on the same street, just a few houses away. The cousin's husband is in Germany, a POW. She is a blue-eyed, ash blond beauty. We sometimes teased the Old Man saying that he had a crush on her; he admitted she was extremely attractive.

Today a neighbor of hers rushed in and asked Rachel to come over immediately, because her cousin's children — a girl of four and a boy of three — were crying and banging at the locked door. Their mother had disappeared. Rachel went and came back enraged, with both kids and a note that their mother left: "I couldn't stand it any longer. A German colonel offered me shelter. Please take care of the children."

The child was feverish, covered with boils. It required a good physician to nurse her back to health. Now she was all right, Maria said. As to prove the veracity of her words, they heard a gay, "Hello Lili, hello Elli." Emmi tossed away the blanket, and in the next moment sat on Lili's knees. She was pink, smiling, and happy. "Aunt Maria told me she was going to bring me to you and Elli; I promise I'll be very good. I didn't like it in Lublin. Uncle Daniel didn't know how to make my bath, and I saw Grandpa Michael using Grandpa Weil's teeth and got very scared."

When Emmi went to bed, Maria told them that Emmi had once seen her grandfather brushing his dentures and, as she had seen such a device used only by her Great-grandfather, she thought Michael had taken them from the Old Man; ever since, she had looked at her grandfather with apprehension. Daniel's hands — calloused from handling the millstones, wires, and other mill stuff — hurt her sensitive skin. Though all in all she had not liked it there, Maria said she was a brave and clever girl, never asking embarrassing questions, always ready for the road. Still, it was a problem to know what to do with her in Chełm.

Maria gave Lili Emmi's baptismal certificate (Noemi converted to Emily could still be called Emmi), and then they discussed the possible alternatives. The choice was very limited. At first they thought she could spend part of the time in the restaurant. The place, however, was still closed when they went to work. Moreover, Lili objected strongly to letting the child stay among drinking and drunken people. A charitable institution, if any could be found, was out of the question because of Emmi's forged certificate. None of the four women from the restaurant could take care of her and these ladies were the only friends they had. The only answer was to leave the child at home. Emmi would have to remain indoors and never go outside because she might get lost or else be faced with confusing questions. Also, she would have to stay in the unheated room; it was too dangerous to have the fire on.

"You wouldn't leave a dog alone for the whole day," burst out Elli.

"A dog with her progenitors, yes," said Lili dryly. "Do you have a better solution, Elli?" She had not.

Emmi adjusted to her new life quickly and without difficulties, it seemed. They left her sleeping in the mornings with her breakfast and noon meal prepared on two plates. It appeared that the small girl ate her meals in reverse order, but this did not matter. It also appeared that the water left for her to wash with, she poured into the chamber pot. It was too cold to wash, she explained. This did not matter either, for every night she had a bath in a big basin, an investment Elli made with her first salary. At night when they came home, she greeted them with unvarying cheer; when asked what she did all day by herself she always gave the same answer, "I was waiting till you came home." Sometimes Jan would drop in during the day and stay with her for a while. When Mr. Rahm was out of town, Elli would run home to see if she was all right. Sunday was Emmi's. After Mass they would take her for a walk, have dinner together in the restaurant, play with her at home. But after a couple of weeks Emmi grew pale and lost her appetite. The lack of air was making her listless. Once, strolling with her on Sunday, they met Mr. Baryński. Elli introduced Emmi to him as a daughter of a late friend since any ties of kinship were taboo and Emmi knew it.

The next day Mr. Baryński, while walking Elli home, said, "Elli, by now you should know that there is nothing in the world I would not do for you. I know I have no right to talk to you like that. I could easily be your father. As you see, I never did speak until I saw this little girl yesterday. I do not want to know whose daughter she is, Lili's or your's. I only want you to know that if it would be helpful to adopt her, I would be happy to do so."

Elli was so stupefied that she did not say a word, not even when he kissed her hand and left. She knew she looked older than her years but it had never occurred to her that somebody might take her for the mother of an almost four-year-old child. Nonsense! Mr. Baryński simply thought the birth date in her documents was false, and consequently distrusted the other data. Hence, the offer to adopt the child. He knew that she was in danger and he wanted to save her child. Was he alone in his suspicions? Or were they all suspicious? Perhaps they discussed her in the office behind her back? Perhaps the rumor had already reached her boss? Perhaps he would call her tomorrow to tell her that he knew she cheated? She stared with empty eyes at Emmi kneeling in front of the huge cross hanging over her bed saying her daily prayers.

That night she awoke with a sudden realization that she had heard the first confession of love in her life.

The first thing the next morning Mr. Rahm's secretary told Elli that the boss wanted to see her immediately. He had not talked to her before as he communicated with his Polish employees only through his secretary. It was known that when he abstained from this practice, something was wrong. Elli knew exactly what it was. She put down the receiver and said to no one in particular, "Mr. Rahm wants to see me." Nobody uttered a word. Mr. Baryński followed her into the hall. She stopped, and on second thought, got the key to their apartment from her handbag, turned to him and said, "The little girl is no relative of mine. She is alone in the house." She started to climb the staircase. It crossed her mind that she still might call and warn Lili but instantly realized it would be too late. Rahm was a good friend of Robert Posch. They were all more efficient than she. She should have told Lili everything last night, and they might all three have escaped early in the morning. She had not wanted to frighten her. It had not occurred to her that it would happen so soon.

"Good morning, Elli," Lena, Mr. Rahm's secretary smiled. "You must wait a minute. Mr. Rahm is talking to one of the Posch brothers. Sit down, please." Lena was a pleasant-looking, smartly dressed girl, about twenty, the guardian angel of Mr. Rahm's Polish staff. She would always spread the news when he left town or even the office, so that they could do errands, take a sick leave, or just breathe freely. She had her ways of convincing him that his watch was too fast when somebody was late or too slow when he caught somebody leaving a minute too early. She always had a drink in her desk for an employee he summoned and would sometimes fill up his calendar so that a talk was postponed for days and eventually forgotten. Of course, thought Elli, she could not have done it for me. The matter was too serious.

"You look so pale, Elli," she heard Lena. "Would you like a drink?" Not waiting for the answer, she poured under cover of her desk a shot glass of vodka and quickly passed it to Elli. "Here, have a sandwich, you certainly had no breakfast."

Elli felt much better after the drink; she even ate the sandwich.

"I tried to find out from him what's the matter," continued Lena, "but he sometimes has that silly grin on his face which can mean everything or nothing. But I'm sure it's nothing serious. He is in a very good mood today."

Mr. Rahm, a minor employee in a Berlin travel agency before the war, had become a big shot in Chełm. His closest friends were the commanders of the local SA, SS, and Gestapo, like himself fervent hunters. The Chełm woods provided deer and Jews, both equally sought after. Mr. Rahm was said to be put into a particularly good mood when he had a chance to flush out the latter.

The phone on Lena's desk rang, she picked up the receiver, said, "Jawohl, Herr Direktor," and motioned Elli to his office. It was a spacious room, magnificently furnished. A thick brightly colored carpet covered the floor; a massive bookcase, a valuable piece of old Gdańsk furniture, occupied the whole length of one wall; a small oval table and two armchairs in soft leather looked frivolous in this place. Mr. Rahm was sitting behind a mahogany desk, under the standard picture of Adolf Hitler. There were no papers before him, just two leather-framed photographs, one of his wife, the other of his little daughter, and a carved silver paper knife. He puffed a cigar as he scrutinized the fingernails of his left hand.

"Fräulein Warska, yes?"

She nodded.

"When I ask a question, I must hear a reply."

"Jawohl, Herr Direktor."

"Yes, what?"

. . .

"I said, are you Miss Warska?"

"Yes, Herr Direktor."

"Is it the only word you can say in German?"

"Yes, Herr Direktor."

"What do you mean by this 'yes'? That this is the only German word you know?"

"Nein, Herr Direktor."

"So, now we have two, *jawohl* and *nein*. It's not much. I'm afraid I made a mistake. I trust people too much. Don't you think so, Miss Warska?" He deliberately aimed the last two words.

"Yes, Herr Direktor."

"It's good you agree with me. I would be desolate if you didn't." He stopped to examine his manicured fingers and looked at her for the first time.

"Yes, Herr Direktor," she said quickly.

"You work in the accountant's division, do you?"

"Yes, Herr Direktor."

"You work or you pretend, just like the rest?"

"I work, Herr Direktor."

"Oh, that's something new. I mean a new word. So your German vocabulary is not limited to only two words, is it?"

"No, Herr Direktor."

"Where did you learn your German?"

"At school, Herr Direktor."

"Did your parents speak German?"

"Yes . . . no . . . Herr Direktor."

"Yes or no?"

"No, Herr Direktor."

"All right. Let's suppose they did not. It's irrelevant. Look here, Miss Warska. I have a letter here concerning you." He got out a white sheet of paper from his desk and waved it in front of Elli. "Do you know who wrote this letter?" he asked.

"No, Herr Direktor."

"Do you know what this letter says?"

"No, Herr Direktor."

"Well, well. Suppose you try to guess."

No response came.

"I was told you are a smart girl."

. . .

"Gut. So, I'll tell you. But first I have an important call to make. If you don't mind," he said with mock politeness. She rose to go, but he motioned her to stay. He picked up the receiver and asked the secretary to connect him with Herr Standartenführer Rauschenbach. Rauschenbach, the commander of Gestapo in Chełm, was the terror of the town. The very sound of his name made people shudder. Wherever this dwarfish man with his ever-present horsewhip appeared, there was disaster and death. He used to race in a black BMW sports car through the narrow streets of the town for the pleasure of terrorizing people. He was known in Chełm as "the devil of death."

Mr. Rahm got his connection. His face brightened as he shouted, "Jawohl, Hans, so wie ich dir gesagt habe. I was damn right, my scent is matchless. What? Sure, alles stimmt. No thanks, old boy, brauchst du nicht, I'll manage. Wie? Nee, hab schon selbst erledigt. That's beyond any doubt. Thanks anyway." After a jubilant "Heil Hitler!" he slammed down the receiver, took a gold fountain pen from his vest pocket, and started to write on the back of the letter he had held in his hand, all the time. He wrote for a while, meditating gravely, his forehead wrinkled, his mouth tight. When he lifted his head, as if trying to remember something, he saw Elli and said with disgust, "Oh, you are still here. We have to finish our conversation, don't we?"

"Yes, Herr Direktor."

"What were we talking about?"

"You have been talking about this letter which you had on your desk and on the back of which you were just writing, Herr Rahm," said Elli clearly and loudly. She was done.

"So my friend was right." He looked at her with slight disbelief. "You can speak German. And not bad German either. That's what Herr Posch wrote me in his letter of recommendation and that's what I have been trying to find out for the past ten minutes. So, it's all set. Tomorrow morning you'll report to my secretary. You are promoted to her assistant. On the first of next month you'll get a raise. Auf Wiedersehen, Fräulein Warska."

May 1, 1940

I had the first lesson with a ten-year-old boy, Olek. Teach him Polish and history. It's much better than knitting. I didn't mind the work but felt terrible when I had to sell my "product." It was even worse than selling meat. After all, in the marketplace nobody knew me while with that stuff I had to go to friends of my uncles and aunts or to friends' friends. This foolish pitying grin, "Aren't you hungry, my dear?" "How's your poor grandfather, my dear?" "Who'd ever think Emmanuel Rostow's daughter would have to peddle, poor thing." God! I'd fling this damn sweater right into that stupid face! But I had to sell it. Such a good lady would turn this sweater over and over, look at it in daylight, in electric light, think, consider, reconsider, try it on, make silly grimaces in the mirror, call her husband, her daughter, her maid, her neighbor, to decide finally that it was either too light, or too dark, too tight or too big, and after all she has some twenty sweaters in her drawer and what she was really interested in was a new hat. Every time I pushed the button in one of these fancy elegant houses, I felt my heart in my throat. I prayed to God nobody was in, and of course, somebody always was. Once, after two hours' deliberation, an old lady bought a sweater, but it was Saturday; she said she couldn't touch money, she couldn't pay me. I came back four times for my money, then the lady moved out and I never saw it.

Olek is very nice and quiet but he never listens to me. I'd talk and talk and talk, and when I ask him a question, he doesn't have the slightest idea what I am talking about. I asked him what is he thinking about all the time, and he said he keeps imagining all kinds of food he'd like to eat. Most of all he'd like to have an apple biscuit with whipped cream.

May 6, 1940

When I have time, I take Emmi for a walk in her stroller. Just around the corner is a huge square, Pole Mokotowskie, which now is green and fragrant. Sometimes Lili and Martin join us.

The baby sleeps, or we put her on a blanket spread on the grass, and talk and play with her. Rachel is only eighteen, beautiful, has lots of friends, and sometimes leaves in the morning to come back before the curfew. If it were not for the war she'd have a nurse for the child and nobody'd blame her as they sometimes do now. Rachel brings all the gossip and all the news about the latest fashions. Last winter turbans were in vogue, and we made some out of shawls. The Old Man was enraged when he found out that Rachel accepted some dresses from a Jewish charity organization. He shouted not to dare to wear them in his house, and she never did.

May 15, 1940

Got my first salary from Olek's mother. After the lesson took him for a walk, and bought him an apple biscuit with whipped cream. He smiled for the first time since I have met him.

Emmi was growing more and more restless in her solitary confinement. A month had passed since she had come to Chełm and though she never complained, often when the girls came home they'd find the food untouched and the child squeezed in a corner. From the moment they entered the room she would desperately cling to them, till she was in bed. Even then she would tightly hold Lili's or Elli's hand until she fell asleep. Elli told Lili about Mr. Baryński's offer. Oddly enough Lili did not see anything suspicious about it. She said that probably he thought Elli had an illegitimate child and wanted to save her reputation. "Men in love do all kinds of crazy things," she said, and added on second thought, "and sometimes dangerous." She saw no advantage to letting Mr. Baryński adopt Emmi, for he had no way of taking care of her himself. Neither an adoption nor a nursery could be arranged without the child's baptismal certificate. They discussed the problem into the small hours of a Saturday night. Sunday was a sunny, clear day. After Mass and dinner they took Emmi for a long walk. Lili was telling her for the hundredth time the story about Sleeping Beauty, when they heard a loud "Halt!"

The guard from the wooden shelter at the camp's gate was waving at them. They stopped. He shouted, "Komm, Fräulein, komm hier!"

Elli grasped Emmi's hand and looked at Lili. Lili said, "Just keep quiet. Let's go over to him."

Holding the child between them, they crossed the street and approached the guard. It was a boy of perhaps twenty, tall, massive, his face red from cold. He seemed a little embarrassed when he asked, "Deutsch — German — sprechen — speak?"

Lili told him she spoke German. His face brightened. He said that he and his friends saw the two "Fräuleins" leaving home every morning, so the child, they guessed, whom they knew from the Sunday strolls, surely stayed alone. Wouldn't it be better if the "Fräuleins" left the girl in the morning in the shelter where they have a small iron oven? Later, when the sun came out she could play in the yard and they would, of course, look after her, take her in when she was cold, and feed her warm soup. The offer was made in an almost pleading tone, as if the soldier were afraid they might turn it down. Hearing no reply, he added that he was speaking on behalf of his colleagues, the other guards, who entrusted him with this mission.

Meantime, another soldier rolled a huge snowball toward them, and in no time a real snowman, something Emmi had never seen before, was standing near her. She dropped the girls' hands and slowly approached the strange creature. She touched it with her fingers, its eyes of coal, its carrot mouth, and burst out laughing happily when the soldier put his cap on the snowman's head.

"Thank you very much," said Lili, her eyes fixed on Emmi. "We appreciate your kind thoughts. Yours and your friends'. We will bring the child tomorrow morning at six o'clock and pick her up between five and six at night. Thank you once more." They had a hard time persuading Emmi that they must go home now, and that she could play with the snowman again in the morning. The soldiers saluted, and they left.

Hans, Klaus, Kurt, Willi, Heinz, and Fritz became within a few days Emmi's beloved topic of conversation. She picked up some German and got along with them splendidly. The color came back to her cheeks, she ate heartily, though mostly with the soldiers. At night, when Lili came to pick her up, they would give a detailed report of her meals like a nurse eager to satisfy the mistress. They boasted about her looks, appetite, and German, and at one point suggested that she might spend Sundays with them too in case the "Fräuleins" should have some plans of their own.

In company Emmi spontaneously referred to them as "my nurse," never mentioning the names. The girls preferred it that way, of course, in order to avoid questions or comments. Only their friends in the restaurant and Jan knew about the arrangement.

One morning a group of Jews leaving the camp passed them as Elli was kissing Emmi goodbye in front of the shelter. One of them, pointing at Emmi, said, "I had a daughter same age as this brat. And a son a little younger. They killed them before my eyes, and this damn goyish bastard is still living."

For the first few days, every time Mr. Rahm entered his outer office, Elli jumped in her seat. Sometimes, when his eyes were narrower than usual and their blue froze into ice gray, her heart would beat wildly. Finally she got accustomed to his frequent passing through the room and would not lift her head from the typewriter. When Lena first handed her a handful of letters, she typed them all neatly only to get them back.

"Each letter must have at the end a double-spaced 'Heil Hitler!'" explained Lena, "not 'hochachtungsvoll!.' They don't use it in official correspondence."

It was the end of her first week on the new job. She typed for perhaps the thirtieth time "Heil Hitler!" when Lena said, "We can call it a day. Leave it, Elli. It's almost six o'clock. Let's go home."

She was surprised to find the house empty. Usually — and always on Saturdays — Lili was home before her with Emmi. She thought for a moment that Lili might have been back and left; but the oven was cold and there was no trace of her or the child. She ran over to the camp to pick up Emmi. Hoping against hope, she asked the child if she had seen Lili. She had not. It was unusual for Lili to be that late; if she met Jan after work or if she had to stay longer she always phoned Elli. The child was already asleep when she heard Jan's familiar knocking at the window. He asked if Lili were home. He had waited for her at the appointed place but she had not come.

His nerve-hung face and eyes like a weary animal's filled Elli with panic. "What is it, Jan?" she grasped his hand. "What happened?"

He sat down heavily. "We'll have to find out. I'll have my boys work on it."

Elli stubbed out her cigarette. "It's Pock-face, yes?"

He nodded. "Yes, I suppose so."

When he left she poured herself a double vodka. Then another. Vodka was very cheap and given on ration cards.

It was still half-dark the next morning when she felt a touch on her cheek. "Where is Lili?" Emmi pointed at the empty bed.

Elli took the child into her bed and softly said that Lili was spending the night at her girl friend's house.

"When will she come back?" It was a new experience for Emmi. Never before had Lili spent the night at a friend's.

"I don't know exactly, Emmi," said Elli. "I don't know. Let's have breakfast." Neither of them could eat. Emmi drank her milk; Elli, a glass of hot strong tea. Emmi knew something bad had happened — or at least unusual. She was silent and refused to go out. Around noon Elli said she must see Natalia, and Emmi let herself be dressed. They dropped in at the church, too late for the Mass, but in time to have their presence noted.

Natalia had heard already from Jan and she did not conceal her distress. "It's bad luck it's a Sunday," she said. "I have already tried some of the people I know but everybody seems to be out of town."

That night Jan came. "She is at the Gestapo HQ," he said. "My boys found it out. She was summoned yesterday from the office and ordered to report immediately. I can think of no other reason than her seeing me."

Elli could.

"They have been after me for months," he continued, "and they would try to find out from her where I live. Haven't they been here?"

"Not that I know of," said Elli, her apprehension growing. For, as a matter of fact, why did they not look for him here, in their house, when he was the one they were after? They drank till the night turned into gray dawn.

The next morning Elli did not leave Emmi at the camp. She took her to Natalia's house and asked, in case she could not come to pick her up at night, that Natalia keep the child until Maria's next visit. She hoped that even with Lili and herself caught, they would not trace Maria or Emmi. In the office she remembered that she had not given Natalia Emmi's baptismal certificate. What's the difference after all, she shrugged her shoulders. Perhaps it was the finger of God? In Natalia's hands Emmi was safer with no certificate than with a forged one.

Lena gave her a big bundle of letters to file. Mr. Rahm had cleaned his drawer, she said, which he did twice a year. Elli mechanically filed the letters when suddenly her eye was caught by the words "top secret." She was not allowed to handle this kind of correspondence, not even those marked "confidential." She made a move to give the letter back to Lena when she saw in the middle the words "Jewish Quarter." She buried the letter among others and when Rahm announced he was leaving and would be back in a couple of hours, she read it. It was a copy of a letter dated November 2, 1942, written by an Obersturmbannführer of the SS Oberkommando in Kreis Cholm to the SS Headquarters in Berlin. It referred to the liquidation of the Jewish Quarter in Chełm and said:

This is to acknowledge the receipt of your letter No. 478/42/TR of October 26, 1942. With all due respect I feel myself wholly justified in denying that the orders I received in September, 1942, via Krakau concerning the a.m. item have allegedly not been executed efficiently. It is true that I encountered some unforeseen difficulties, listed below, though I must emphasize that these were overcome as quickly as possible and at present the area previously inhabited by Jews is entirely cleared.

The reasons which caused the delay in performing the operation were as follows:

1. The Jewish population living in Cholm did not report to the dispatch point in the number previously estimated, thus disobeying Order No. 71 of October 2, 1942; there is substantial evidence that the news concerning the destination of the trucks was spread here by refugees from the Warschau Jewish Quarter, six of whom were caught and shot.

2. According to reports from the staff, there were some unfounded rumors circulating among the Jewish population to the effect that

the trucks were destined for labor camps or even gas chambers, which are lies purposely spread by propaganda hostile to our Führer and the German Reich.

3. Some members of the Jewish population, contrary to their usual behavior, managed to escape to the woods east of Cholm. Investigations were duly conducted.

4. Those members of the Jewish population who succeeded in hiding in Cholm outside the Jewish Quarter (ten men, ages 18 to 34; eighteen women, ages 17 to 62; seven children, ages 1 to 8) were detected within four days following the date indicated for the liquidation of the Jewish Quarter and according to orders shot on the spot.

5. Some of my subordinates (four in total) got drunk the night the liquidation of the Jewish Quarter was due to take place. Although they were court-martialed the following day, their improper conduct in the troop charged with the liquidation of the Cholm Jewish Quarter damaged to some extent the heroic spirit with which every German soldier is inspired.

As it is evident from the a.m. facts, it was neither lack of control nor inefficiency which caused obstacles in the execution of the orders. As for point 5 — which was a regrettable occurrence unique in our close ranks when following with love and respect the ideas of our beloved Führer — alone I am responsible and am ready to account for it.

I take the liberty to point out that the obstacles, hitherto unknown, encountered in the liquidation of the Cholm Jewish Quarter, can be put to a good use in future actions of this kind and thus prove useful for the consolidation of the powerful Third Reich. Heil Sieg!

The "Heil Sieg" was still dancing before her eyes when she heard Lena say she had a phone call. An unknown voice said evenly, "Lili was set free half an hour ago. We brought her home. The doctor will call at seven o'clock."

Who were "we"? Why had she to be brought home? Why a doctor? She told Lena she must go and without further explanation grabbed her coat and rushed out. She decided to leave

Emmi at Natalia's. She did not want the child to see Lili in a state in which she was unable to walk by herself.

Lili was lying on the bed in her coat. She was unconscious. Her disheveled long hair was clotted with dry blood. Her upper lip had a deep cut still wet with blood. When she unbuttoned her coat, Elli saw the navy blue dress torn to pieces. The skirt was fastened with a safety pin; another safety pin held the blouse together over her breasts. She made a fire and warmed a kettle of water. She undressed the inert body as gently as she could, but was afraid to touch the underwear sticking to the bloodied skin. She washed Lili's face, hands, and feet, and waited. At the stroke of seven somebody knocked the agreed signal at the window and she let in a short, plump man. He ordered her to heat as much water as possible and give him clean towels and sheets. Lili moaned softly.

He was finished at ten o'clock. "She is still unconscious," he said. "It's better that way. You'll give her these pain-killing pills when she regains consciousness. Not more than one in two hours. It's nothing serious. All skin-deep wounds. I'll be back tomorrow at the same time to change the dressings."

Past midnight Lili began to toss on the bed. "I don't know, Mr. Wendel," she murmured. "I can't tell . . . I don't know . . ."

Elli froze. Wendel, Rauschenbach's deputy, was an expert in making people talk. She put a fresh cold compress on Lili's head.

"I saw him once . . . maybe twice . . . from Warsaw . . . Krotoszyn . . . they died . . . Catholic . . . Roman Catholic . . ." It was graying when she jumped and sat straight up in the bed. She said in a clear voice, "No. I never was in any ghetto. No. I have told you already. My mother is dead. Dead, dead, dead," she cried spasmodically, fell back on the pillow, and breathed heavily. Elli was putting her coat on when Lili's voice reached her.

"No, Mr. Wendel, thank you. I have nothing else to say." She sounded very polite. "I can't accept your offer, Mr. Wendel

. . . I regret the truth is so disappointing for you . . . truth usually is . . ."

It was a load off her mind when Lena told her that Rahm left for Kraków and would be back in three days. Elli told her Lili had had an accident and she must go back home. Lena promised to sign the attendance record for her for the following two days. She dropped in to ask Natalia to keep the child for a couple of days. Natalia told her Jan got away and wanted Elli to know that his boys would take care of Pock-face. They had proof that he reported on Lili. Elli half-listened to Natalia's words, trying to calm Emmi, who begged to go home.

"Lili is sick, dear," she said softly. "Please try to understand. She mustn't be disturbed."

Emmi looked at her, her blue eyes reproachful. "But, Elli, I won't disturb her. I will nurse her, please believe me. She taught me once how to nurse my doll when it was sick. I know how to do it." She felt deeply insulted and tears rolled down her cheeks when Elli refused. "You don't believe me," she cried. "Lili certainly would. Would you please ask *her* if she wants me to nurse her?"

Elli promised she would and left in a hurry. She found Lili moaning and for the rest of the day kept giving her the pills. In the afternoon Lili said firmly, "No, Mr. Wendel. No, thank you. No, I have nothing to add." Around six she called Elli. Elli leaned over her. She was conscious, but her eyes had a strange blank detached look. She lay, holding Elli's hand, wordless. At seven the doctor came, changed the dressings, left some more pills and said he would be back in two days.

September 14, 1940

Lili said today that, if I still don't believe in the ghetto, she'd like to show me something which might make me change my opinion. I went with her and Martin. They took me to a

*part of Warsaw I've never seen before. I knew about Nowolipki
and Nalewki streets from the books of Pola Gojawiczyńska. Now
I've seen them. Also, I've never before seen so many Jews
dressed in Hasidic robes. They looked phantasmagoric, running
through the streets, the black coattails flying in the air like ugly
birds. They talk with their hands and heads and bodies; they
scream and shout, all in Yiddish. They really look dirty, and the
streets and houses are filthy. And then Lili showed me a red
brick wall under construction. This, she said, is the wall which
will surround the ghetto. Nine feet high, eleven miles long.
I couldn't say a word. Her smile was detestable when she said,
"Now do you believe? Or perhaps it's just the reconstruction of
the old city walls, my dear little historian."*

It so happened that it was Emmi who finally nursed Lili back
to life. After all, she was the only one who could stay home. She
would walk around as if on the tips of her fingers; she knew a
patient needed silence. She would change the compresses on
her head and felt very embarrassed when Elli showed her that
the pillow was drenched with water dripping from the compress.
She promised to wring it out "with all my strength," but her
tiny fingers could not manage. She kept sitting, silent as a mouse,
all day long near Lili's bed, serving her tea, a biscuit, some soup.
Lili seldom said a word. Most of the time she lay silent, her blank
eyes fixed at some distant point. The day Lili first got up, Mrs.
Kowalik rushed into their room — for the first time since they
had lived there — screaming madly, "They killed him! They
killed him! My beloved! My sweetheart! These bandits! They
killed my man!"

She had found him with a hole in his head behind the house.
He held in his cold hand a note, which she now tossed furiously
on the floor. The note bore a round stamp and a signature. It

said: "On behalf of the Headquarters of the Armia Krajowa. Death to the traitors."

They never learned whether Mrs. Kowalik connected them with the assassination of Ignacy Kosiński or whether despair drove her mad. From that day on their life in her house became unbearable. She would run into their room several times at night, wailing, crying, cursing. Emmi became nervous and jumpy. Elli was dead tired in the morning and half-asleep in the office. Only Lili showed no sign of annoyance. It was as if she neither saw nor heard the woman. It would be dangerous for them to move to another place, to go again through the registration procedure, to change the landlady, to meet new people. But the situation worsened from day to day. The bereaved old woman had gone out of her mind. After she rushed in once, threw herself upon the remote Lili screaming, "You slut, they should have killed you," Elli decided that they must move out. For the time being Emmi, deprived of her baby-camp, was not a problem since Lili had a sick leave. Within three days Lena found a room for them. It was a neighbor of hers, an older widow who, Lena said, wanted to sublet the room immediately. Without seeing either the room or the landlady, Elli packed their meager belongings, left the rent on the table, and shortly before the curfew they arrived at the new place. Lili did not ask a single question when Elli was packing; she merely sat in the chair, smoking a cigarette, staring at nothing. Emmi helped, eagerly humming, "Let's go; let's go; let's go; and leave the witch behind."

The new house was in a nice neighborhood, close to Elli's office. The nightmarish trip home, the cemetery, the camp, came to an end. And the ghastly nights. The new landlady, Mrs. Banasik, greeted them very warmly, happy, as she said, that friends of Miss Lena, the secretary to Herr Treuhänder himself, would be her tenants. She let them into their room, invited them to have tea with her, switched on the light, and left. The room with its three windows was much more pleasant than the old one, simply but nicely furnished. There were only two beds but Mrs. Banasik promised to get a small couch for Emmi.

On one of the beds Elli saw a pink lace nightgown and a pair of pink fuzzy slippers beside the bed table. She took the glasses out of her handbag and gave the room a closer look. In an open wardrobe hung several bright dresses. On the table lay half a pack of cigarettes; an ashtray was full of lipstick-stained butts. Earrings, necklaces, bracelets, artificial but in good taste, were scattered on the table. Every drawer in the bureau was pulled out, fancy lingerie, silk stockings, scarfs, gloves, small bottles of perfume, all mingled together. An elegant young woman, probably fond of dresses, must have left this room in a hurry. Too tired to face Mrs. Banasik again, Elli gave some bread to Lili and Emmi, sneaked into the kitchen to bring water, helped them both to wash and go to bed. The moment her head touched the pillow she fell into a heavy restless slumber.

Mrs. Banasik greeted her with a friendly "good morning," and inquired about their first night in her home. She said it was very important to remember the dreams Elli had, for those in a new place always turn true. "Mrs. Banasik," said Elli wearily, "could you please tell me who had left this terrible mess in our room?"

"Oh, I am sorry, miss," exclaimed Mrs. Banasik. "I am really sorry. But you moved in so quickly that I haven't had the time to clean it. I'll do it later. Or," she added on second thought, "if you don't mind, simply put all she has left in one of the drawers. She will never come back."

"Who?" asked Elli.

"This girl had lived here hardly two weeks when they found out she was Jewish. People say somebody reported her. Anyway, the other night the Germans came and took her. Do you think she might come back?"

"No," said Elli.

"That's what I thought too. And that's why I rented the room.
I also wanted to do it quickly, to show my neighbors I had no
idea who she was, to show them that I would let only Poles into
my house, Catholics, as you are. So, I asked Miss Lena to recom-
mend this room to some quiet, religious girls, and I was happy
when she told me the other day that her own assistant was looking for a place." Mrs. Banasik put a kettle on the oven and went
on, "A pretty girl she was, and nice too, who would think she'd
be that mean? She was perhaps twenty. So young and yet so
corrupt, would you believe it? She said she came from Warsaw,
but now I don't believe a word she said. People say that it was
also her excellent German that made her suspicious. Otherwise
she was blond, though dark-eyed, but when I think of it now, she
had a very long nose."

"Had she?" said Elli.

"Oh, sure. The more I think about it the more angry I am at
her. Mind you, to expose me to such a danger! To lie so im-
pudently, so shamelessly! I realize now that she always left the
door of her room open to make me see that she was saying her
prayers." The woman's face was turning red. "A cheater, arrogant, selfish, ruthless, like all Jews! They'd do anything, insult
God and man to have their own way. She didn't care that the
Germans might think I was hiding her, this damn bitch." She
crossed herself quickly and invoked God as her witness that she
was neither a violent nor an angry woman. "But you'll agree
with me that a thing like that, the danger she willfully put me
in, would make anybody mad." She looked at Elli for approval.

"Yes, of course, Mrs. Banasik," said Elli.

The same day she asked Ola if she knew about a room. She
asked her friends in the restaurant and even Mr. Baryński whom
she had avoided from the day he gave her back the key to their
apartment. But the thought of spending another night in
this room made her sick. When she came home, she found the

room sealed off by the police. The former tenant had been sentenced to death and her property confiscated, they said. Lili and Emmi were sitting in the kitchen on suitcases. Mrs. Banasik suggested they spend the night there, but Elli politely refused. The next six days they lived in the basement of Lena's house. It was there that Lili mentioned for the first time that it might be a good idea to talk to Mr. Wendel.

Mr. Baryński found them a room that belonged to his friend who had been temporarily transferred to Lublin. His landlady, Mrs. Palinska, agreed that the girls could live there until he came back in May. She had grown very fond of Emmi and suggested she would keep an eye on the child when Lili went back to work. She also had a niece living nearby, with two children Emmi's age, and they could play together in the small garden at her niece's house, she said.

Lili was silent and withdrawn; her eyes retained the blank look; her auburn hair lost all its shine. She walked stooping, her eyes down. It seemed as if she grew smaller, as if she wanted to pass unnoticed. When she spoke, it was mostly to Emmi; with Elli she often grew impatient, sometimes rude. Her moods became unpredictable. One day she would play and sing with Emmi, the next lie on her bed, chain-smoking in utter silence. Days passed when they simply exchanged greetings and communicated when it was absolutely necessary.

In the end of March their landlady announced that she was leaving for a couple of weeks to visit her family in the country. Again, Emmi would have to stay home alone. Automatically typing a letter, Elli was racking her brains concerning the child when Lena lightly touched her shoulder and said that somebody was waiting for her downstairs.

It was Miriam. She said that Maria had obtained a letter of

recommendation for her from Mr. Posch to the Treuhänder in Zamość who needed a German-speaking secretary. Smiling, she told Elli that she found out from Mr. Posch that the Treuhänder in Zamość was a good friend of Elli's boss, and she thought it might be a good idea if Elli introduced her to Mr. Rahm as her cousin.

"You are mad," said Elli. "Get it out of your mind. What have you done with your child?"

Miriam frowned. "I had to leave it," she said quietly.

"Leave it? Where?"

"Well, there was nothing I could do about it," Miriam said slowly. "I would have perished together with her."

"What have you done with her?" Elli whispered angrily.

"I told you I left her." Miriam tried to free her hand from Elli's grip.

"Where did you leave her? With whom?"

"With nobody in particular," Miriam dropped her head. "I left her at the gate of a big elegant apartment house in Warsaw. I am sure some good people will take care of her. I have the address, I'll find her after the war. She was such a sweet baby. I know it was not the right thing to do," she wiped her eyes, "but there was no way out."

"And you . . ."

Mr. Rahm was crossing the hall. He cast a look at Miriam, then at Elli, and went upstairs.

"I guess I'd better go," said Miriam. "Goodbye, Elli."

December 19, 1941

Aunt Adela, Miriam, and Nathan arrived today. Miriam is pregnant. She refused to have an abortion in Lublin, although my mother and her own husband implored her to do it. She said she absolutely must have this child, she must prove herself in motherhood, otherwise she would not be a perfect female. "You are a perfect fool," cried David. "Don't you see my child is starving?" "That's your child," she answered smiling. "Mine will be naturally different, because I am different. I'll feed it with my vital juices, I'll transfuse in it my resistance and strength, and it'll be as happy as I am." "And as crazy," cried David.

The day their landlady left for the country Rahm casually asked, "Fräulein Warska, do you know that girl, whom you were talking to the other day in the hall, very well?"

Elli knew he knew. "No, Herr Direktor," she said. "It was the first time I ever met her."

As he signed the letters she had brought, he said without looking at her, "That's interesting. She claimed she was your cousin. That's what she told my close friend in Zamosc. He phoned me this morning to warn me." He got up, walked to the window, and with his back turned to her said, "Yes, Fräulein Warska, to warn me. She told him she was a Jew." He sat down on one of the leather armchairs and went on, "She escaped at night but that's beside the point. Our men will get her. I just wanted to find out what your relationship is?" He was watching her closely.

"I saw her for the first time in my life the day she was here, Herr Direktor," said Elli.

"Well," Rahm quietly puffed his cigar. "Her end will be anything but enviable. Our men will see to that. You surely know what I mean. Do you?"

"Yes, I do, Herr Rahm." Elli was looking at the bluish circles of smoke he puffed out.

"Your complete indifference certainly does you credit. It might convince even me. Do tell me, however, Fräulein Warska, how did it happen that she came to see you, a perfect stranger?" Elli waved her hand. "Oh," she said lightly, "she just came from Warsaw where she met my girl friend who knows I am working here. With no friends here, she thought she might sometime come over here on Sunday and spend the day with me and my sister. At least that's what she said."

Rahm got up. "You can take the mail, Fräulein Warska. It is signed."

7

THE HEAVY SILVER SAMOVAR smashed into small pieces as if it were made of thin glass. "Elli, Elli," said her father softly, "How could you do it to me?" She ran to tell him that she just wanted to get the razor out of it; she embraced him warmly but he kept repeating, "Elli, Elli," and his hands were ice-cold.

"Elli, Elli," the whisper rang in her ears while she struggled back to consciousness. It was almost completely dark in the room. The phosphorescent hands of the alarm clock showed half-past four. "Elli, Elli." She felt a wet cheek on hers and two cold little hands around her neck. She pulled the small shivering body under her cover.

"What is it, darling?" she whispered. "Did you have a bad dream?" The child sobbed without restraint. "Elli, don't leave me alone, please, please, don't leave me alone at home." Elli hugged and kissed her. "Sleep, dearest, sleep," she said soothingly. "I'll try to work something out. You must not think about it now. Try to sleep, darling." She rocked her in her arms, humming quietly a lullaby, a remote, long-forgotten song about an old man, chased by angry dogs, drenched, cold and hungry, saved by a child's loving heart. Emmi finally fell asleep but now and again she would quiver and squirm. Nor did she loosen for a moment the tight grip on Elli's neck.

At five Lili lighted a cigarette. Elli saw her often smoking at night, but Lili wouldn't even answer when asked about her new restlessness. Now she lay, her eyes fixed on the ceiling. She did not budge when Elli sat on the edge of her bed and asked hesitantly, "Lili, when will you be back home today?"

"I don't know."

"Listen, dear, I must stay in the office overtime. Emmi will be alone all day long. She is frightfully upset. Maybe I can manage to drop in at noon, but I'll have to go back. Couldn't you come around four?"

"No. I can't. I have an appointment." Lili's voice was detached.

"Couldn't you postpone it until tomorrow, Lili?"

"No. I have an appointment with Mr. Wendel."

"Lili! You can't be serious! Did he tell you to come?"

"No."

"So, why this appointment?"

"Why not?" She lit another cigarette.

"You mean it is you who want to see him?"

"Precisely."

"But Lili, you are exposing yourself." Elli trembled all over. "And all of us."

"I am not. I will save you. You will see."

"Lili, be reasonable. What are you talking about, for heaven's sake? This German will destroy you. He already tried."

"What do you know?" Lili smiled coolly. "He certainly will not. He will help us all."

"Lili, you are not going to tell him, are you?" She grasped Lili's hand, which Lili impatiently pulled back. "He is the most dangerous Gestapo man in the town," she said imploringly. "Everybody knows that. You don't know what you are doing!"

"I know perfectly well. Please leave me alone."

"But you can't possibly talk to him. It's sheer madness, Lili."

"OK. I am mad. Let's leave it like that. Mad or not I am going to meet him."

"Lili, you can't really mean it. Say you don't."

"But I do. He is a quite decent man. I know he is. We are doomed anyway. If anybody can help us he can. Don't worry. I'll make a deal with him."

"Please, please, Lili, don't go today. We'll talk it over tonight. I must run now. I am already late. Please, promise you won't go, you won't meet this man."

"You silly girl." The vague, inscrutable smile appeared again on her lips. "You have no idea what power this man has."

Elli washed and dressed quickly, got the breakfast ready for Emmi, and left. Passing her boss with a polite Guten Morgen (he did not like gloomy faces, especially in the morning), she realized, as she did every day entering the office, that she had a whole day ahead of her, a twelve-hour day, every hour made of sixty minutes and every minute of sixty seconds. What could happen in every one of these hours, minutes, seconds?

It was ten o'clock, and Elli was finishing the third letter with the double-spaced "Heil Hitler!" when Mr. Rahm entered the room. She was alone because Lena had gone to do some errands for his wife who had to stay home with small Hilda. He turned to her, "Get your coat; you will come with me." He did not even say "Fräulein Warska," thought Elli. He has found out. He did not believe me about Miriam. He is taking me to the Gestapo HQ. What will happen to Emmi? Did Lili talk to Wendel? Impossible, it was too early. She said she would meet him later in the afternoon. And even if she did, she would not tell him. I am crazy. What will happen to Maria? Will they find out about her? What will Lili do when I don't come back tonight? Will they go at once to Posch's office? Will she have time to take the child and escape? She looked at the clock on the desk. Five past ten. She took her coat from the hanger. Mr. Rahm in his fur coat of excellent cut was tapping the glass-topped desk impatiently, with his impeccably manicured fingers. "Let's go," he said.

When they left the office building and turned left, Elli knew for certain they were heading for the Gestapo Headquarters. It was a frosty but sunny day. Is it possible that I will never see the sun again? Poor mother, she did miracles to protect us and here it is. What will she do? When will she know? Dear God, let me not tell them. Following Mr. Rahm, looking at his handsome figure, she suddenly felt her paralyzing fear melting away and her mind perfectly clear. In some way she felt relieved. The nightmare will end. No more fear, no more humiliation. Still, her heart sank at the thought of her mother, the child, and Lili, at the sight of the sun, of the bare trees which would soon turn green and fragrant without her ever seeing them again.

Mr. Rahm passed the entrance to the Gestapo HQ and stopped at the door of the next house. He rang the bell. A young woman opened the door. "Tell her I want to see the mink coats she has to sell," said Rahm to Elli. She translated his request into Polish, still not believing this was the purpose of their trip. But it was.

The woman had two mink coats to sell which she promptly brought to the corridor and displayed on a hanger where they could be seen in the light streaming from the room. One was light gray, a large, the other dark brown, smaller, both in excellent condition. The silken labels, which Rahm studied with great attention, indicated a Viennese furrier. As it often happened, these two luxurious coats might have been either exchanged for bread by some Jew or left with this woman "till better times come."

Rahm smoothed the shining hair of the gray mink, carefully inspected its rich soft collar, obviously pleased with its freshness and elegance. He took a close look at the cup-shaped sleeves of the brown one, examined the armholes, outside, inside, but found no fault. Instead, in an inside pocket of the shimmering moiré lining he found a matching mink bonnet with a funny golden pin — a dwarf with a tiny ruby eye — and his face brightened with childish joy. This piece, obviously just now discovered, seemed to give him more pleasure than the coats themselves.

He looked inquiringly at the woman who immediately grasped the international language of "how much?" Elli repeated in German the ridiculously low price. Rahm ordered the woman to bring a fresh sheet, wrapped the coats in it, and told her via Elli that his driver would collect the parcel sometime that night. "Tell her I'll let her know about her husband in a few days," he concluded the deal.

The usual barter business. For two mink coats, I'll tell you where your husband is, should he still be among the living. If not, you will at least know there is no use waiting for him.

January 19, 1942

All day long we ripped fur from coats, jackets, and whatever had a piece of hair on it; the rabbit skin from Emmi's coat, the kid lining from the Old Man's coat, the trimming from Lili's robe-manteau (and what remained of the past glory?). All that made but a small bundle.

Late in the afternoon I went with Danny to the Judenrat to give them that Winterhilfe for their German masters. I felt abomination and shame looking at the two rows of people patiently waiting in freezing weather to give away freely the poor

remnants of what could keep them a little warmer, bringing
upon themselves more cold, more disease. If it were snatched
from us, if we were robbed of it — but no — like trained dogs,
we report here on order. Not the wretched paupers — they have
no furs — but those who still preserved the look of human
beings. Why didn't we burn these damn scraps of fur? Why are
we so obedient? so servile? I winked to Danny and we left the
row. In a small back street I told him I wouldn't do it. I didn't
have to repeat it twice. For more than an hour we looked for a
place where no one could see us. Behind a wooden barracks we
found a ruined latrine. The bundle fell down with a loud splash.

When Elli returned to her office it was eleven o'clock. Barely
an hour had passed instead of the eternity she endured. Lena
still was not in so she could not run home to see Emmi. At
noon Lili called. "Sois tranquille. Je n'y vais pas." Obviously
she did not want the office girls to understand. Confused, Elli
could find no answer, and Lili hastily added, "I mean it. I will
be home at four or even earlier. I'll feed Emmi and go for a
walk with her."

At last Elli said, "Fine, Lili. I'll see you around seven. And
thanks a lot for calling, dear." She put down the receiver and
resumed her work. Of course, Lili was just kidding in the morning, a little angry because Elli was pestering her that early. God,
how could she be so silly to take her sister's words seriously?

Emmi was sound asleep when Elli came home. Lili, smoking a
cigarette, was reading on her bed. "I had a beautiful long
walk with Emmi," she said. "The child was gay as a lark and
awfully hungry when we came back home."

Neither mentioned Wendel. It had been a long day. "Und
wieder geht ein schöner Tag zu Ende . . ." The popular German song sounded in Elli's ears as she was falling asleep. Drunk

German soldiers were enjoying themselves in the nearby brothel before going to the Russian front.

Two weeks later, early in the morning, Lili said, "If you want me to bring the bread, give me the passes and the ration cards." She was ready to leave. She started work at eight o'clock but recently was leaving as early as six. She said that she spent this time in the church. "I'm sorry, Lili. It entirely escaped me yesterday, but I'll certainly bring the bread today," said Elli guiltily, for provision was her department.

As soon as she had finished work, Elli went to the bakery.

May 2, 1941

On the way back from classes I bought a bagel for Emmi, which I held in my hand. On the corner of Karmelicka and Leszno, the half-wit, singing his usual, "oi,oi,moira,moira," tore it from my hand and swallowed it together with the wrapping paper.

She opened her bag to give the ration cards and passes to the baker. Because she could not feel the papers, she opened the bag wider and looked into it. She could not see them. Frantically she emptied the bag on the counter: some money, glasses, Arbeitsausweis, a comb, Emmi's tiny teddy bear, cigarettes, matches. She felt like collapsing. "You must have left the cards at home," said the baker, seeing her growing paler and obviously thinking she would miss the bread badly if she had lost the cards. Elli did not mind the ration cards at all; they would somehow survive without them. But the passes, the priceless passes were missing! Anyone could be stopped in the street at any time and ordered to produce his Kennkarte. All knew who it was who did not possess them. They could not even report the loss. A Pole could and would eventually get another one, but not they. Was it possible that she had lost all the documents? When? Where? Did somebody steal them from her bag? What for? For the bread ration cards? Here they were not *that* precious. Someone would rather steal the money she had. She ran home, her brain feverishly churning. She let herself in and began to look everywhere for the documents. She pulled out all the drawers, searched in the beds, under the beds, among Emmi's toys, and all in vain. She drank a cup of cold water and went to the restaurant where Lili and Emmi were waiting for her.

When she entered the restaurant, she saw Emmi playing under the table at which Lili sat, quickly writing on a sheet of paper. Two other sheets covered with her handwriting lay beside the first.

"Lili, have you seen our passes?" she asked quietly.

"No." Lili kept writing.

"Have you any idea what might have happened to them?"

"I have."

"What? You know where our passes are?"

"I do."

"Tell me, Lili, please."

"Two days ago when we were having dinner at the table in the other corner, you left your handbag hanging over the arm of the chair," Lili said in a dull, indifferent voice. "A man who was sitting at the next table opened it and took out the documents." She resumed her writing.

"Did you see it?"

"Yes." She did not lift her head.

"Why didn't you tell me?"

"What for? What could you have done? He must have known the documents were forged, and has taken them to get his reward from the Germans."

"Lili, please, be serious. Did you really see this man take the documents out of my bag?"

"I have already told you." Lili started the next page.

So that is the end. Why haven't they come yet? It is two days already. Maybe they are just waiting in our room? Elli decided to leave Emmi with Natalia. She left her soup untouched and walked over to Natalia. "Natalia, I have had some misunderstanding with Rahm today. He threatened that he would have me arrested. I don't want the child at home. They might take Lili too, you never know. Could Emmi stay here? And in case they take us both, would you take care of Emmi?" A "misunderstanding" with a German boss was no joke at all.

"Sure, Elli, she can stay," said Natalia gently. "But let's hope to God he was only threatening. That's their usual way. Emmi certainly can stay with me till Maria comes."

"She might not come for a month or two," said Elli aware that she might not come at all in case they should dig further.

"It doesn't matter." Natalia smiled reassuringly. "You know I like the kid. I might find some girl from the country to help out if worse comes to worst. But I am sure you will come tonight and take her home. Besides, if I don't see you by tomorrow, I'll pull the proper strings. It can't be that serious; I am pretty sure my 'friends' can help."

Elli kissed the child without bidding her goodbye in order to avoid questions. But Emmi felt something was going on. "Elli," she begged, "please take me home."

"I am not going home, darling," lied Elli. "I must meet some people."

The child was desperate. "Oh, please, I'll be good, I promise, just don't leave me here. I haven't seen you all day. Lili didn't even talk to me, she is writing all the time. Elli, please, don't leave me alone." Courageously, she tried to hold back her tears.

"No, Emmi," said Elli firmly. "You are my little darling girl, but you must stay here." Before she left she told Lili that she was going back home and that Emmi would stay with Natalia. She also asked her to stay overnight with one of the other women. Lili, still busy with her writing, did not seem to pay any attention to Elli's words.

Elli moved quickly along the street and started to climb the staircase. She could hear nothing. Usually one could hear their harsh voices at a mile's distance. There was no one in the room. The mess she had left behind was intact. She sat on her bed, her mind blank. She was no longer afraid, only tired. She waited for them to come for an hour, for two hours. Shortly before eight o'clock Lili came back with Emmi. Elli did not even ask her why she brought the child. She was too exhausted to say a word.

Next day she waited for them to come to the office. She waited from seven in the morning for ten long hours. But they did not come. She expected them to be waiting at home. They were not. Four days had passed since the mysterious man had stolen the documents. It was agony to wait for them when they took so long to come. Perhaps they were checking Maria to get all three at once? On the fifth day, when she was typing the second page of a monthly report, the office charwoman entered the room. "Miss Elli," she said, "I am terribly sorry I kept your bread card so long. My boy was sick and I couldn't leave him alone." And she handed Elli a loaf of bread along with the passes and cards. Elli looked blankly at the documents. Slowly it dawned upon her that she had given the passes and the cards to this woman to get their rations from the bakery. "You look so pale, Miss Elli; you are certainly hungry," continued the woman. "Let me give you a piece of bread. I can't tell you how sorry I am."

Elli smiled absentmindedly, munching the bread the woman had given her.

Back home Elli fed the child, washed her, and put her to bed.

Lili came precisely at eight o'clock, as she had now for a week. She looked composed. She prepared herself a supper of bread and beetroot marmalade, not interested in where the bread had come from. For several hours Elli had been racking her brains to know the reason that Lili had invented that fantastic story. But the fiction made no sense.

"Lili, why did you tell me you had seen a man stealing our documents?" she asked. "I have them."

"You have. Fine." Lili slowly sipped her tea.

"Why did you do it?"

"Just for fun."

"How mean! Don't you see I'm a nervous wreck?"

"It's your problem." She was pouring more tea into her cup.

"Lili, please tell me, why, for heaven's sake, why?"

"Because I hate you." She lighted a cigarette and started to read a book.

October 25, 1940

Autumn is so beautiful this year. We spent two hours in Park Ujazdowski with Lili, Martin, and Emmi. The sun was still warm, the leaves of gold and red and yellow dazzling. Emmi slept, Martin was reading, I was talking with Lili about our studies after the war. Lili would like to go to France and study medicine as already arranged by Papa with Uncle Boris when he came here last year from Paris. I told her I'd like to be an architect. Lili said I'd do much better as a gardener because flowers are probably the only thing I wouldn't be afraid of. She saw how hurt I was, quickly took it back, and said I'd make a perfect architect. But I'm sure it was only to comfort me.

The heavy winter, with slight frosts even in April, definitely ended. One more winter was behind them. Spring was now in full bloom. In spring everything seemed more cheerful, although Elli sometimes wondered if it was to be her last. The German soldiers were singing in the streets, "Es geht alles vorüber, es geht alles vorbei, nach jedem Dezember kommt wieder ein Mai." For whom? For them? Will Abel see another May, will Daniel? Will she?

While Lena was on leave, Elli replaced her in the office. She hated to work so close to Rahm, to answer his friends' calls, take messages from them, listen to their trivial jokes. She thought with relief that it was the last day of Lena's vacation. Tomorrow she would be back at her typewriter in the corner. The phone rang again on her desk. "Guten Morgen, Fräulein. Ich möchte mit Genosse Rahm sprechen. Oberst Johannsen am Apparat."

"Guten Tag, Herr Oberst. Ein Moment, bitte. Ich leite sie weiter," answered Elli.

"Warten sie, Fräulein, keine Eile, haben sie Zeit heute Abend? Ich möchte gern ein Wodka mit ihnen trinken."

It was the fourth time Johannsen asked her to have vodka with him. "Es tut mir furchtbar leid, Herr Oberst, aber ich bin erkältet, ich möchte nach Hause gehen." She was afraid he would be angry, and he was.

"Kann kaum verstehen, warum Genosse Rahm kränkliche Leute in seinem Büro beschäftigt. Unglaublich! Das vierte Mal in zwei Wochen sind sie krank. In einem Arbeiterlager werden sie sich wohl besser fühlen." Bang! Herr Oberst slammed down the receiver.

At this moment somebody timidly opened the door. A woman, poorly dressed, tall, heavily built, in the last months of her pregnancy came in. The name she gave, the black straight hair and dark eyes indicated her Ukrainian descent. "I would like to see Mr. Rahm," she said in a small voice.

"Can you speak German?" asked Elli.

"No, I can't. But I must tell him something very important," replied the woman.

"I will see if Director Rahm can see you. Please, wait a moment." Another mink coat. She went to Rahm and asked if he would talk to the woman.

"Bring her in," he snapped. Awkwardly, the woman entered his imposing office and humbly bowed. "Ask her what she wants, Miss Warska," Rahm said. Elli repeated the question to the woman.

"I found out," the woman said a little louder, "that some Jews are hiding in the attic of the house next to mine. I thought Mr. Rahm would like to know it. I can show him the place."

Automatically Elli translated her words into German.

"Fine, let's go," said Rahm. He opened his desk and took out a gun. While he was checking the cartridges, the door abruptly opened and little Hilda rushed in.

"Vati," she cried, "Mutti said she'd buy me a little puppy a man just brought, if you agree. Oh, please, Vati, please, say yes."

He put the gun in his hip pocket, took the girl on his knees, kissed her, and said, "Why, of course, Hilda, I agree. You know your father loves you. Go and tell your mother you can have the puppy."

The child planted two loud kisses on each of his cheeks, jumped down, and cried standing in the door, "Thank you, thank you, you are the best father in the world."

Elli left the room right after her and sat down heavily at her typewriter. Suddenly she felt a hand on her shoulder, "You will go with us, Miss Warska. I can't understand her."

She followed them. They walked for two blocks. The woman, no longer timid, stopped in front of a shabby house.

"It is here," she shouted, "on the fourth floor." Leading the way, she started to climb the narrow staircase, moving with difficulty, the impatient Rahm panting behind her.

Where am I going? pounded in Elli's head. What stuff am I made of? Here I am, a companion to the murderers of my people, feeling relief it's not me, it's not my mother, not my sister. Why don't I tell him, go ahead, shoot me, I belong to them? Would that make any difference to them? to Rahm? to God? That God who makes me hate myself for being alive? No fooling anymore. I'm damned, rotten. He expects me to appreciate, to be grateful to Him it's not me. Is this the price He set on my head? What kind of bargain is that?

They reached the attic. The woman indicated with her hand "here." Rahm with the gun in his hand opened a small wooden door and shouted, "Heraus, verfluchte Juden!" A gray-haired woman in her middle sixties was the first to come out followed by another, dark-haired, perhaps thirty years old. Then three children came out: a girl about ten; another about six; and a boy, three or four years old. Blinded by the sudden daylight, they shaded their eyes. Dirty rags were hanging loosely on their skinny bodies. None of them uttered a word. Only the boy cried silently. The older girl took him in her arms, hugged him to her breast to hide the spectacle. The younger woman gave her an approving look and held out her hand to the older, the mother to the two generations. The procession made its slow trek downstairs.

Here Rahm dismissed Elli and the pregnant woman, who followed the group with eager eyes. Elli went back to the office. Sitting behind her desk, she heard five shots.

Lena was telling Elli about a boy she had met on her holiday and fallen in love with, when SS Hauptsturmführer Brammer flung the door open and shouted gaily, "Guten Morgen, Fräuleins! Wie gehts? Lena zurück vom Urlaub? Sieht aus wie ein Röslein. Verliebt, was? Ha, ha, ha! Ist der Chef da?" Not waiting for an answer and without knocking, he rushed into Rahm's office. After a while the phone rang. Elli picked up the receiver.

"Bringen sie bitte zwei Tassen Kaffee und zwei Schnapsglaser."
Lena had disappeared meantime, so Elli made the coffee, put
the pot, cups, and the glasses on the tray, knocked at the door,
and entered.

"Nee, unglaublich," Rahm shook with laughter. "You can't
be serious, Helmut." They were sitting at the small table, hilari-
ous.

"Doch, Kurt, doch," Brammer assured him. "I received the
report this morning. You could have knocked me down with
a feather but that's what it said." She took the cups from the
tray and put each in front of them.

"You telling me these Maccabeans know how to handle a
gun!" roared Rahm. "It's the best joke I have ever heard." She
was pouring the coffee, carefully, not to let a drop fall on the
saucer. Mr. Rahm hated wet saucers.

"That's what I thought too, Kurt," Brammer got a paper out
of his pocket, "till I saw this. Look here: '. . . betrifft Ghettoak-
tion in Warschau . . . die Widerstandsnester wurden durch
eine Kampfgruppe der Wehrmacht niedergekämpft' . . . now
here: 'die Verluste des Gegners' — the language they use, these
blockheads in Warschau, to call these rats 'the enemy,' as if it
were a battlefield — anyway, 'die Verluste des Gegners sind nur
unbestimmt zu ermitteln . . . unsere Verluste zwei Tote, sieben
Verwundete' . . . Yes, believe it or not, they fight . . ." Elli
put the brandy on the table and softly closed the door behind
her.

As soon as Brammer left, she went to Rahm. She told him she
had had a hemorrhage at night and must go to Warsaw to be
examined by a good gynecologist. She said that she had had
this trouble before and had been treated by this physician. Rahm
answered there was no need for her to go to Warsaw; he would
arrange a visit for her to a good German doctor on the spot.
She argued for a moment, but he was not easily dissuaded. "A

Polish doctor cannot be better than a German," he concluded.

She waited till he left the office, told the same story to Lena, said she had decided to go without Rahm's permission because the doctor in Warsaw was the only one she trusted, and left.

On her way home she dropped in on Natalia, hoping she would find out something more. She again repeated her story, and when Natalia heard she wanted to go to Warsaw, she advised against it. A few days ago, she said, an insurrection in the Warsaw ghetto had started; and no one knew how things would turn out. That was all Elli wanted to know. She asked Natalia to keep an eye on Emmi and said she hoped she would be back shortly but, she repeated Natalia's words, in this situation "No one knows how things will turn out."

"Maria wouldn't like you to go, Elli," said Natalia. "We can certainly find a doctor here. It might be dangerous there. Better think it over."

At home Elli packed a small handbag, told Mrs. Palinska that Rahm had sent her to Lublin with no definite return date, and implored her to take care of Emmi. She left the ration cards on the table and a short note to Lili saying she was going to Lublin. If she were lucky she could catch the 6:30 train for Warsaw.

8

Wᴇɴ sʜᴇ ꜰᴇʟʟ ᴅᴏᴡɴ, breathless, heavy, all wet, Benjamin's words again sounded in her ears, "Don't try to get out at the cemetery gate; they watch it day and night; be careful not to get lost there." Which she had been. Now she left them far behind. Those people and the gate. And Benjamin too, it struck her suddenly.

From the very beginning he tried to persuade her to renounce the "absurd" idea of leaving the ghetto other than through the sewers. He had a clear liking for the word *absurd* and pronounced it, deliberately drawling, with a contemptuous grimace on his handsome face. He insisted the underground way was the only safe one left; any other was absurd. However, after Sara came back — the only survivor of fourteen who tried to get out through the sewers — Elli knew she would never make it. She was completely terrified listening to Sara's scattered account of the forty-two hours of hopeless struggle in darkness against the waves of thick, quaggy drainage. More than of people, or bullets, or fire, Elli was afraid of choking.

She wanted to get out as she had come in eleven days before — through the wall. The wall worked now the other way around:

it kept off the Germans who wouldn't enter the ghetto except through cleared paths and in close order; and it became instead a bulwark and passage for the insurgents. All she needed was darkness. Shelled and battered, the bricks were easy to remove; and any outlet in the open excluded suffocation.

Benjamin argued that within the last six days four out of thirty people who had tried the wall got out alive, whereas over sixty out of eighty got out through the canals. The last unfortunate group did not make him change his mind. He said bluntly that Elli was hysterical about this choking business and that it was better to choke than to fall into their hands.

Only one sewerage outlet was reported from outside to be still safe; it was the one farthest east which took at least sixteen hours to get through. Two others — one coming out right in the middle of a marketplace, the other in a distant suburb, safe only a few days ago — were already useless. Watched day and night by German guards and volunteering hoodlums, they had turned into actual traps. Abel reported from outside that both the guards and the Poles could now rarely be bribed. He said they enjoyed the game more than the money and strongly advised against taking this chance. The fun of the game, he explained impatiently to the amazed Benjamin, lay in surprising the people emerging from the ditch; they called it "pull-push." The point was to give a helping hand to the emerging person, pull him out, and at the moment he grasped the situation, to push him back and snap the iron lid down.

Benjamin insisted that Elli join the group of four, Leo and his wife Klara, Ala and Noah, and try the east sewer. He felt it was a far better chance for her than to go by herself through the deserted streets, where any errant bullet could hit her. Half-heartedly Elli agreed; and then Sara came back. That was when Benjamin told her, "Let me think for you, let me be reasonable for you." He was right that her brains did not work any longer. If she still knew anything, it was that her mind was a complete blank. She could almost physically feel the vacuum in her head. She reacted to Benjamin's arguments like an automaton, repeating dully, "I would choke, I would choke," so that at last Benjamin gave up. He told her she would never get out alive; and if she felt her instinct was right, she was mistaken. She did not know whether she felt anything, instinct or not, and she nodded approvingly when he shouted angrily that she could have just as well chosen a less absurd way of committing suicide.

The group of four left at dusk. Without Elli. It was a cloudy but warm May day. Moshe, the eleven-year-old guide, brought them to the sewer outlet. He was back late in the afternoon. He reported that the usual twenty-minutes' distance took them almost three hours; they had to wait twice for "enemy patrols" to pass, then a mortar shell exploded almost under their feet. Then, they again had to wait to make sure nobody was within hearing distance. This was not simple at all; Moshe scratched his head, his red-rimmed eyes weary and serious in his freckled sweating face. Explosions, detonations and fire, and howling dogs and hungry rats, could mislead the most sensitive ear. Finally, he saw them descend into the inlet. On his way back he was stopped only once by the sound of a shellfire he could not place. It was clear Moshe was very concerned with Benjamin's estimation of his assignment and reconnaissance. Benjamin looked at him sternly, shook his hand when the boy finished, then told Sara to feed him. He did not say anything to Elli but looked at her with bitter and accusing eyes while the boy was talking. Then they sat silent on the basement floor, leaning against the damp wall. Elli was dozing, her head on Benjamin's shoulder, while he scribbled something on small sheets of crumpled paper in the dim light of the candle.

At quarter-past three it grew light. Elli got up, stiff and cold from sitting motionless on the concrete, wrapped herself tighter in her coat, and said to Benjamin, "I will go now, Benjamin. I know my coming here and my leaving are equally senseless but I never had much sense. Don't be angry, please."

She did not wish him good luck; every word implying his survival would have sounded like an insult. He did not wish her good luck either. He told her to keep close to the walls, to stop at full daylight, wait in hiding until dusk. Then he said, "Don't try to get out near the cemetery gate; they watch it day and night. Be careful not to get lost there." He squeezed the crumpled sheets of papers into her hand, hugged her, lightly kissed her on the lips, and pushed her toward the door.

She left and never looked back, not even once. Not that she was afraid she might yield and change her mind, or might once more experience the compulsion of going back to stay with them till the very end. She was only afraid she might see somebody following her. She was more frightened of facing a man than of what he could do to her. A bullet in her neck was all he could do. She preferred to get it unannounced.

The moment she heard the basement door slam behind her, her mind started to work. She experienced a funny feeling, as if something clicked in her head and put her brain back in motion. She felt it defrosting, receptive. Again she was able to think clearly, the first time since Benjamin told them the fight was lost. Completely alert, she repeated silently his last instructions, jumping over scattered glass, broken pieces of furniture, half-burned bricks. She tried to keep as close as possible to the shattered houses; whenever this shelter — which was like a live thing moving, squeaking, swaggering — became too noisy, hinting danger, she would move farther toward the open, straining her ears and eyes. She felt defenseless and awkward without her glasses which had gotten smashed in battle two days before; her blinking, shortsighted eyes twice spotted at a far distance a green-gray uniform. Once it turned out to be a curtain dangling from a broken sash; once, a green-painted bathtub shamelessly exposed on the fourth floor of a split house. Waiting for each to aim at her, she lost at least half an hour both times.

It was six by her watch when she decided to stop. The day was bright and sunny, much too bright and much too sunny; a cloudy one would have given her one hour more in the morning and one at night. She had to wait now about twelve hours. She could not make out where she was; she had never been in this part of the ghetto before; and besides, the streets were a jungle of stones and bricks, impossible to tell one from the other. She guessed she had come about two-thirds of the way. Benjamin told her the trip should take her no more than four hours; deducting the lost sixty minutes, she had been walking for about two hours. She planned to start around seven at night; at nine she should reach the Aryan side.

She hid behind an iron gate in a huge, burned-out, red brick apartment building. From behind the iron bars she looked outside. For the first time she took a closer look at the area through which she had passed blind, attentive only to danger. She did not realize before how dead a dead city can be. Now she fixed her eyes upon the monstrous piles of charred bricks, melted iron, broken pipes, smoldering wood. And she prayed and demanded that this fiery desert reduced to dust and ashes had never been a man's home. Or, at least, not for a very, very long time. A year, or a half year, or, oh God, a month. Until she saw the first corpse, then a second, then a third. She closed her eyes and cried listlessly.

Then she fell asleep and upon waking, feeling her hand being touched, almost fainted. Her scream came short and shrill. She opened her eyes and saw a small boy standing close to her, gently stroking her hand. Before she came to her senses, the boy said in one breath, "I'm nine; I only look so small; my name is Isaak. Can you give me something to eat?" Dumbfounded, she reached into her pocket and gave him the parcel which Sara had put there last night.

But he was more experienced. "Let's divide it," he said. "You will be hungry too and you will find nothing to eat here. I have searched all over already. You know, I have lived here for a long time, and for the last two days I couldn't find a thing. Nothing, would you believe it, nothing at all."

He said all this so unemotionally that it made her blood run cold. His eyes shone with sincerity; his little face was patient, earnest. She felt nothing but a cold hurt despair; she was numb, heavy with dull pain. The boy, meanwhile, slowly unfolded the newspaper, with his dirty thin fingers gathered the overflowing marmalade from both sides of the crust, smeared it over the piece of bread lying on the palm of his left hand, meticulously measured it with the thumb and forefinger of the right, marked it in the middle with his nail, and broke it in two. One half he put in the pocket of a soiled, torn, adult-sized jacket, hanging loosely on him, the other he wrapped again in the newspaper to give back to Elli. He stood for a while, the small parcel in his outstretched hand. Seeing he was waiting vainly, he put it in the pocket of her coat. Elli stood, unable to move, to utter a word. The boy did not seem to be bothered by her.

Once more he gently touched her hand and said, "I must go now. I left my little brother over there." He pointed with his hand toward the nearby ruins. "Must feed him. He is always hungry and crying. You know how it is with children, they never understand a thing." He did not look at her; nor did he seem to expect any answer. Suddenly he knelt down, picked up Elli's glove, and tucked it into the other pocket of her coat. He turned toward the inner yard and started to go. Elli wanted to call him back, to say something to him, to give him the rest of the bread, but she could not utter a word. When still a child, she had experienced this feeling of frustrating impotence: she had been drowning and could not make herself cry for help. Now also she opened and closed her mouth like a fish searching for water, but no sound came from her throat. The sight of the tiny creature disappearing from the yard made her somehow move. She started to go slowly, then she ran after him. She had the sticky parcel in her outstretched hand. The boy did not turn. He could not see her. She could not call him. She saw the small figure diving into what might have been a store on the ground floor; then he emerged, desperately small now, on a heap of iron pipes. He stopped there for a minute, as if gathering breath, then jumped down and disappeared completely.

Unsure of what to do next, Elli stopped. Then she went slowly across the yard up to the smashed store entrance. Inside, water was dripping from a broken faucet; the floor was covered several inches deep. She turned and went back to the iron gate. She still could not voice a sound. Collapsed on the ground, she tried hard to say something aloud. She tried with "mother," then with "God," then with "father." Her lips moved but no sound came out. Then she recalled that the first word children say is "mama," and she tried this. Again she failed.

At half-past six Elli got up, combed her hair, straightened the crumpled coat. She took the piece of bread out of her pocket, put the small parcel exactly in the same place where the boy found her, and fastened it with a brick. To make sure he would find it, she took the beige glove he had picked up, put it on the brick, and placed a stone on the top. She left the gate, turned left, stopped, went back to the gate, and silently stared at the funny small pyramid. It was so silent that she could hear the dripping water across the yard. Suddenly her fingers felt something hard in her pocket and she knew it was the mint Abel had given her before he left. She put it into the glove, once more fastened it with the stone, and left.

She had been walking for perhaps an hour when she saw something glittering in the fading sunshine. Uneasy, nervously blinking, she moved forward a little. Right in front of her, at a distance of perhaps one hundred yards, there was a barbed-wire-edged cemetery fencing. At the same time she heard loud voices, laughter, shouting. And a trumpet in her head, "Be careful not to get lost there." Her palms and armpits were cold and wet. The pit of her stomach was hollow. She was afraid. Rigid, stiff, hardly breathing, there she stood, facing the gate, till it grew completely dark. Sometime later, perhaps as long as an hour, the voices died away. When she became aware of the silence she started to go.

She took a few steps, stopped, made sure nobody was following her, and then, delirious, lunatic, blind, took flight. She kept running until she fell down, Benjamin's words in her ears.

An acute pain in the elbow and in the knee brought her back to life. She touched the knee. It was swollen and sticky but she could straighten her leg. She was dying to light the last cigarette she had, but frightened it might draw somebody's attention. She lifted her head and saw a lamppost; this was what she had fallen upon. She crawled to it, leaned her aching back against it, and looked around. No ruins, no flames, no smoke, nothing she was familiar with. What part of the ghetto was she in? Which part was still intact? Benjamin said not one street was left, not one house; he must have been wrong. Her confusion growing, she stared at the smooth asphalt road glittering in the moonlight. A small kite was dangling on a birch. Not far behind stood a one-family house, then another, and another. None of this belonged to the dead city. She realized she had crossed its border.

Elli spent the rest of the night sitting on a log under the birch tree. When she sat down, she instantly fell asleep. Later in the night the cold and barking dogs woke her up. A nauseous feeling in her stomach reminded her that she had eaten for the last time when Moshe came back to the basement. She did not feel hungry, but rather dizzy. She stretched out flat on the ground, and with her face touching the earth lit the cigarette, carefully shading the flame with the palm of her hand. She was careful not to inhale too deeply on an empty stomach. She still had half of the cigarette, the glowing end down, in her folded palm, when the well-known, heavy pace of nailed boots reached her. She crushed the cigarette in her palm and lay still. When the patrol passed, she said aloud and absentmindedly, "Oh, mama." After a long while she realized that her hand was badly burned and that she could talk.

9

AT DAWN Elli boarded a green streetcar. She still could not make out in which part of the town she was. After half an hour's ride she recognized a familiar street. She got out and soon found a small dairy. A bell rang as she opened the door. Inside, it was white, warm, smelling of freshly baked bread. She bought a glass of hot milk. The plain-looking, friendly, smiling shopgirl and the warm drink made her feel safe and confident.

Sipping the milk, she deliberated whether to ask the girl to show her the way or to ask somebody in the street. She decided that the girl might be safer for she smiled at her and did not ask questions, though Elli's untidy hair, dirty hands, bloodstained stockings, and the mud on her crumpled coat might easily have provoked some. When she finished drinking, she asked the girl how to get to Boduen Street. To avoid questions, she explained in a somewhat hurried, husky voice, she had come from the country, had spent the whole night on the train, in order to visit an aunt whose apartment she had found locked; she was trying to discover her whereabouts from some people who lived on Boduen Street. The girl, busy draining glasses while Elli was speaking, took a white paper napkin from the buffet, bent over Elli's table in order to draw a rather complicated route, and explained where to change trains. Elli thanked her and paid for the milk.

She had her hand on the doorknob, her back to the girl, when she heard, "Be careful, we have roundups here from morning till night. They are raving, checking everybody, looking for runaways." A pause, and then, "You better get washed and get your coat cleaned." Elli slowly opened the door. The bell rang again.

Elli changed trains twice. It was well past eight when she finally found the house. Abel had given her the address before he left and she had memorized it, but now she stood stunned in front of an elegant, imposing apartment house. It seemed incredible to her that people living in this house could have anything in common with those from behind the wall, even for money. Good housing was still associated in her mind with wealth, security. Irrelevant now, she realized, a bluff, like my being here. Still she felt embarrassed touching the shining brass doorknob with her dirty hand. Shyly she opened the entrance door, careful not to soil the luster of the polish. Her embarrassment grew as she entered the spacious downstairs hall, all mirrors and nickel. Red-carpeted marble steps led upstairs. It was inconceivable. How did Abel ever find a hiding place right here, amid all this luxury? He was with ten or more people. She could imagine them hiding in an overcrowded tenement house, in some attic or basement, but not in a place like this.

Apartment number eight was on the fourth floor. She gently pushed the shining button. After a prolonged silence she heard footsteps and a female voice saying, "Don't get up, I will answer the door." A very attractive woman in her late twenties stood in the door looking at her questioningly. A huge mass of ash-blond hair contrasted strikingly with big, dark eyes, rimmed with long black eyelashes. She had the small, very red, and capricious mouth of a spoiled child. Her parted lips showed very white, sharp teeth. She was clad in a pink peignoir stitched in silver. She seemed to be more preoccupied with adjusting its folds with her shapely bejeweled hand than with Elli's answer, when at last she asked her jauntily, "May I help you?"

Elli was almost sure now she had come to the wrong place, and she did not know what to do. The looks of this woman, this house, this atmosphere of comfort and tranquillity that she had not imagined still existed — all this left her completely confused. She stared at the beautiful creature leaning against the oaken frame, waiting patiently for her answer, and mumbled, "I don't know, I think I have the wrong address."

The woman said quietly, "My name is Rena Zawadzka," and waited.

This was the name Abel had given her. She had made no mistake. "I would like to see Adam," she said.

Now the woman hesitated. "Who is that?" she asked.

"Adam and his wife Eve." This was the password.

"Please, come in." Rena Zawadzka let her in and closed the door behind her.

The hall matched the exterior. The fluffy, reddish-pink carpet; big, oval, gilt-framed mirror; crystal chandelier with matching side lamps; a set of ivory-colored furniture; everything too fine, too glamorous, perfectly suited to the landlady. In less than five minutes, Rena came back and motioned Elli to follow her. She led the way through an over-decorated, mahogany furnished dining room into a long corridor. They passed three pairs of closed doors and entered a room resembling the boudoir of an eighteenth-century French cocotte. Everything here was immersed in waves of wine-colored plush and white tulle. While Rena looked for the proper key, and tried one which did not fit the tapestry door in the right corner of the room, Elli had time to look around. She saw a huge bed with a lace canopy, adorned with four chubby angels, a bright soft carpet covering the whole floor, a three-winged mirrored vanity table, a chaise lounge with innumerable embroidered cushions. The flowery wallpaper was lined with all kinds of knickknacks; gold-stitched dragons on the heavy, velvet red curtains and on the matching screen were surrounded by small black birds. Meanwhile Rena turned upside down all the drawers in her bureau and in the vanity table and finally found the key on the bed table under a richly ornamented bedside lamp. All this time she did not say a word to Elli. Now she disappeared behind the door but soon was back. She motioned Elli inside and locked the door behind her.

In total darkness she heard Abel's soft voice, "It's good to have you here, Elli, I'm happy you made it." She strained her eyes in vain. She did not see him but felt his hand on her arm. "You must move very carefully here," he said. "Hold my hand, I'll get you through, don't trample on them."

Elli tiptoed behind him, tightly holding his hand. Once or twice she stumbled over a body lying on the floor but no one moved; she bumped into Abel and breathed a sharp odor of alcohol. After a while she got accustomed to the blackness. Abel's shadowy body towered right before her; hands and feet were waxen against the black floor. Abel helped her out of her coat, made her sit on the floor against the wall, removed a pair of feet, and squeezed close to her. "They are all still sleeping, won't awake soon. We had a hard time yesterday and lots of vodka at night. I'll let you in on everything later. First, tell me how Benjamin and the others are and how you got out."

Her report was dry and terse with no adjectives and no comments. So many killed, so many wounded, no arms, no medicines, no food, no water.

"So, they are lost." His voice was leaden. It had a strange, strangled quality. "Benjamin and the others." He stopped, and then, "I tried everything. I was even admitted to the emissary of the Polish Government-in-Exile in London. He kept me waiting for four hours; had an important conference. Benjamin asked them to kindly abstain from delivering useless weapons and machine guns without ammunition. 'We did all we could,' this man told me. 'We don't have spare ammunition.' Spare, mind you," he repeated angrily. "At this important conference they probably decided to write us off. Three, no, four days ago, I told them I do not want guns, all I want is help to get Benjamin's unit out. Since then, no one has answered my calls. No one has called me." The last words came out sharp, shrill. She never told him how she got out.

For a while they sat silent. The air in the room was heavy with the foul odor of alcohol, stale offal, and unwashed bodies. Still holding her hand, Abel said, calm again, "You must be hungry, but I have nothing to eat here. She will bring food first around noon, at least, I hope she will. You see, we ran out of money, and every time this happens, he will not let her bring food for us. He knows perfectly well he will get his money sooner or later, but he will keep us hungry till your mother comes and brings it. Twice in the last two months he has raised the price, and yesterday he came here again with all kinds of wild demands and threats. By God, Elli, you don't even know who I'm talking about," his laugh had an unpleasant note. "It's Rena's husband, Alfred. He is the rarest son of a bitch you ever met. You will have the dubious pleasure of meeting him. He'll certainly be back today. He kept pumping us from the very beginning, though not exactly at this pace." His voice became gruff, tense. "Max, who discovered him and is the oldest tenant here, told me that Alfred behaved quite decently for the first six months. Maybe he is afraid now that the war will end before he gets everything Max has. The news from the Eastern front has upset him, there is no doubt about that." Now Abel spoke hurriedly, it was plain he was boiling, and this eruption was a relief. "He knew Max before the war. He knows that Max's mother saved her jewelry, her fabulous jewelry, and he would like to have all of it as soon as possible. He does not even bother to conceal that, as soon as he gets hold of it, he'll get rid of us. God, how I hate this man. I could kill him with my bare hands." His face wore a hard, ugly look; it was contorted but at the same time sober. Elli shrank back with an unconscious look of dismay. "He comes here every now and then for no other reason than to tell us he feels uneasy lying in bed with his wife over there, with us shut right behind them, so he has to denounce us. He knows we know that if he does, they will not punish him. The first few times we believed him; it was hell; Abram tried twice to hang himself. Then we found out that he just enjoys this little trick. He rarely does it now. It's not amusing any longer since he cannot see us panic-stricken. For the last two months or so he has found another entertainment. To spite Rena, who really does not mind it — she is in love with a high-ranking underground officer — Alfred would come and take Marta or Ida for five or ten minutes and screw them behind this door. Abram, Marta's husband, begged him on his knees to leave her alone; Max, who sleeps with Ida, attacked him; but then, everyone got used to it. What could they do, after all? They know that we are in his hands. Now, when he comes to get one of them, no one pays any attention, save the girls maybe, though I really cannot tell if they still feel anything." Abel's face relaxed. "Rena hates him, though for reasons of her own. She is a very strange creature, you'll see. A bedable woman, isn't she?" he laughed harshly, "but a wildcat, too. Alfred bought her this apartment and furnished it with Max's money. He is mad about her, perhaps even more mad about her than about money. He knows she is with him because of that money and drowns his sorrows in liquor. He is drunk most of the time. Rena smuggles his vodka in here just to spite him. She'd certainly do the same with food, but he'd smell it somehow and raise hell. She is afraid that the neighbors might hear and that we'd be lost and they too. Don't know why he doesn't mind that we drink his vodka. Sort of comradeship, I guess, fraternity, headlined we are all human, we all have our weaknesses, our troubles, goddamn his guts." He choked with rage. After a while, quietly, "Now you know, more or less, what's going on here, though I could spare you this experience, I guess. Why did you come here, Elli?" he grew nervous again. "You aren't going to stay here, are you? Why didn't you go back to Chełm?"

Without a word she unbuttoned her dress, unfastened two safety pins in her bra, and got out a small parcel wrapped in a dirty handkerchief. Feeling its contents with his fingers, Abel said with excitement, "That's from Benjamin; it's very important, it's good you brought it now. Next week they'll have it in Switzerland . . ." And suddenly with his head down, "As if this could help . . . but still . . . I don't know . . . it can . . . non omnis moriar . . . Do you think, Elli," he sounded animated again, "do you think these facts and figures will shake the world out of its lethargy? Tell me, Elli," he grew impatient, "you think they will." It was hardly a question; it was a statement.

"No, Abel, they will not," she said softly. "And besides, you know as well as I do, it is not lethargy." She stopped. I must shut up, she thought, now immediately, but she went on, "It is plain indifference, a fear of getting involved, to derange the unperturbed emptiness in which they immerse their souls, their little immaculate souls unaffected by the human condition." She looked straight into his angry eyes. "You may say they are afraid of feelings, but it's more than that. Worse. Let's not kid each other, Abel. I shouldn't have taken the risk of coming here because of these papers; you shouldn't take the risk of sending them."

His face was distorted; his eyes gleamed with spite and despair. "You little idiot," he snapped at her, "you frightened, cynical idiot, shit on all that crap about souls. If everybody'd care about his own ass and nothing else, I wonder what'd become of all of us. You 'shouldn't take the risk,' I 'shouldn't take the risk.' Sure, our historical mission will be fulfilled if, processed into lampshades, we pass the message by softening the light at their bedsides. What time is left to you you can spend making designs for them. Just think of it, you offer the design, together with the raw material and the spiritual message. All-Elli-Top-Quality." He stopped, glared at her, and dropped his head. He must have realized he had overdone it because he changed the tone. "If your mother said it's no business of hers to sell Max's jewelry and bring the money here, what do you think will happen to these twelve people here?" This was a question.

Elli frowned and decided to ignore his outburst. "Abel," she said, "Abel, don't get excited. Why do you ask me questions if you don't want to hear the answer? You refuse to hear the truth; you cannot stand it; you are afraid to face it. You would like me to contradict what you already know. You would like me to give you the faith you lack. I cannot; I do not have it." She inhaled deeply the cigarette he had given her. "My mother is here," she explained as she had explained things to Emmi, when once the child asked her how a flower looked, or a bush. "She is one of us. She comes here, yes, exposing herself and her children, and what's left of her family. She does it, I guess, because she feels what we feel and because she cannot escape. Neither can you, Abel, nor I." She moved closer to him. "And that is not because we are locked together by fate and not because we have no way to escape — we know the ways and we know many who use them — but because we must save what is still human inside us. For later, in case there is a later. That's the trouble with us, I guess." She hesitated for a long moment before she whispered, "These people to whom you send your figures, hoping against hope, against reason that they will respond to them, will not do a thing because they do not understand. And I doubt very much if they ever would, if they ever could. Maybe, if we could talk to them, if they could see all this with their own eyes, I don't know. But a sheet of paper, covered with figures so wild that they offend any sound judgment, how can you possibly expect people to react to them? To imagine human beings behind those small black marks, even if you wrote them with your heart's blood? What can you prove by figures, Abel? You can go on multiplying them, bringing them up to date, adding those killed yesterday. But they will remain numbers for those who read them. You said there are twelve people here. What difference would it make in Switzerland if you add twelve to a six-figure number? And yet it makes a hell of a difference for us. That is the gap you try to bridge, Abel, can you understand?"

He pushed her away. "I think that the best thing for you to do is to leave here as soon as possible," he answered in a wooden voice. "These people here believe help will come any day from abroad, and only this hope keeps them from final madness. They are not sane, but I can still handle them. Twelve people, ten men, two women jumping at each other when sober, crying when drunk. Twelve people without light, without air, condemned to each other; women who lost children, men who lost dignity. I'd really prefer, Elli, that you go. You have it much better there anyway; you can breathe, you can move, you can see the daylight."

"But, of course, Abel, I'll go. I never meant to stay here. You know why I came; I carried out an order. I have nothing more to do here. Do you want me to leave right now? If so, call this Rena of yours to let me out." She rose.

"Don't be childish, Elli." Abel made her sit again and put his arm around her. "We should not have started this silly argument. I should not have started," he corrected himself. "Of course, you can stay here as long as you want. I'd be happy to have you here. At least you are somebody I can talk to, and I like," he added, hugging her closer, "yes, very much."

She stiffened. "I don't know if I can go back to Chełm, or when," she said quickly. "I'll have to find out. I left my office without permission. I was dying to see you all," her voice softened, and she held him close again, "to go back."

"Are you still?"

"No, Abel, I am not. But I had to do something about it. I was back in the ghetto the moment I overheard my boss laughing with his friend about these Maccabeans who know how to handle a gun. He asked him how he liked that, the best joke he ever heard. I knew I must go back. It was a compulsion, I don't know, I can't explain it. I knew I would be of no help. I did not know then how to handle a gun, how to dress a wound. I felt guilty from the day I left the ghetto. Rats always desert a sinking ship. I was obsessed by it; I could not get rid of it. It's silly, I know. I once told my grandfather that I'd rather stay there. He told me that what is hard is to live, not to die, that I should not take the line of least resistance. I left."

". . . And you went back . . ."

"Yes, I did."

"And you got rid of your guilty feeling." Half mockingly.

"I don't know. I do not think so. Now I think that staying there wouldn't have amounted to the line of least resistance. But then I thought my grandfather was right. He believed they'd slaughter us like sheep. It looked like that at that time. Some people were apathetic, others frantically trying to get outside; but nobody, at least nobody I knew, considered staying in order to fight. Why, tell me, Abel, why? Why didn't we do it a year ago? Why did we take every insult? Why did we wait so long?"

"I thought a long time about it, Elli, but I don't know that I have the right answer or that anybody will ever have one. It is very simple, of course, to blame us for lack of courage, dignity, physical fitness, for submissiveness, passivity, resignation. It's all fake; it's a dirty lie. Any group of people, systematically humiliated, cruelly treated, deprived of dignity, mentally and physically tormented, hungry, sick, cold, can be reduced to submission. Maybe there are some exceptional men, whom suffering makes stronger, but I think it breaks the average man. We are neither worse nor better than other people. We are not belligerent and not bloodthirsty. These are our faults and we pay for them. There is no unity among Jews. We pay for that too. Our history is full of informers, of traitors. They started by selling Joseph into Egypt and are still doing the same. All over the world.

"Our passive resistance was an activity to which nothing can be compared. We fought every day by the mere fact of living behind the wall and this is a higher degree of resistance than the use of weapons. We can use force too," his voice was firm. "Now that the world knows it, it will probably be said that it was a desperate act of a handful of desperados. This is not true. We started to fight as soon as we got arms. Why did it take the Poles so long to close the deal? It was the seller's market, sure. A machine-gun, forty thousand zlotys. We paid it. Our persistent and humiliating soliciting lasted till most of those who could fight were killed. We declared war bare-handed, equipped with bricks and stones. Let those answer who are responsible for that. We were annihilated not by Germans only but by all people, here and everywhere, who let us down, who were silent. You come from a lawyer's family, Elli; you must know that there are cases when inaction is considered a criminal act just as action is."

After a long silence she said, "You know, Abel, my grandfather told me once, when things were going very badly, that he was haunted by a ghastly idea. I think he was very much depressed at that time and was trying to find an explanation of this — what you called — inaction. He said it is a painstaking task to live as a Jew, that for some Jews it is mortifying. They fight against this curse, a fight that becomes a curse itself. They think that by not getting involved now they are less conspicuously Jewish. They want to prove that they are already a different breed; that you can be so profoundly American, or English, or Swiss that being a Jew does not matter any longer. They desperately try to destroy that part of their Jewishness which they define as "suffering." They believe that once this image of the suffering east-European Jew, the filthy, backward, alien arousing hatred and contempt — that once this image is wiped from the surface of the world — the 'Jewish question' will cease to exist. Or, it would become palatable, less ugly, when not tied to this particular image.

"I remember the dark look in his eyes when he finished. Perhaps he was angry that he said it to me. I, for one, was never really upset by what he told me. I do not care what those who live a different life in a different world think, or feel, or do. If what he said is true, these people will never escape; and that would take care of the days and nights they have to live through, they and their children.

"Still, I do not myself believe it is so. I'd rather believe they are either misinformed; or don't believe what they are told; or both. I am sure that once all this is over, these people will prove they did not consciously abandon us. I believe they will come here, many of them, hundreds of thousands, to bury the dead, and take care of the living. I believe they will never forget what happened to us. They will tell it to their children and impose on them a burden never to forget."

Elli sat still, feeling terribly exposed, close to tears. She knew her words sounded pathetic, trivial, out of place here. She saw Abel's shoulders shake in mocking laughter.

Sometime later the floor began to bulge and heave. A loud yawn was followed by grunting and puffing, the aftermath of a profound, unhealthy sleep. Half-spoken curses, angry murmurs, hissing, sniffing, sighing filled the room. Elli saw clumsy shadows rise from the floor, rolling, stumbling, falling on each other. The bodies swelled in the darkness and the odor they emitted grew more and more dense. She saw a match struck; Abel put a carbide lamp made of a tin can on a wooden fruit case. Nobody paid any attention to her. In the flickering light she saw drowsy, unshaven faces, morbid, swollen eyes, limp bodies. After a while she recognized Max and Abram. The two women were still sleeping or perhaps just lying there. Neither the men she knew nor the others seemed to be surprised by her presence. Abram said casually, "Good morning, Elli," as if he had last seen her a few hours ago; Max murmured something to her, probably a greeting. The men started to adjust their shirts and trousers, with movements clumsy and lazy. They did not talk, nor did they look at each other.

Now Elli could see the hiding place better. It was a cubicle without windows, the only door leading to Rena's bedroom. A former dressing room of hers, it still had a wall-length closet, with rows of empty hangers dangling inside. On the wooden shelves covered with caked grease and clotted hair were scattered combs, toothbrushes, dirty jars and glasses, rusty tin cans, pieces of cotton. A broken mirror reflected the yellowish light of the lamp. In one corner near the door, empty vodka bottles were piled; in another stood a battered chamber pot surrounded with cigarette butts and balls of crumpled newspaper. Pieces of clothing were scattered all over, some dangling on iron hooks fastened to the soiled wall. A torn, faded map was hanging from the ceiling on a thin piece of rope. A greasy pack of playing cards lay on the floor next to a half-empty bottle of vodka. Over a broken oil lamp on one of the shelves was pinned a photo of a small child. Next to it on a piece of wire hung a knitted, red, woolen baby cap. Shoes, socks, and stockings, shreds of paper and cloth, pieces of glass, and filth were piled against the walls.

Suddenly Elli felt somebody grip her hand. A slim girl was standing beside her. Elli had not seen her get up. She must have done it quickly and noiselessly just as she approached Elli. A mass of untidy, long hair, like streaming gold, was hanging down her back. This thick, warm, glittering hair was so incredibly beautiful that Elli wanted to bury her face in it. She felt the grip harden and heard a hurried whisper, "That's you who found her, isn't it. Was she all right? She slept when I left her. I tucked her in the blanket to keep her warm till somebody finds her. She is a sweet girl, isn't she? Never made me any trouble, even when hungry. Is she missing me? Tell me, does she speak about me? Have you your own children? Does she play with them?" The girl held fast to Elli's hand and stared imploringly at her. Elli looked into the dilated, dark blue eyes, sick and filmy, and said half aloud, "Oh, yes, of course, she is a sweet girl; everybody adores her."

As suddenly as she had come, the girl disappeared. Elli saw her next seated on the chamber pot, her feet wide apart, singing softly. "I should have told you about Ida," she heard Abel next to her. "Her husband was an officer. He was killed in the September campaign; she was pregnant then. She left the ghetto with Dina, but nobody would take her with a child with jet-black curly hair, black eyes, and a dark complexion. It's rare for a child to be so unlike her parents. Her father, a son of a rabbi, had the looks of a Polish knight. When Max met Ida, she had already changed her hiding place nine times in two months. She told him she used to take Dina in tightly wrapped so that nobody could see her immediately, and they could rest and warm up before they were thrown out. People were afraid to keep the little black devil, as Ida said they called her. Max met her in the street, in freezing weather, desperate, hungry, penniless, with no place to go. He brought them here, the child was sick and cried day and night. Alfred threatened he'd throw us all out unless we got rid of her. Ida wanted to go with her. Max did not let her. He worked on her, with two other men here, for two days and two nights. Finally, she took Dina out one day and came back alone. Ever since she has been like that. She says that any other mother who found Dina would come and tell her; that a mother would understand her despair. You had the bad luck to be the first woman to come here."

He said all this half aloud, obviously unconcerned that Ida might overhear him. Meanwhile Ida brushed her magnificent hair, talking to herself, now softly, now angrily, then changed from her long, white nightgown into a plain, black dress, and squatted down near the chamber pot, playing with the red, woolen cap, whispering incessantly. "She'll sit like that day after day," said Abel. "If it hadn't been for Max's money, these two — " he pointed toward two men, one red-haired with a hooked nose and big white hands, nervously gesticulating, the other, elderly, bald, with a deep-wrinkled face, and attentive, wise eyes — "Rudolf and Arnold, would have thrown her out. Rudolf was in big business before the war, Arnold was a well-known scholar, a university professor. They are always quarreling like hell, but somehow agreed on that point. She cemented their friendship, poor girl," he smiled bitterly. "Before she came here, they were literally at each other's throats."

"Is that Professor Arnold Mannstein?" asked Elli.

"Yes, indeed. You know him?"

"His younger daughter and Lili were good friends. I met him several times at their home. He wouldn't recognize me, though; I guess I have changed a lot, and besides he was always so distracted that he hardly saw people at all. We used to laugh at him. Do you know, Abel, what happened to his family?"

"Sure. One daughter was killed in Umschlagplatz, back in

August; she refused to get into the train, but I don't know if that was the younger one. The other was killed in action a month ago in the ghetto. She had refused to join him here. He kept sending message after message to her. I delivered two myself. A great girl, bold as hell, and twice as stubborn . . ."

"That must have been Monika, Lili's friend. She was always like that. Odd, before I left, she told me I'd come back . . ."

". . . and his wife was killed in front of their house. She was limping, and they noticed it. He still has a son in England; he was studying law at Oxford, now is a pilot in the Royal Air Force." Abel stopped, and then said, "I should tell you about the other people here, too, so that you know who you are living with."

She shrank. "Oh, no," she protested and abruptly covered his mouth with her hand. "Please don't; I don't want to hear it." His mocking eyes calmed her down. "I really don't think I'm going to stay here, Abel. Every one of them is a bundle of despair. What more do I need to know about them?"

He lifted her chin and looked in her eyes. "You might, Elli. Else who will tell the world about twelve men, bold and proud, who lived like dwarfs and died like rats." His smile was detached, slightly ironic. She did not know whether he was serious or joking.

"The fellow you see over there," he pointed toward a very handsome boy, eighteen or twenty years old, who bent before the mirror and, grimacing, examined the thick, dark hair on his face, "was one of the leaders of the insurrection in the ghetto. He was badly wounded in action. Below his waist everything removable has been removed. He was seized by a regular fit of rage when he first regained consciousness and found that we had shipped him out of the ghetto. Fool, there was no help for him there; here they saved his life."

Abel stopped, scratched his head. "Maybe Judah was right after all; maybe we should have left him there."

"The man who holds the mirror for him is his most zealous political opponent." Elli looked in the same direction and saw a man whose age was hard to tell, for his beautifully shaped head was covered with a silver helmet of thick, abundant hair. It was glittering and shining in the semidarkness of the room. When he changed position to adjust the mirror for Judah, who apparently had decided to shave, Elli saw a dark face with brown eyes and a pleasant smile. "My God, it's Ian," she whispered. "Abel, it's Ian." She made a quick move toward him, but Abel held her arm firmly.

"You know him too?"

"Why, of course, I know him. I was given to him in holy wedlock," she laughed softly. "Just think of it. He was my cousin Danny's best friend. Remember, in July there was a rumor they wouldn't take married women, followed by this wild wave of marriages. How could we ever have believed it? Still, we did. And Ian married me. We were very good friends, anyway. I lost him in August and never knew what had happened to him. I am happy he is here. Let me go and give him a legitimate, wifely kiss."

"Better not, Elli. Wait a moment. You certainly see some change in him, don't you?" Abel sounded hesitant.

"Why, yes. He has white hair; his hair was as auburn as any girl would dream of having. I used to tease him that it was a real waste for a man to have that kind of hair. But he must have been through a lot. You don't need to tell me."

"I think I do. Ian is blind. Much as he was against the idea of armed opposition, out of reasons I never could really understand, he worked with two of our people producing grenades and explosives. There was an accident there. The other people said he was always very careless. Anyway, that's how it is. I didn't want you to find it out for yourself. Ian somehow knows when he makes this shocking impression and hates it."

"Yes, Abel," she said, "yes, I understand. I'd rather wait. Go ahead." She looked at the close-cropped silvery head. The deep-sunken eyes were fixed upon her, dead, inaccessible. She felt sick of Abel's monotonous account, sick of this place, of these people. She felt trapped in a lunatic asylum, helpless against the plot to drag her in. She still did not know whether Abel really meant that she should know who lived here in case they got killed or whether he just wanted to kill time. Anyway she wanted the recitation finished. Or rather, she wanted to run away — now, immediately — from this ugliness, madness, utter misery. Instead, Abel's voice bored right through her head.

"You know Marta, don't you? You've certainly heard about her. Right before the war she published two books of poetry, very successful, bleeding with Polish green lush meadows, weeping willows, Chopin's nocturnes, et cetera. Her fellow poets laughed and said she wrote it on a government's order, to hold up the nation's dwindling morale, see . . . Well, she was, or perhaps still is, what you call a true patriot. That's why I let her deal with Alfred when he comes here. Though with him she is not half that successful." He smiled maliciously.

Elli started to count for the hundredth time how many people were still left. There were three; she thought she could take it better now that she had Ian here. Meanwhile Judah finished shaving, took the mirror from Ian's hands, and put it back on the shelf. He jumped over Ida who was still playing with the cap, then stamped over Marta; but neither minded. Trampling over each other has become natural for them, thought Elli; they have been trampled upon for years and years and don't mind it anymore. Ian noved quite freely here, a hell of a place for a blind man. He passed Marta, lying on the floor with wide-open eyes fixed on the ceiling, and aimed toward Professor Mannstein. In passing, he slightly rubbed against Elli and stopped, confused. She could see the tension mounting in him; his face stiffened, it was pale, apprehensive. Then, a faint smile appeared on his lips;

he relaxed, and without a word made his way onward. Elli knew that he recognized her, but chose not to show it. Mad, like all of them, she thought. Why do they have to keep acting? here? now? Abel is pretending, too. With that assumed pose of tranquillity, he is driving them all mad. God, let him finish, please, please, let him finish; I can't stand it any longer; I'll scream . . .

"The tall, handsome fellow, talking to Marta, is Berek. He is not a Jew. He is Aryan, as good as the Holy Father, but more Christian. We call him Berek, but his real name is Ziemowit. His family claims descent from Prince Ziemowit. As an expert on history," Abel smiled to Elli, who cast him an angry look, "you certainly realize it is nine hundred years of recorded history. It adds glory to all of us, doesn't it? His poor ancestor, it would make him turn in his grave to see his offspring here. Do you want to know why he is here?" Had Abel waited for her answer, he would have heard "No," but he did not. "To protest against the indifference, to say the least, of his fellow countrymen, to prove the nobility of his spirit. To himself, of course." The jeering mockery was back in his voice. "Berek is a Polish nobleman to the tips of his fingers. The others did not want to have him here. At the beginning he made them feel uneasy. They even shaved every day, gritting their teeth, and tried to keep this pigsty clean. Because he did. Wanted to prove to him, mind you, that Jews are not necessarily dirty. But, thank God, he knew better, or perhaps realized that using a razor here might not be, at times, altogether safe. Anyway he stopped shaving and cleaning, and somehow the difference between races faded away." Abel laughed briefly and unpleasantly. "A modern Christ, mind you, waiting till we crucify him one of these days." He made a meaningful pause, as actors do on the stage; then in all seriousness, "Which we might as well do. And then the salvation will be his."

Elli felt her stomach turn upside down. She was sure now

that Abel was deliberately shocking her. Was he jealous of her being free to go, to breathe fresh air, to see the daylight, to die outside this hell? Did he want to tie her with some bonds of perverted loyalty to them, to this place? Did he think, once she came back, she was committed to them?

"What are you thinking about so hard, Elli?" She could smell the odor of Abel's breath. "I'm sorry if I scared you. I didn't want to. You look so pale. I would never have thought that after what you've seen, you'd mind my words so much. I have finished, I promise."

"I am tired, Abel. I do not mind your using these words or any others. I just did not realize . . ." Words failed her.

"I know," he said softly, stroking her hand. "I admit that I didn't make it any easier for you. I'm just an old ass, that's what I am — believe me I did not mean to frighten you."

"This place is . . ." Again, she could not talk.

"I know, it's odd, isn't it. You may as well say it. I don't mind. I don't think there is anything I still mind, save when they start jumping at each other. You can't blame them, either. Every day is like mounting a slippery hill to find at its top a pile of shit. The worst of it is neither the mounting nor the shit, but the urge to go all this way over and over again. If I could give them a grain of hope, a tiny faith. But I can't, I can't . . ." He squeezed Elli's hand so tightly that she almost cried; she felt his fingernails deep in her flesh. "The only thing I can still do," Abel let her hand fall, "is to pretend we live a normal life here, and to make them pretend, too, not to let themselves go. That's all I can do."

"Abel." Elli preferred the mocking Abel to the exposed one and the Elli wanting to vomit rather than the Elli wanting to cry. "Abel, you still did not tell me about the two boys."

"You are right, Elli; now I let myself go. Revenons à nos moutons. The two boys . . . They aren't boys; they are two respectable gentlemen, see them?" He pointed toward two men, standing behind Ida, talking very quietly. Now, as Elli gave them a closer look, she saw that they were both in their sixties, both of moderate height, one slim, the other corpulent. "They are both warm, affectionate creatures," continued Abel. "I owe them a lot. They are the only men here who don't take delight in dragging out their wretchedness, taking it in hand to feel it, lick it, taste it, and talk, talk, talk. The smaller, Josef, owned a chain of steelmills here and abroad; the fatty, Stefan, was a worker in one of them. It's quite a story how they met. Stefan found Josef literally in a gutter, with a fractured skull, and nursed him out of it, all by himself. Don't know how. By that time neither of them had any family left. Stefan did not know, of course, what a precious skull he was nursing, but Josef told me that he was not very impressed, and when told, showed no surprise. Do you think, Elli, there is anything left that might surprise any of us?"

The door, manipulated from outside, opened just far enough to take Rena's width, and she squeezed herself into the room. "Here comes your answer," Elli almost said aloud. At no later time could she find a logical reason for those unspoken words.

10

RENA LOOKED quite different now. She was clearly excited and hungrily smoking a cigarette. Her scarlet fingernails matched the lipstick on her full mouth. The heavy makeup made her look years older. The ash-blond hair now was artfully set high above her smooth, white forehead. She was dressed up in a green mink-trimmed spring outfit, mink hat, and glistening black patent knee-high boots. In her left hand she held white kid gloves and a big black crocodile bag. She was fragrant with strong perfume.

With no sideway glance, she quickly made her way toward Abel, and burst out breathlessly, "Abel, you must help me. I cannot stand this son of a bitch any longer . . . He is drunk all the time . . . He threatens me . . . I mean, he threatens you, all of you. He threatens he will denounce you . . . I swear . . . You must do something about it, Abel, you must, else you'll all be lost." She looked at him imploringly.

"And you came to warn us, didn't you, Rena." There was undisguised mockery in Abel's voice.

She smiled stiffly. "Why, of course, haven't I done it before? But he becomes more and more dangerous, and . . ."

". . . And you two just had a wild row, didn't you, Rena?" Abel grinned at her.

"Yes, we did, but that's not important. We have rows all the time, you know that." She met his eyes with an effort. "Abel, do believe me, I came to help you . . ."

"Oh, come, Rena. You just said you want me to help you. Maybe you better make up your mind who is to be helped by whom." They faced each other with open hostility.

"I want to help you, Abel, I really do," she repeated stubbornly. "He just told me he is going to the police if he doesn't get his money by noon." A quick glance at her small golden wristwatch was followed by an almost triumphant, "It is quarter to twelve. You can't have the money in time, you . . ."

". . . We are all lost. You said it already. No use to repeat it. Now, come on, Rena, be a good girl and tell Abel the truth. What was the row about?" He was examining her with mild interest.

"About you." Her face was flushed with anger. She stubbed out her cigarette and stamped it on the floor.

"Look here, Rena," Abel said dryly, "you know I'll help you, even if it's not about us; but tell me the truth. What was the row about? Did Alfred find out who your boyfriend is?" He looked at her inquiringly.

"Well, yes, no, that is . . . That's really meaningless, Abel, it has no connection with you." She smiled at him pleadingly.

"All right, Rena. If you insist I believe, I do believe. You are free to go for your date now." A friendly nod. "You are a good girl; you came here to warn us. I really appreciate it, just as all my roommates do." He made a wide circle with his hand, then looked at her attentively, expectantly. He clearly waited for her to say something. When she did not speak, he said, "Goodbye, have a nice time."

"But, Abel, you certainly don't want to let him get you all murdered." Her voice became shrill again; tears appeared in her eyes. "You must do something, now, immediately." She took from her bag a small, white handkerchief and lightly touched the corners of her eyes, careful not to smear the mascara. "You expect me to go and leave you all in mortal danger? You cannot be serious. You cannot demand that of me . . . I'm not a monster . . . I know Alfred threatened you before and has never done anything, but today he was really furious. Aren't you afraid?"

"I am not," said Abel clearly.

"You are inhuman."

"So what?"

"He did find out, Abel, he did," she said bleakly, giving up the struggle. "I thought it was irrelevant, but since you insist . . . And he made this row . . . He was in a rage. I've never seen him like this before."

"It's hardly a great revelation, Rena." He looked at her resentfully. "He makes rackets all the time and has fits of rage and all that."

"But I told you that he found out about my friend," she insisted meekly.

"You told me that before." Abel was, or pretended to be, bored. "As long as he doesn't know who he is and where he lives, you are both safe. I think you better go now, Rena. You'll be late for your date."

"But he does know," Rena said in a dull voice.

"What?"

"Who he is and where he lives." Her voice had gone completely blank. "He found an old notebook of mine."

"Oh, that's the big news, is it?" Abel sounded sarcastic. "Why didn't you say so? That's exactly what you should have started with, isn't it, Rena?"

"Oh, well . . ."

"There is no 'oh,' and no 'well' about it. It is or it is not?"

"I guess it is," she agreed.

"Now what do you want me to do? You don't expect me to get this damn notebook from him, do you?"

"It wouldn't help. He knows the name."

"So, what can I do? What is it you want me to do?"

"To silence him once and forever." She was quiet and earnest.

"See, see, now all the chips are down, eh, Rena? Who'd have thought this pretty head breeds such lousy thoughts."

"Abel, please, stop it. You wanted to know, so I told you. Now you must help me. He'll have his cronies kill my man before you can say one-two-three. If he does, I'll leave him, and . . ." she was not sure whether she should go on or not, but she did, "and, of course, I'll leave you all."

"Well, well, you are threatening, aren't you, Rena. You should have known better. Living so long under the same roof with your husband makes me immune to that sort of crap. You should realize that."

"I don't mean to threaten you, Abel, I really don't. It's just, it's just . . . that . . . I couldn't go on living here." She was crying.

Abel shouted at the top of his voice, "We'll feel perfectly safe with Alfred, understand? Don't you worry about us."

Rena screamed, "But I must not let him get this man."

"That's your problem."

"So you refuse?"

"I certainly do."

"You better think it over. You better discuss it with them; it's their lives too."

"There is nothing to think over. My answer is no, no, noooo," he yelled at her, wildly flinging his fists right before her funny little nose.

The people in the room obviously heard only the last earsplitting part of the argument. Until it grew very loud nobody paid any attention to Abel and Rena. Even now they watched the two people with only mild interest. Rudolf and Professor Mannstein continued their conversation; Ida did not change her position. The rest stood and stared impassively. Rena looked around, as if weighing her chances with the others, then turned to the door, and quickly left. No question was asked; no explanation demanded.

At two o'clock Rena came back attired in a long, red velvet robe, and brought them food. She took from a brown paper bag a loaf of clayish bread, a jar of carrot marmalade, and six baked potatoes, and wordlessly put them on a shelf. In a few minutes she was back with a kettle of hot water and the cleaned chamber pot. She put it on the floor and, with her high heels clicking, left.

Abel cut the bread and spread it with marmalade. He whistled when he was ready, and one by one they came to get their ration. Marta took Ida's piece of bread, and Abel followed her with his eyes till he saw her put it in Ida's hand. As in a labor camp, thought Elli with resentment. Why does he impose that drill on them? He must have noticed her grimace, for, biting a morsel of bread with his strong, white teeth, he smiled at her and whispered, "I have no choice, they are too hungry. They'd cheat on each other. They have already tried it on Ida."

Elli was napping in her corner when the door banged abruptly. A tall man, thick-boned, heavy, almost lumpish, with a robust face of a peasant, pale, lusterless hair, and small piercing bluish eyes, was standing in the middle of the room. What first occurred to Elli was that he must certainly be drunk. She knew, of course, that it was Alfred. But Alfred was completely sober. He smiled in a friendly way at Elli and said, "How are you? Pretty tired,

I guess. You must have had a tough time over there. Better get a good rest, miss. Did they give you something to eat?" His voice was deep, melodious, not to say, charming, a most stunning contrast to his boorish looks. "Abel, did you give her something to eat?" he asked with concern. "If you don't have food, I'll go and bring her something." Abel was busy fixing his shoe, bent over it on the floor. He did not lift his head; nor did he answer Alfred's question.

Elli said quickly, "Thank you very much, I am not hungry." She would not say she had had some bread, afraid to expose Rena. She was more terrified than amazed by this man, of whom she expected anything save composure and concern.

"Is it very difficult over there?" he asked softly.

"Well, I don't know . . . I don't think so . . ." She stammered, not sure she should confirm that she had been behind the wall.

"It's incredible what these bastards do to your people," continued Alfred undiscouraged. "They should all hang, every one of them. They will one day. You take my word for it." He took a cigarette from a big, square, gold cigarette case, offered one to Elli, and lit both.

Elli was annoyed and angry that Abel left her to talk to this man. The others, absolutely unconcerned, were lying or sitting on the floor. Judah, Max, and the professor played cards; Marta was lying close to Berek, whispering into his ear; Ida sat motionless leaning against the wall, like a limp doll. Josef, Stefan, and Ian were busy with a crossword puzzle. Abel still mended the shoe.

"Did you meet my wife?" asked Alfred, smiling. The pains he took to keep up a polite conversation made no sense to Elli. What was he driving at? What did he want? If he yelled, cursed, threatened, she would feel more at ease. Every word he said might be a trap.

"Oh, well . . ." she said, and stopped.

"Isn't she beautiful?" There was a caressing note in his voice. "She is the most beautiful woman I ever met. Don't you agree with me?" he asked, insisting, as if her opinion was a matter of prime importance to him.

"I do, of course. She is very beautiful."

"Would you ever believe," he said gently, "such a pretty woman is a dedicated whore." Elli did not know if that were a statement or a question. She thought she had better let it pass. But it was a question.

"Would you?" he repeated, his voice modulated, with a melodramatic undertone. She did not answer. "Would you?" he insisted, scrutinizing her coldly, shrewdly, with a look which said, "You'd better answer my question."

"Oh, yes," Elli said quickly. She wanted to scream to Abel to come and free her from this man.

"Do you know," she was happy he talked, for it was better to hear his voice than to see his eyes, "do you know the difference between a professional whore and a dedicated one? The last one is the real, authentic whore." His voice grew cold but he did not raise it a bit. "That is what my wife is." After a while, "Did you meet my wife?"

He must be insane, shivered Elli; he is out of his mind. She answered, "Yes, I did." He turned abruptly from her to Abel.

"Abel, my dear boy, do you have the money for me?"

"You know I can't get it today. You'll have it in two or three days." Abel was bent over his shoe.

"Oh, well. It doesn't matter really," Alfred said pleasantly. "Even if you gave it to me today, it wouldn't matter. I just dropped in to say goodbye . . ." And he paused. As he expected, Abel swallowed the bait. He lifted his head and looked at him perplexed. Alfred framed his words with obvious delight. ". . . And I thought you might want to give me the two weeks'

overdue money . . ." Again a long, theatrical pause, and then,
". . . before you leave." It all sounded like a rehearsed part, but
Alfred looked extremely pleased with himself.

"What do you mean, before I leave? I am not going to leave.
I'll stay here and give you back your money," said Abel irritably.

"I meant before you all leave," Alfred lit a new cigarette, and
offered one to Elli.

"But we are not going to leave." Abel's irritation grew.

"But you are, my boy, though you might not yet be aware of
it. I thought Rena told you. I am sorry if she didn't." He
sounded profoundly sorry.

"No, she did not. Why should she?" Abel realized he had
been taken in.

"I just thought she did. It really doesn't matter. As I said,
I just dropped in to say goodbye to all of you and to wish you
good luck." Alfred turned toward the door.

"Are you crazy, Alfred?" Abel lost his composure. He shouted,
"Where are you going?"

"It is you who is going, Abel; I am staying. It was nice to have
you here, old man, but I've told you many times already, it gets
on my nerves. I'm fed up with it."

"Like hell you are," shouted Abel, "goddamn you."

"Stop shouting, Abel. It's of no use. You know I am a friend,"
his voice was full of warm affection, "perhaps the only real
friend you ever had. So, let us part friends, boy. I am sure I
will not see you here by tomorrow morning." He put his hand
on Abel's shoulder.

"Oh, well, Alfred," Abel smiled at him. "You are right. I
apologize. If we have to part, let us part friends. I hope you
won't refuse a special treat later tonight. Surely you'll agree
that our parting calls for a celebration."

"Sure, Abel. You want me to bring the booze?"

"Oh, no, you'll be our guest tonight. You were our host all

this time; let us be hosts just for one night, the last." Abel looked like a man determined to smile in the shadow of the gallows.

"Right you are, Abel. I'll be back around nine, old man." He slapped Abel's shoulder affectionately, walked toward the door, manipulated the tiny lock under the doorknob, and left.

Elli wondered if, save for Abel and herself, anybody understood what was going on. If they did, either their composure or their resignation accounted for a total lack of reaction. Rather, she believed that they missed the point. The moment Abel invited Alfred for the night's celebration, Elli understood that the decision Rena could not force on him a short time earlier was already made. She froze with tension, clinging to a faint hope she knew was betrayal. She felt waves of weariness taking hold of her; her consciousness was blurred; she was in a state of near collapse. Then the protective mechanism started to work in her: first the piercing pain of the current switching on in the back of her head, then the throb of the vibration gearing up, and finally the familiar relief of the rapid whirl. She could function again. She saw Abel, sitting cross-legged on the floor, his face calm and assured, repeating softly, "Well, well," and again, "well, well." Then he lifted his head and stared at Elli with his deep-sunken, sad eyes. There was in them a desperate call for help and understanding. She responded to him, abandoning her hope. His eyes betrayed his loneliness and fear, long and carefully disguised. She looked at him again waiting for some clue, some hint. Suddenly he made eyes at her like a regular schoolboy in old schooltimes. The tension was gone. He knew, she knew, and he showed her with his eyes that the others did not.

A few minutes later Abel walked to the shelf with the broken mirror, knelt down, and knocked two times lightly on the wall, paused, and knocked again three times. In a little while the door opened. Rena slipped in, went straight to Abel, and stood like a soldier awaiting orders from his senior officer. She had a haggard look, her former vivacity and aggressiveness all gone. "I need six bottles of vodka here, by eight o'clock at the latest," said Abel to her expressionlessly. "All right," she answered and rushed out. She knew too.

At a quarter to eight she brought in eight bottles of vodka in a white pillowcase. She put it in the left corner of the room, together with a big jar of water and several bottles of beer, and left. At half-past eight, Abel whistled lightly the tune of "Meyn Shtetele Belz," and like trained hunting dogs, all quickly gathered around him. The faces were attentive, expectant.

"Ladies and gentlemen," started Abel standing amid the people seated on the floor. "We had a guest this afternoon whom I presume all of you saw, but none listened to. It is hardly a great loss, I hasten to add, since what this gentleman had to announce could hardly be considered a great revelation. I would not dare to take your precious time going into details, though I consider it my duty to convey to all of you that he came here to bid us goodbye. Without consulting you, for which I sincerely apologize, I took the liberty of inviting him here on behalf of all of you for a farewell party." He mopped his head, knelt down, and said slowly, seriously, "I need your help. It is going to be a farewell party, and I mean every word that I say." He looked like a strategist at a war council, making his choice for assignments. "Stefan, you will be in charge of the vodka. My order is that everybody drinks, but only one gets drunk. Is that clear?" All nodded. Stefan grasped Abel's hand and shook it vigorously with affection. "Elli, Marta, Ida, Josef, and Arnold, turn the party into a real social event. I mean, take good care that our guest has the time of his life." He looked around and repeated, "The time of his life. Clear?" "Damn clear," said Marta. "Now, Ian, Judah, and Max will stay near me all the time. Rudolf and Abram will guard the door. That is all."

Again no questions were asked; no comments made. It was

a complete puzzle to Elli, by means of what magic these people, passive, bored, quarrelsome, slack, underwent this miraculous transformation. They were animated, responsive, but at the same time calm and serious.

"What about me, Abel?" she heard suddenly. It was Berek, standing near the carbide lamp, just opposite Abel, staring keenly at him. "Did you forget me?"

"No, Berek, I did not." Abel intercepted his glance. "You must stay out of it."

"But why, Abel? Why this difference? Am I not one of you? Haven't I proved it?" A child's pleading was in his voice.

"Look, Berek. I would rather not go into lengthy explanations. It is just my feeling that you should stay out of it, and let it be that way."

"That hardly answers my question, Abel." He sounded firm. "You minimize what is a life problem for me. You have no right to do so."

"Berek, I want you to remember that, though very unlikely, there might be an after. We might have the bad luck to survive. We will have to answer then for what is going to happen here. There will be no justification for you. You cannot identify yourself with us nor seek redemption in doing so."

"Shit on your intellectual crap, brother. I've already made my choice."

"You stay out of it, Prince Rodziński."

"Is that an order, Major?"

"It is an order, Prince."

They all stood in a semicircle, Berek facing them. A jarring roar of shrill, hysterical laughter suddenly came out of him, and a monkey-grimace distorted his face as he thrust the full length of his tongue out at them.

Alfred came at ten o'clock. They spent an agonizing hour waiting for him. Somebody said that at least Rena could have come and told them what had happened to him, but Abel said she certainly did not know herself. Anything could have happened to that bum. Shrugging his shoulders, he suggested that Alfred might be drinking someplace; he might be sleeping dead-drunk in the street; or he might have run into a patrol after the curfew. The possibility that Alfred would not come never entered Abel's monologue. He showed neither emotion when Alfred finally came nor relief.

Alfred was breathing heavily. His face was crimson and sweating, eyes bulging, legs unsteady. "Good evening," the charming voice was gone; now it was growling and hoarse, "Good evening, Abel, good evening, everybody." He stopped, looked around, and burst out laughing. "Why are you staring at me as if I rose from the dead? I was just about to bring my buddies, Otto Kraut and Hanz Lehmke, with me, but you know Rena when she sees a handsome boy. There was a new restaurant opened today downtown, 'Penguin,' and we three went to have a look at the place. An extraordinary place, you can believe me, they have the former president's cook, and he knows his job. Boeuf à la Strogonoff, you'd lick your chops. They'll make big money, these people. They know their business. The waitresses, none more than twenty, know their job, too, the sweetest dessert, you can believe me," he repeated with the persistence of a drunk. "What was it I started to tell you . . ." He scratched his head. "Hmmm . . . that I almost brought Otto and Franz, well, yes, I told them I must go, I was invited to a farewell party. At first they wouldn't let me go and then grew wild to join us. Okay, boys, I said, let's go, let's celebrate together, and eh, eh, we came. Rena is a quick girl, she made us a good drink, but then fell down in the kitchen and injured her leg. She asked Otto to go and bring a bandage, and Franz is right now admiring the new chandelier I bought for Rena's bedroom . . ."

He sat down on a chair, drew Ida nearer to him, kissed her on the neck, long, loudly, and moistly, then made her sit on his knee, and put his red fleshy hand deep under her skirt. Ida, a vague smile on her lips, unbuttoned his shirt, and gently caressed his white, hairless chest. Then she put her hand in the pocket of his trousers, twisted her mouth, in surprise or disappointment, and got out a parcel wrapped in greasy paper. Alfred sprang to his feet so abruptly that she landed on the floor, snatched the parcel away from her, and shouted with laughter.

"See, what I've got. I bet you forgot what real bacon looks like. Know a friend. Here." Triumphantly he took a piece of salt bacon in two fingers, and one by one put it under everybody's nose. Abel blinked angrily at their stony faces, until Marta squeaked with joy, "Oh, Alfred, you are wonderful, you are the most ingenious man I ever met. Hey, there," she shouted, "I need a real good big drink. Let's toast our best friend, Alfred." She embraced him and kissed him on the lips.

The party started. Those assigned to keep him company would not let him rest. Marta created the saloon atmosphere; she sat half-naked on his knees, hot and voluptuous; giggling and laughing shrilly, she made him drink from her glass, caressed his ear, kissed him passionately. When this ended in his crying on her shoulder over his whorish wife, his wasted life, and cirrhosis, Josef took over; and there they were engaged in a fervent discussion over the skill involved in making big money. On a piece of paper, which Alfred later carefully folded and put in his wallet, Josef designed for him a postwar real estate project, the quickest and surest way, he pointed out, to make money in a war-ridden country. Then Arnold made a show of his intellect and wit, arguing the historical inevitability of wars. When he skipped to recent political events, Josef cut the map from the rope, and soon all three were bent over it on the floor, recapturing occupied territories, wiping out armies, demarcating new borders. When they finally landed in the German capital, Elli replaced the two men.

"Alfred," she whined, holding a bottle of vodka in her hand, "Alfred, won't you have a drink with me. I'm dry as hell, and these boors don't have the guts to make a girl high. They wouldn't know what to do with her, either," she giggled.

"I sure do," roared Alfred, dragging her down to him. She knelt down, filled two glasses, and heard his hoarse whisper, "You smell like fresh air, they stink like a carcass, both of them, goddamn them. Come, come, nearer, here, let me get deep into you," and he started to unbutton his fly. He could not manage the buttons though, and she helped him out of his trousers. His clumsy fingers tried in vain to rub the limp penis to erection. Infuriated by this vain effort he screamed at her, "You lousy bitch," and heavily rose from the floor.

When he got up, the upper part of his body all dressed up over white cotton drawers tucked in black boots, they could see that the liquor spent on him was not wasted. There was a moment full of anxiety, at about eleven o'clock, when he seemed sober for a short time, and then said to Stefan that they would run short of booze before they made him drunk. For the next ten or fifteen minutes he kept track of Stefan manipulating the bottle to make sure everybody was drinking. He toasted each of them, carefully watching as they drained their glasses. But with Stefan next to him all the time he never had his own glass empty. When he was rising from the floor, Stefan whispered to Abel that only one bottle was left.

"What's the big secret?" shouted Alfred to them. "What are you two plotting now?" Obviously, he had forgotten about his recent disappointment, and was cordially laughing again. Rolling, he made his way to Abel. "Now . . . you must . . . drink with me . . . old man," he retched. "To the future . . . to our freedom . . . and yours . . . to our beloved country . . . Stefan . . . more vodka . . ." Stefan filled his glass from the last bottle and Abel's from one filled in the meantime with water. "Let me see . . . what . . . you have . . . in your glass . . . old man . . ." choked out Alfred. Before anyone could prevent him, he grabbed the glass from Abel's hand, spilled half of it on the floor, and put it to his mouth. He sobered up.

"That's . . . how you drink . . . with an old friend . . . with the best friend . . . you ever had . . . you insult a man . . . who risks his life for you . . . you son of a bitch . . . you refuse to drink to the . . . future of Poland . . . you stinky kike. . . Hey, there," he screamed, "everybody drinks to our beloved country . . . To Poland from the Baltic to the Black Sea . . . independent . . . powerful . . . free from . . . Germans . . . Bolsheviks . . . Jews . . ." He followed Stefan with his bloodshot eyes till all glasses were filled, and then drank himself to everybody. When he finished the round, he raised his glass again. "Farewell, Abel . . ." he blubbered, "farewell, friends . . ." He was standing now just opposite Abel, keeping his balance with effort. "A time to part . . ." he was looking straight in Abel's face, "let us part friends . . . when we must part . . . let's part friends . . ."

Three things happened precisely at the same time: Alfred's eyes grew wild with apprehension, Judah threw the white pillowcase over his head, and Rena appeared in the door.

They worked on him with precision, passion, and determination. He bellowed only once, then he moaned, and then he was still. They kept working on him long after his wildly flinging limbs stiffened and his head in the blood-and-vomit stained pillowcase, ceased to move. No one knew at what point the thing they worked upon had become a dead body. They went on and on and on, until their fear and misery and wrath were gone.

Rena kicked away the broken glass and the wallet which

had fallen from his pocket and pushed aside Max who blocked her way. Without a word, she lifted the big red hand and let it fall. It fell like a log, with a hollow sound. "Ready," she said. She left the room and quickly returned with a big pot of hot black coffee and mugs. "A strange girl," indeed. Abel's words came back to Elli, to keep the coffee hot all that time. The coffee, she soon found out, was only a part of the arrangement.

With Rena's help, Judah and Ian moved the body against the wall. She asked them quietly to sit down, and obediently they did so. They looked like puppets without strings, thrown away after the show was over. Rena, the string puller, put a mug in each hand, poured in the coffee, and like a good hostess invited them to drink. When her mild persuasion did not work and they kept sitting, dull and dizzy, she knelt down and made them drink one by one. She must have burned somebody's lips, for angry hissing and swearing broke the silence. She pumped the flickering flame of the carbide lamp, and it was now lighter in the room than ever before. Then she brought more coffee, and again filled the mugs. From the traveling bag she brought out ham and smoked bacon sandwiches and a couple of cigarette boxes. They stretched out hands for food, and soon were eating and drinking and smoking like a work gang after a hard day. Now she had the situation under control. Their dizziness faded away, the empty stomachs responded to her efforts. They behaved just as she must have imagined they would. The first to speak was Abram, who said he could not remember the time when he had had such excellent coffee. Then Rudolf praised the tasty sandwiches; the professor, the juicy ham. They talked off their anxiety and rage. Abel and Ian sipped their coffee, but did not eat or take part in the conversation.

Elli's watch pointed to half-past two when Rena got up and cheerfully said, "Well, boys, and what are we going to do now?" Nobody answered. She made herself clear, "I mean, with the body." Silence. She still smiled pleasantly. "You don't want him to stay here, do you?" All eyes were fixed on the floor. Only Abel looked at her ironically, and Ian's blind eyes would not move from her.

All at once she grew furious. "Damn you, Abel, don't stare at me with that silly smile. I did not kill him, did I? I want to help; you should at least appreciate this. I could as well leave him here, couldn't I, and he, even as he is now, sure as hell could drain the life out of you." There was spite and a note of triumph in her voice. She waited a short while, but obviously was not as unconcerned as she wanted to appear. "Come on, Abel." It was amazing how quickly she could change; her voice was now pleading, humble; her countenance, that of a wronged child, helplessly seeking protection; big tears rolled down her cheeks. "Oh, Abel, you helped me, and all I want to do now, is to . . ."

Abel abruptly rose to his feet and said with indignation, "We did not help you; you get it out of your dirty mind, you bitch; you forget it once and forever. We would not lift a finger to help you, is that clear?" He shook his fists in her face. "Is that clear?" he shouted madly. "Answer me, is that clear?"

She shrank back with a fearful look and whispered, "Yes, clear." Her back turned to the door, she backed up toward it, but his loud, "No, you stay here," halted her. "Sit down," he commanded. She sat on the floor between Marta and Josef. "What is your advice, madam?" Abel bowed with courtesy.

"I . . . I . . . I really don't know . . . I never thought about it, how could I possibly," she muttered helplessly.

"Don't be so smart," Abel said wryly. "You schemed this out right from the beginning till the very end in the smallest detail. Come out with it, and make it quick." And she did. She said that it was, of course, impossible to get rid of the body in its present state; it would be too dangerous, and then, she could not lift it herself. Nor could any of them leave the apartment to help her. Thus the only thing to do was, she continued, to quarter it. Or rather, she corrected herself, to cut it into small pieces, because big parts could not be safely carried out. She had a chopper, she said, which they used to quarter pigs, and she also had a couple of big sharp knifes. The body must be cut in small pieces, the flesh must be taken off the bones, the bones burned in the kitchen stove, the flesh packed in small parcels, which she would carry out. She presented her plan impassively in a monotonous voice of a schoolgirl reciting a well-prepared, but boring text.

"All right," said Abel. "That sounds reasonable. What do you think, Judah?" Judah nodded. "You, Ian?" Ian smiled lightly. "All right, Abel," he said. "Who has a better solution?" Abel looked around. Nobody had. "So let's get working," he ordered. "Bring your tools, Rena, and before you go, you might as well finish undressing your husband. We would not think of depriving you of performing the last rites for him." She eyed him with resentment, but obediently knelt down and started to undress the body. Josef and Stefan helped her with the heavy boots; Abram and Max held the torso while she stripped him naked. She wrapped the boots in the clothes and, still furious, left.

Sometime later she came back with the tools. The huge cleaver slipped with a bang out of her hands onto the broken glass. The two knives were stuck under her right arm.

Judah slowly picked up the ax, balanced it in his strong, hairy hands, felt the edge of the blade with his fingers, abruptly cut the air, and said, "Just imagine, in this age of supreme killing techniques, this cute little device is still not outmoded."

Max said angrily, "We are not going to kill anybody."

And Judah smiled, "Forgive me, Max, it was a slip of the tongue. What I actually meant was the technique of getting rid of corpses."

Abel turned to the men and said, "We need a table here;

Rena has one in her dining room, but it's heavy oak. She agreed two of you can go with her and bring it. What?" he turned to Rena, "Four? right. She says two won't do; she wants four. Go ahead, Judah, Ian, Max, Abram, and be careful not to scratch the furniture; one problem a day is enough for a frail woman."

It was a table which, though huge and massive, could be dismantled. Abram's face was red and wet with perspiration, when he dragged in the first heavy leg ornamented with bronze oak leaves. Never in her life had Elli seen such a fancy table. She asked Rena where she got it. It was made on special order, she explained, just a month ago; she had seen such oak-leaf ornaments on some old armor in a museum while still a girl and ever since had been mad to have some in her home. Full of concern, she asked Elli if she thought they would rust now, especially those on the edges. Elli assured her that she could polish them later quite easily.

The four legs were already propped against the wall, and the men were dragging in, in twos now, parts of the top, six altogether. When they put it together, panting and swearing, the table just fitted the closet, barring the entrance entirely. There was hardly room enough for them to stand around the table. Next, they had to put the body on its surface. It was a real challenge to lift it from the floor and get it on the table. Once it was there, nobody quite knew what to do next. They stood silent and limp, looking at Abel. For the first time that night, Abel averted his eyes. Rena picked up the chopper and put it on the table, next to the head still wrapped in the pillowcase. Then she placed the two long knives, one close to each hand. Her eyes seemed to say, look, what would become of you if he got up a knife in each hand. Still they stood apathetic, heads and hands hanging down.

*

Before they recovered from the sudden pounding bang, the head bounced to the end of the table, hit against Marta, who jumped aside, bumped hard on the floor, and rolled until it stopped by the wall. Thick, black blood spilled from the ugly hole. Clots, like black currant jelly, splashed upon the table. The blow was precise; no shreds hanging, no splinters fallen. The pillowcase, too, was evenly cut, not tattered or torn. Soaked with blood, it stuck hard to the opening, a stiff collar. The body lay as before, a load of strong pink flesh, only several inches shorter.

No one looked at Berek. Gently, slowly, he placed the chopper on the table, right on the spot he had just made vacant. He took in both hands one of the knives, lifted it high above his head, thrust it fiercely into the chest, and ripped downward. Judah grasped the ax and chopped off the right arm, then the left; then the right leg, then the left. Abel gathered the limbs and put them on the floor. Marta and Elli brought blankets and made a kind of fence around the stumps, to keep the blood from spilling around. Abel returned to the table and began to work on the lower part of the torso. At some point a dozen or so silver table knives appeared on the table; Rena picked up a hand from the floor, put it on the right corner of the table and started to peel it.

When Elli first lifted her eyes from the foot she was working on, she saw what reminded her of Rembrandt's *The Lesson of Anatomy.* A poorly lit room, dark heavy shadows, and men standing around a table over a supine corpse. It was the atmosphere only that reminded her of this picture, an atmosphere of earnestness and dread. The work of art, however, showed man's meditation over the mystery of death; its grotesque counterpart reflected man, generations apart, to whom death was a mystery no longer.

The faces showed neither zeal nor interest nor satisfaction; but the former apathy and irresolution were gone. Hands were moving hastily, as if they had not a moment to spare. Knives were glittering, manipulated firmly and efficiently. The table was covered with blood, dried and fresh — as were the hands and the faces and the arms — and with scraps of skin, pieces of flesh, and chips of bones. At some point Berek chopped the arms and legs, each in three pieces, and flung them onto the table.

Later Judah halved the torso with one blow between the back and the buttocks. The women worked on the tender parts, cutting the flesh in pieces, no bigger than veal cutlets. The men worked on the bones and the sinewy parts of the body at the crotch and genitals. From time to time somebody would go to the shelf, where beside the broken mirror Rena had put a whetstone. The jangling of the sharpened knife rang harsh and dissonant amidst the sound of chopping and hacking.

At six in the morning Rena brought a fresh pot of black coffee, two loaves of bread, and a large piece of slightly smoked ham, pink as the meat on the table. She also brought a bottle of vodka. She served the food with hands brown with dried blood but no one blinked. Greedy fingers tore off chunks of bread and half-raw meat to stuff into their mouths. It seemed that they might next grab the meat from the table and devour it with equal voracity.

January 24, 1940

Now the food Mama smuggled from Lublin must be sold. I thought I'd die standing in the marketplace with a chunk of meat in my hand watching out for the police who arrest the "wild" vendors and praying for customers to come. Everyone was staring at me. I'd rather have black hair and stay home.

They finished the meal and immediately got back to work, a drilled platoon, conscious of its duty, frantic to have it done.

Some of them were still munching and chewing, afraid to be left behind. Again, hands moved fast; knives glittered, bones cracked, flesh splashed. For hours, and hours, and hours.

Rena inspected the finished pieces as they were put aside. Some she considered too large. She took them from the pile and threw them in the middle of the table for further processing. She examined the bones too, and flung back those with too much meat. That happened to almost all the ribs. After breakfast, she washed and changed, and subsequently did nothing but supervise their work. All clean and cool, her hair nicely set, the heavy makeup replaced with a lighter kind, in a little navy blue dress with white collar and cuffs, there was something prim but pleasant about her. In a large pocket, she had white paper napkins and whenever she stained her rubber-gloved hands, she carefully wiped off the blood and threw the napkin on the floor. Now and again she would stop before the mirror and adjust an escaping curl, or pump the carbide lamp when it grew too dark to work. Slim and erect, she passed the people in the narrow space left between the table and the walls without as much as touching them. When she thought she might have, she would examine her dress or shoe for a spot. Elli observed her, gracefully moving in her high-heeled shoes, and felt like flinging a bloody chunk into this dollish face. The clicking of Rena's heels amid the sounds of a slaughterhouse was more than she could bear. Her watch had stopped; she had lost track of the time. She thought it must be around noon when Rena brought the next meal on a big silver tray. At that time the middle of the table was empty, save for the intestines, contorted and spread, with small clogs of grease around them. When the meal was over, Rena swept the bowels with a big piece of cotton cloth into the empty meat pot, covered it with a lid, and put it on the floor near the door. The tray in her hands, she click-clacked in the opposite direction. She put the tray on the table, picked up the head, lying there since it had fallen, and placed it on the tray. Then she lifted it, her fingers firm on both handles, and slowly shoved one hand toward the middle, till she had it balanced. She turned in a half-circle, the tray high, but no reaction followed. Rena, visibly disappointed, put the tray in the middle of the table.

Either they did not look at her, or, if they did, they missed the point. They cared only about the head; not who brought it or how it was served.

It was lying now, or rather standing, propped on the chin, and on the jawbones. The hair was in bloody clumps, at its back and over the ears, but the top was smooth, shining with hair oil. The glassy eyes, wide open, looked like pieces of dull shale. One ear only, the left, was stained with vomit. Save for that, the face was almost clean. The tongue, huge and black, protruded heavily from between the purple lips; from the bluish nose a snot hung down to the chin. The face was covered with short, sharp, pale hair. In the flickering light of the lamp the sticky clumps of hair seemed to dance and tremble on the shining silver of the tray. The dancing stopped when Judah chopped the head in two. After he had hacked each part in small pieces the silver still shone through the multicolored pulp. Then, like logs, they collapsed around the table and slept for hours without end.

When they woke up, the table was clean-washed, the remains neatly piled on waxed paper spread over the table. Together with the food Rena brought another roll of waxed paper, a rationed, scarce article. She put the coffeepot, the bread, and the rolls on the table, and then brought two pails and several various-sized candy and chocolate boxes. Dressed in a tomato-red, clinging light-woolen dress with golden buttons and red knee-high leather boots, she served them the coffee. No one answered her cheerful "good morning," but they learned that a new day had begun. She said that the day was bright and lovely and that the only thing to do now, was to get rid of the stinking trash. It would take them an hour — or at most two — to get the parcels ready. She would be happy to help out, she smiled, to be done with it as quickly as possible. "You wouldn't like to spend another night with him, would you?" she grinned, looking around, a little annoyed with the lack of response. Suddenly, as if realizing the reason, she knocked her forehead with her cherry-colored fingernails, quickly approached Abel, put her hands on his shoulders, and said with a sweet, disarming smile, "Oh, Abel, how silly of me. I should have thought of it before, I didn't even thank you for all your . . ." Abel looked at her, taken aback. Judah said, scarcely audibly, "Shut up, you brainless idiot," took her hands off Abel's shoulders, and shook her vehemently, as though he wanted to shake the life out of her.

It took them two and a half hours to separate the bones for burning, and the soft parts for packing. There was really only one unpleasant moment when one eye slipped from Marta's hands and rolled, pursued by all living eyes, along the floor, a dead-yellowish slimy mollusk, until it hit against the wall. The professor quietly picked it up, slightly flattened and dripping with fluid, took its opposite number from the tray, and put both into a chocolate box half filled with teeth and fingers. Then he pushed it toward Rena. Rena was busy lining the empty boxes with waxed paper, and finishing off the full ones. She fitted the lids, and bound them with ribbons, green, red, yellow, white, which she tied in big colorful bows, so that, ready, they could pass for birthday presents. Smacking her lips, concentrated on her work, she grasped every full box pushed toward her like a long-awaited gift. There was some consternation when all the boxes were full and much meat still remained, but Rena quickly ran to her bedroom and brought two big hatboxes.

She wanted to tie these boxes too with ribbons, but Judah snatched them away from her with a look in his eyes as if he wanted to strangle her with the bits of silk.

Then, all were standing, looking at the boxes piled against the wall, and she was standing, too. Finally, Judah asked in a strained voice, "Rena, what are you waiting for? Why don't you take it and go?" She said grinning as before, "I am not going to go alone. I am afraid. After all, it is my husband, isn't it . . ." She took a cigarette case from her pocket and put a cigarette in her mouth.

"But, Rena . . ." It was the professor, helpless and nervous.

"Yes, I mean it." To be more convincing she wiped the smile from her face. "Why should I, of all people, take the whole risk? What if they caught me? You get what I mean? With one of you, they'll get you; alone I'd be lost. I will not go alone." She was firm though polite.

"Are you mad?" said Abel angrily. "Are you out of your mind? You know perfectly well that none of us has documents. You go alone and quickly."

She burst out laughing, "Now, what does this mean? You giving me orders. And what if I refuse? I can just lock you up here, and you'll rot together with him." And she made a quick move toward the door.

But Abel was quicker. He blocked the door with his huge body, and said, very softly, "Look here, you goddamn bitch. Look here and listen carefully. We already know how to do it, and when we ourselves carry the boxes out of here, there will be twice as many of them. Then it will be worthwhile to take the chance."

She grew pale and started to cry. "But, Abel, I am really afraid, believe me; you must believe me, I'm scared to death. I'd do it if I could, but I can't, I can't, I can't," she sobbed.

Then Elli said, "I will go with her, Abel. I have my documents."

They made three round trips that day, each to a different part of the city. Each time Rena hired a riksha, stopped it in front of some big apartment building, and then they walked four or five blocks to a less populated and poorer area. There they looked for an abandoned sewer and, with one of them standing guard, the other threw in the parcels. Rena dressed Elli in her clothes, a light black-and-white checked coat with matching hat, shoes, bag, and gloves. The ribbon-bound boxes in their hands they looked like two girls going to an aunt's birthday party. Out of town they would cover their heads with scarfs and put the boxes in shopping bags. Shortly before the curfew they were back from the last trip. All night long they burned the bones in the huge kitchen stove, and Elli had the taste of it in her mouth long after she left the house. She left it next day, early in the morning. In the pale rays of the rising sun two glistening jade-green glass eyes of a stuffed fox stared at her through a store window. She leaned against a wall and vomited.

March 2, 1940

A terrible thing happened. I'll never recover from it, never. Pickwick disappeared. I let him out last night, as usual, and he never came back. We all went to look for him, Daniel, David, Danny, Lili, but we couldn't find him. He was a purebred, worth much money, somebody must have stolen him. I couldn't sleep all night, neither could Lili. In the morning the Old Man gave us money to place an advertisement, he even wrote the text himself and offered a reward. He was awfully sweet about it. Perhaps Pickwick lost his way and somebody found him?

11

Elli PHONED LENA from the station. The Warsaw-Chełm night train was two hours late. She was cold, hungry, exhausted. Lena greeted her cheerfully, asked what the doctor had said, if she was all right? At the office everything was fine, Elli could come back to work. "His lordship was furious," she laughed, "but he has already calmed down. It's even better you didn't come sooner; it always takes him time. I told him I found you that day in the washroom with another hemorrhage and I persuaded you to go to the doctor who had treated you before. Go to bed now, Elli, have a good rest, and I'll see you tomorrow."

She had very mixed feelings when several days later Rahm asked her to his office and told her that his friend, the director of four industrial plants in the Chełm district, needed a secretary, and he had offered him Elli. "You have been working here long enough to know the secretarial work, your German is good, and that's what Herr Labisch needs. You'll start there on June first," he finished. On the one hand Elli was happy to part with Rahm; on the other, his decision was as unexpected as it was strange.

It was not usual for the Germans to deprive themselves of useful workers. And Elli had never heard before that this Labisch was a friend of Rahm's. Something was certainly wrong. She suspected he had wanted to get rid of her since the incident with Miriam; her Warsaw trip did not improve their relations either. He never mentioned it, but behaved as if she did not exist. Maria, who came a few days later, agreed that Rahm might have been suspicious about Miriam; he probably did not want to antagonize Posch; but neither did he want to keep her in his office. He welcomed the first opportunity to get rid of her and still keep up appearances.

Elli told Maria briefly about her trip to Warsaw — the first part of it. Maria did not ask her any questions.

"I understand, my child," she said. "I know how you felt."

Maria had not seen Lili since her arrest. Elli had informed her about it in a carefully worded note, when Lili had first been brought home. Now she said that Lili was not her own self yet and that it would probably take more time until she wholly recovered; but she said very little about Lili's real condition. During Maria's visit, which lasted four or five hours, Lili behaved entirely differently. She did not show any of her moods, was cheerful and smiling. Elli regretted that she had even suggested to Maria there was anything odd about Lili's behavior; Maria could not possibly have noticed it herself. Perhaps Maria's presence cut Lili off from the sickening experience. Perhaps it prompted or even completed the process of convalescence.

"Would you mind closing the door? I hate drafts." The sarcastic, impolite voice came from the ceiling. A man, standing on a ladder with his back turned toward Elli, was stacking fat files on the uppermost shelf. She closed the door and stood still. "Why are you standing there like Lot's wife? Can't you come in?"

She took a few steps and stopped. She had been told by Rahm to report to the director of Die Verwaltung der Klinkerwerke on June first at eight o'clock in the morning. She was pleasantly surprised when she found out that the office was on the first floor of the same house as Natalia's restaurant. Lena also told her that there were some apartments available for the employees of this office and advised her to ask for one during the first interview. The matter was pressing, for Mr. Baryński's friend had already come back and was sleeping in the kitchen while waiting for them to move. But this was hardly a hopeful welcome. Save for this rude man no one seemed to be around this strange place. The room was big, full of sunshine, with four French windows, probably a former reception hall converted into an office. In the left corner stood a desk piled with papers, and a typewriter on a small table. Behind the desk a huge map was hanging; multi-colored headpins curved in mysterious lines on it.

"Why don't you sit down?" the voice said in the same arrogant manner.

Suddenly angry, she retorted, "Because you didn't offer me a chair."

The man jumped down lightly and, not even giving her a look, rushed to another room, brought a chair, put it in the middle of the vast room, bowed deeply, "Mademoiselle," and climbed the ladder again. He was tall, slender, dark-haired, with a narrow and intense face. She took the chair, put it against the wall, sat down, and got out a cigarette. "Matches?" asked the voice with a note of amusement. "No, thanks," she snapped.

A small, gray-haired man bounced into the room. He went straight to the map. Looking at a newspaper that he had put on the desk, he took several pins out of the map and started to reset them. Then he said in German, "Where is everybody? It's two minutes to eight."

The voice said, "At your service, Herr Direktor. And there

is also a young lady waiting for you. If she is endowed with Sisyphus' patience, she'd perhaps put an end to this bordel."

The small man reddened. "Mr. Zbarski, I have asked you many times to spare me your dirty language. I won't put up with such jokes."

"Jawohl, Herr Direktor," came from the ceiling.

Director Labisch turned toward Elli, "Fräulein Warska?"

Within fifteen minutes he had introduced her to her duties. The former secretary, a German girl, had left a month ago; and they could not get another from the Vaterland, Labisch said. He decided to hire a Polish one but, of course, did not expect her to be as efficient and industrious as Fräulein Bemke, although Genosse Rahm had assured him Elli was reliable and quick. Their staff was small, he explained, because they administered only the factories located in the district. Save for him there was his deputy Herr Quibus, an accountant Herr Urban, and four Polish employees including her — Adam Zbarski in charge of the administration division, his assistant Miss Ilona Skowrońska, and the cook Helena Rak. Elli would be also in charge of the personnel files, he said, and of the kitchen. He preferred the staff to lunch together in order to save time. The working hours were from eight to six with a lunch-break. He had no doubts, he finished the interview, that anyone who had worked for Genosse Rahm was well aware of die deutsche Ordnung und Disziplin. He told her to start the work right away, first of all to answer overdue letters.

Standing in the door of his office, she timidly asked about the room.

"Yes, you can have one," he said. "There is a spare room in Herr Quibus' apartment. And I like to have my people within reach. Sometimes there is work late in the night, and in this way I have no trouble with night permits."

The apartment house was in the rear of the front building.

Zbarski had an apartment on the ground floor; Quibus' was on the first floor. To live with a German family seemed far from attractive, but perhaps living right in the lion's den was not bad either. Elli asked for permission to finish work early this day in order to move in right away. The permission was granted, though Labisch said firmly that she should stay later that night to make up for the lost time.

The room was so small that with three beds, it took an acrobat to move around. Mrs. Quibus, however, appeared to be a very pleasant and sympathetic woman. She provided a small bed for Emmi and, when the bigger one was removed, a little table fitted in. She did not use the wardrobe in the hall, she said, so they could have that. When she saw Emmi, she suggested she could play with her two sons, four and six years old, while the girls were at work.

Back at night in the office, with Lili and Emmi safe in their new home, Elli felt relieved for the first time in months. She lighted a cigarette and stretched her legs on the desk; neither the piles of papers that she did not know what to do with nor this rude man spoiled her hopes for the future.

October 6, 1941

An order was issued that leaving the ghetto without a permit is punishable by death.

October 15, 1941

I got a book from the outside. No sender indicated. Tolstoy's The Kreutzer Sonata *which I like so much. Certainly one of my Polish classmates sent it. I tried to read it. I can't. It seems so*

*unreal, detached from life. Lili said I am all wrong in thinking
that the only reality is the street I pass every day. It might be
real for me right now but to press into "your tiny box," she said,
"all beauty man created, all that really counts in life is unjust
and narrow-minded. I thought you had more common sense."
Evidently, I do not, because her high-pitched words didn't help
me a damn. I couldn't read the book.*

For two weeks she worked day and night and finally cleared
up the mess. The staff was polite and helpful, save for Zbarski
whose manner was sometimes hard to bear. Whenever she had
finished her work, he would appear with a pile of letters to type,
all "urgent," and put them on her desk with an angelic smile.
His assistant Ilona was a beautiful blonde, with a cascade of rich
hair hanging heavily to her shoulders and the china-blue eyes of
a doll. She was twenty, kittenish, and lazy; "A delightful disaster," Zbarski described her, "delightful outside, a disaster in the
office." Mr. Urban — Georg — a former Pole from Silesia, now
a Volksdeutsch, was a handsome man in his late twenties. The
first time they had vodka together, he told Elli that it cost his
father a fortune to keep him on this job, which he preferred to
one on the Russian or on any other front. The deputy director,
Mr. Quibus, was taciturn, polite, and sometimes clearly embarrassed by the manners of his boss. Helena, the cook, a young
woman with a two-year-old girl who clung to her mother, almost never opened her mouth. Doing accounts with Elli, she
would stand silent, her dark head lowered, her eyes fixed on
the floor. Only once, when Elli came to the office late at night to
finish some work, she stopped her with a softly spoken "Don't
go there." After a few minutes Ilona emerged from Labisch's
office buttoning her blouse. Zbarski followed immediately after.

∗

At the end of July Lili called Elli at the office and suggested that they meet in the restaurant and take Emmi for a walk. When Elli came she found Lili at a table feverishly writing; Emmi, on Natalia's knees. She kissed the child and went over to Lili.

"What are you writing?" she asked.

"A letter." Lili did not lift her head. One of Maria's strict rules was not to write. No letters, no journals, no notes, nothing. In a flash Elli recalled that the day she was so desperately looking for the lost documents, she had found Lili here, writing with the same furious attention. Then she had been too upset to ask what she was writing, and later it escaped her mind.

"Lili, to whom are you writing?"

"It's none of your business." Lili continued to write.

"It is. You know Maria had forbidden us to write any letters."

"Please leave me alone." Lili started a new page.

"Lili, tell me, are you writing to Maria?"

"I am writing a letter to Wendel."

Elli could not argue with her in the restaurant, crowded as it was that time of the day. Hurriedly, she finished her soup, took Emmi, and left. The weather was beautiful. They went for a long walk. The child craved fresh air. She held Elli's hand tightly. The long months of seclusion had impressed her with a fear of being alone. Elli was too preoccupied to talk to the child, but Emmi did not mind at all. She did the talking. She told Elli that she was very busy the whole day, telling fairy tales to her teddy bear who was sick. "You know, Elli, he caught a bad cold. I gave him two tablespoons of my syrup, and he stopped coughing."

"It was a good thing to do, darling," Elli pretended to listen.

"But he is now all stained and sticky," the child tried to catch her attention.

"I know, dear."

"Will you buy me another one?"

"Yes, of course, Emmi."

After midnight, when she heard both her roommates quietly breathing, Elli slipped from her bed and tiptoed to Lili's. Shivering, she took Lili's small bag from under the pillow and opened it. The envelope that she found inside was addressed to Wendel at his Gestapo Headquarters. She opened it and started to read the letter. It contained a straightforward confession, including their origin, real names, prewar address, their mother's present domicile. The letter, as Lili mentioned in the beginning, was an answer to those questions that she had refused to answer when cross-examined by him. He had promised then, she reminded him very politely, to save her and her family, if she told him the truth. So, here it was: truth, truth, nothing but the truth.

Elli trembled all over, her teeth chattering. She turned off the light. She was unable to think clearly. She lighted a cigarette, then a second. What was to be done? She could destroy the letter, but this would not prevent Lili from writing another one. She could try to talk to her, but Lili grew more short-tempered every day. And nothing seemed to deter her from her mad obsession. Elli decided to destroy the letter. She tore it to pieces and flushed it down the toilet. Tomorrow she would decide what to do.

When they met the next afternoon, Lili did not mention the letter. Nor did Elli.

Days slowly passed. Elli lived in constant fear that Lili had written again, perhaps even mailed her confession to Wendel. She did not dare to ask.

On a Sunday morning in early September they were dressing to go to church. All of a sudden Lili said in her even voice, "I am moving tomorrow."

"What?"

"I am moving tomorrow."

"Where?"

"I have found a room for myself."

"But you know Maria would not like it. It is very risky to go through the whole procedure of registration, to meet new people. We have already done it too often."

"I don't care."

"Oh, please be reasonable. And why do you want to move?"

"Do not ask me. You know perfectly well."

"Come on, Lili, I have no idea."

"You are lying."

"Lili, I swear."

"You little liar." She smiled with disdain.

"Tell me, please, why?"

"Because you attempted to murder me in this room. You silly. You thought that I would not know. You thought that I would not smell the gas you pour around at night. You are their instrument. They have promised you that they will spare your life if you kill me. I know everything. Now, isn't it so, dear?" she finished quietly, as if she were asking a casual question.

A horrible thought penetrated Elli's mind. Lili suffered from delusions; she did not know what she was saying. No, no, that is absurd; she must be kidding and is putting on this detached air to make the joke believable. Elli did not say another word. She quickly finished dressing Emmi, who stared curiously at both of them. All three went to church.

February 15, 1940

Lili's birthday. She is sixteen. With the money I earned knitting sweaters I bought her a silk scarf. Her new boyfriend, Mar-

tin, *a refugee from Vienna, came for the birthday party. He is nineteen and very bright.*

April 10, 1941

The only place where some trees are growing is the garden surrounding the church for converts. I took Emmi for a walk there. They don't let in people who don't belong to the church but I sneaked in because I wanted the child to see what a tree looks like and how it smells. The first tiny green leaves had just come out. Emmi wanted me to give her a branch or a leaf; she wanted to touch it, but I was afraid to pick it. We left after half an hour; a priest, surrounded by solemn-looking matrons, came into the garden.

The idea of a church in a Jewish ghetto would be dramatic in any other world; here it is melodramatic.

Lili did move the next day. She did not call them for a whole week; she did not come to the restaurant. The only way to keep track of her was to phone her office and ask if she were in. Elli did so every morning without trying to talk to Lili. She could not believe Lili was serious that Sunday morning. She knew it must be a joke, albeit a grim one. Later Ilona told her she had met Lili two or three times with a very handsome young man. Everything became clear. All Lili wanted was a little privacy.

It was then that she accepted Zbarski's invitation to come at night for a drink. He said Ilona and Georg would come too. She was obsessed with the thought that Lili's new boyfriend would turn out to be an informer. She could not stop thinking about it and thought company and a drink were just what she needed. Zbarski's attitude toward her remained one of aloofness and a kind of mistrust. He never missed an opportunity to make a malicious remark about Georg's assisting her — occasionally true — her frequent visits to the restaurant downstairs, her ignorance of cooking (he insisted the food was much better when Fräulein Bemke was in charge of the menu), her "excellent" German. Women he considered generally inferior, suited only for washing dishes and cooking. "But you are a hopeless case; you can't even do that," he would say. She learned from his papers that he had been born to a post office clerk in a small town and had never graduated from high school, that he was thirty-seven and divorced. She said once to Georg that Zbarski was exceptionally bright and well read for a man with no formal education. They were sitting in the restaurant, late at night, and Georg had had several drinks.

"Adam has had more formal education than anybody I know," he smiled enigmatically. "That's why he is here." He volunteered no more information and Elli did not press him not because she was not interested but because she did not wish to exchange confidences. Her first thoughts were to speculate how Georg had found out that Adam's papers were inexact, and if he checked them professionally, if he were apt to investigate hers. She changed the topic.

Adam was a regular guest in Natalia's restaurant. He always came alone, sat at a table in the dark corner over a shot glass of vodka, chain-smoking. There he first met Emmi with whom he engaged in long conversations. Emmi alone was permitted to his table. Whenever he saw the child coming, he quickly exchanged the vodka for a glass of tea.

Elli drank a lot that night. "Elli, what is the matter with you? Is there anything I can do for you?" She looked at Adam in sheer amazement. Never had she heard that soft note in his voice. She had thought him incapable of any warm feelings. He treated Ilona with the same unveiled disdain as he treated her; and she sometimes wondered what made this young beautiful girl yield to a man who showed her nothing but contempt. After

Georg's information she could see the reason for his drinking; but his manners still bothered her and she tried to keep away from him. Neither rudeness nor drunken moods amused her and she was now convinced that the latter explained his unexpected interest in her.

"No, Adam, thank you," she said. "I am perfectly all right."

"You are not. It doesn't take much to see it."

"Because I drink?"

"No. Not because you drink."

"Suppose I like to drink just as you do?"

"I am twice your age."

"I didn't realize that the older you get the more you drink."

"Come on, Elli. You don't have to tell me what's eating you. Tell me if I can help you."

"Yes. Give me another drink."

"No more drinks, baby. Come on, tell me what's the matter."

"Look, Adam, why won't you go comfort Ilona?"

"She is a slut."

"That doesn't answer my question."

"True, she is good in bed. Lots of warm breathing flesh. But she is brainless."

"Like all women."

"No. My wife was not."

"That's why you divorced her."

"I did not. She left me."

"I am sorry, Adam."

"Don't be sorry. The only thing she could do well was to count. She even counted my orgasms."

"She had brains."

"That's right. You can't have it both ways. Either one like Ilona or my ex."

"I must rely on your expert opinion."

"Why?"

"Because you are twice my age."

He smiled. This smile was like a revelation. His eyes lost their chilled sourness and deepened. The tight face relaxed as he took her hand and lifted it to his lips. "I need you, Elli," he said wearily.

Next day he came to the office smelling of vodka, staggering. Georg took care of him before Labisch showed up. Ilona told her that when Georg drove her home at three o'clock in the morning Adam was just opening a new bottle of vodka. "Which he certainly drained all by himself," she laughed happily. There was an inspection from Kraków that day and Labisch was furious when Georg told him that Adam had suddenly fallen ill. "Overdose of vodka, eh?" he railed, a roaring voice giving stature to his small frame. "I wouldn't be surprised if he ended up where they'll make him work." Georg assured him it was influenza; but as far as Labisch was concerned it could as well be cholera. Adam excelled in organizing receptions, which he explained by his having been a waiter sometime in the past, and what Labisch needed right now was a banquet for his guests before they toured the factories. When he announced that he would go and see what influenza looked like, Elli pretended that she had often given receptions for Rahm's guests; so Labisch gravely said he would give her a try. She ran to Natalia, explained the situation, and implored her to make a dinner for Labisch's party. The dinner was a success.

March 10, 1940

Uncle Abram moved in the day before yesterday. He sleeps in the front room; Danny moved to the kitchen. Uncle Abram is very quiet and never stares through the window. He reads or plays bridge with the Old Man and the boys. He is a very sweet man, and I don't blame him for not being able to stand Aunt Midas any longer.

March 12, 1940

Uncle Abram said today that there is no place for chidren in this world; that they should be spared the experience of living through hell. Daniel argued with him for a long time. Uncle Abram just kept looking at Emmi, lying on the bed, clapping her tiny hands, and repeated. "If she knew what's in store for her."

March 14, 1940

Yesterday Uncle Abram said that he saw some Germans standing downstairs, pointing at our windows. He said they were after him, they had found him. The Old Man told him that nobody knows he is living here and that he is quite safe. But he answered that they know everything, and there's no way to escape from them. He cried. I have never before seen an adult man crying like that.

March 15, 1940

David made a terrible row and requested Uncle Abram to leave at once. It all happened at night. He found Uncle Abram bent over Emmi's crib, a kitchen knife in his hand. The boys tied him with a rope until later the Old Man ordered them to untie him. In the morning Mama and Daniel took him to a doctor. What Uncle Abram needs is a reassuring, pleasant atmosphere, no talk about penury or danger. He must be under constant surveillance. He stayed with us; at night the boys keep guard at his bed.

March 28, 1940

Before dark Uncle Abram disappeared. The boys went to look for him in the streets; later at night Aunt Midas called to say that he had come home.

March 29, 1940

Uncle Abram hanged himself this afternoon while Aunt Wilhelmina and Rita were out for tea with some friends.

A week later Lili paid them a visit. She played with Emmi, took her for a walk, and left at seven-thirty. She continued to call on them for the next two weeks. Twice she found Adam there. He had taken to dropping in, playing with Emmi who adored him, and leaving without saying a word to Elli. Lili could not stand him. The first time she saw him she told Elli that he was a German agent. Elli spent a sleepless night; she decided he was not but was prepared to be more on guard in his presence. Lili would usually come before Elli was back home and leave shortly after. Obviously she was avoiding any conversation with her sister. One evening, at the beginning of November, Elli came home earlier than usual and found Lili and Emmi busy dressing a doll. Emmi told her that they had just returned from a walk. Elli was happy to see them both gaily talking, enjoying each other. She felt that everything would be all right; Lili would eventually come back to stay with them. She took her bag to get a cigarette and saw none were left. Since she still had some on her cigarette ration card, she put on her coat to go to the store.

"Don't go," she heard Lili's quiet voice.

"I'll be back soon. I must get some cigarettes," she said, taking her bag.

"Don't go." Lili was bent over the doll lying on the floor.

"Why, for heaven's sake?"

"They are waiting outside."

"Who is waiting?"

"They are." She buttoned the doll's dress.

"You mean the Germans?"

"Yes, that's what I mean."

"Whom are they waiting for?"

"You, silly."

"How do you know, Lili?"

"They were already here when I came back with Emmi." Lili was tying the doll's ribbon.

"Where?"

"In front of the house."

"But, Lili, I came after you and didn't see a single German."

"You didn't?" Lili took the doll's bonnet from the table.

"Lili, perhaps they were just passing by?"

"No, you idiot." She handed Emmi the doll and continued in a dull voice. "They keep watching us all the time. For weeks they have kept phoning my office almost every morning to check on me. Now they have come, six of them in a black Mercedes limousine. Your lover is with them too, you little bitch. He denounced you, all right. I knew he was working for them. I've told you so. But you wouldn't listen. Now you'll get what you've asked for." She smiled vaguely. "No exit."

"Ten minutes ago there was not a living soul downstairs," said Elli faintly.

"All right. Go ahead. I have warned you." Lili took Emmi's other doll, and they both started to dress it.

Elli was confused. Maybe she really did not see them. Perhaps they were really waiting for her to leave? But suppose they were; how long were they going to wait? Since she never went out that late how could they know that she would change her routine today? How could they know that she would run out of cigarettes? Why didn't they arrest her downstairs? She did not, of course, want to have them take her from the room with the child as a witness. Better if the epilogue took place outside. Distressed, already in her coat, she sat down heavily on her bed. Lili and Emmi dressed the other doll. The child was ebullient — she had not understood the German dialogue between the sisters — Lili laughed with her, not concerned anymore with Elli.

Elli went to the front door, listened, tried to distinguish voices on the staircase. There was absolute silence. She opened the door slightly and stuck her head outside. She could see nobody. She ran down the staircase. Still nobody appeared. She crossed the yard, then passed through the gate. No car, no Germans. The street was completely deserted. She bought the cigarettes and returned home. After a short while Lili bade her a polite good night and left.

In the morning Elli phoned Maria. In case of immediate danger she could ignore the prohibition against calls. This was immediate danger. Lili was no longer responsible for herself. In few words Elli told Maria that Lili was sick. Her words might have had a double meaning for in their code malady meant peril. But Maria already suspected. Elli saw how much she knew when they met at the station. Maria had hollow, glassy eyes; her hair had turned gray overnight.

Georg offered to drive them home because the train arrived after the curfew. They were twice stopped by night patrols; but it was a German car so they went on. Inside the vehicle they did not exchange a word. At home Elli reconstructed the whole story from the day of Lili's arrest. Her fanatic desire to go to Wendel, her fixed idea to save the whole family — an idea which had gradually degenerated into an obsession to save herself; the dangers of being trapped and murdered, a fear that mounted daily; a hatred toward Elli that was consuming her. "You have been the image and constant reminder of what she has suffered to save you," Maria said slowly. "And now she wants to get you out of her sight, as if instinctively she recognizes that by going away she will be able to dam up the tide of hatred which will make her destroy you and us." Maria looked twenty years older than she had the last time Elli had seen her. She said she would go to a friend who worked in the municipal government to obtain a travel pass for Lili and would then take her to Warsaw. There Doctor Darski would help to place Lili in an asylum.

By afternoon Maria had all the documents. Together they went to wait for Lili in front of her office. At four o'clock Lili came out, looking strangely beautiful that day. Her head lifted up, her magnificent auburn hair streaming behind, her eyes smiling; her posture erect as it had not been all that time. She did not seem surprised to see Maria. She kissed her tenderly and asked if Maria had come to take her back to Warsaw. She was tired of living here, she said.

They had dinner with Emmi in the restaurant, Maria and Elli nibbling at their food, Lili and Emmi eating heartily and chatting. Lili promised to send her a big new doll from Warsaw as soon as she could find a job and earn some money. There was even a small argument between them concerning the doll's hair: Emmi insisting on dark; Lili, on blond. "Blond is much better," Lili assured the child. "Believe me, it really is. It would be just like yours."

March 20, 1941

Lili is more beautiful every day. The other day I met her downstairs with her new boyfriend, Abel, who must be at least ten years her senior. She was dressed in a navy blue robe-manteau trimmed with fur (David calls the dresses we still have from home "the remains of past glory"), had a little matching hat on her shimmering hair and high-heeled shoes. Her first pair. She is tall, but Abel is a giant. With her head leaning upon his shoulder they made a perfect couple. My hair is dull blond, and I have always had freckles. Why don't I cut my plaits? It would certainly improve my looks.

At six o'clock Georg drove them to the station. Elli saw Adam standing at the kiosk. He motioned that he would wait in Georg's car. Lili kissed Emmi, waved Elli goodbye, and boarded the train with Maria. A few minutes before the train's departure, as if on second thought, Lili leaned out the half-opened compartment window, smiled warmly to Elli, and reached out to her, holding something clutched in her hand. Elli stretched out her hand into which Lili squeezed an envelope and asked gently, "Will you please mail it for me, Elli?"

The letter was addressed to Wendel.

12

The mountaineering suddenly ended. With the "Small" ghetto liquidated, the bridge is not necessary any longer.

After dark I went with Daniel to look at the new ghetto border. He is very upset about David, or rather, about Rachel and Mark. I tried to explain to him that David comes home so dog-tired that even if there were anything, he certainly doesn't see it. And if he does, perhaps he doesn't mind. Daniel said that I don't know life any more than I know David. Maybe. Then he asked me if I have a boyfriend, if I sleep with a boy. He seemed surprised when I told him I have not.

Many of my girl friends sleep with boys, because as Stella puts it, "Who knows what will happen tomorrow?" Nothing will happen tomorrow; we might be hungrier, or colder, but one day all this will end, and we will live a normal life again. I wouldn't like to die without finding out what sexual intercourse involves. I know it's something more than occupying the same bed but I do not know how it actually happens. Books don't help me very much with my total lack of imagination. Don't dare to ask anybody lest I make a fool of myself. I pretend of course that I know everything, laugh when the boys tell jokes, nod knowingly when the girls exchange their experiences. What I can see is that it's not exactly love they care about. What is it?

When I come to think about it I feel that having an experience with a man I do not love can't mean much. That's like replacing the original with a bad reprint. I wait. Perhaps I'm wrong? Will I miss more if I give myself to the wrong man, or if I die in total ignorance? I don't know. I was always sick when I had to make a decision, and then how can one make any decision in a matter like that?

Daniel, holding me closer, whispered that he has keys to his friend's room. As sorry as I was that this bitch, Rose, let him down, I didn't go with him.

She was running along a dark, deserted street. As she reached the bridge the voices grew louder. The yelling of the front runners became wild. They shouted back to the crowd that now they had her. Stark naked, she felt terribly exposed and crossed her hands over her breasts as she ran. If she could reach the woods, the moonless night still gave her a chance. They were closer and closer. She could single out voices and the howling of dogs. Finally she was there, she passed the first trees. Then the sky was lit with a million little glaring, dazzling suns. The crowd was drunk with joy. She felt the first stones on her back. "Elli," a voice reached her through the uproar. Blinded by the light, hot and red on her eyeballs, she could not open her eyes.

"Elli, dearest, wake up." She felt a warm breath on her face. "You had a bad dream, my little Nike. What's the matter with you?"

"Adam," she said with effort. "Adam, did I say anything?" He lit two cigarettes and put one between her lips. "Did I say anything, Adam?"

"Yes. You said you love me." He drew her closer. "You never

say it when you are awake. I had to put you to sleep to hear it."

How did it happen? She tried so hard never to fall asleep in his presence. She curled up inside his arm. She could have fallen asleep again and lain within these comforting arms until she could tell him she loved him, she wanted him to have her. God, she thought, I can't stand it any longer. I'm at the end of my rope. He must think I'm a pervert, a monster. But if he knew? Would he touch me? I can't live with him without telling him the truth. Perhaps I should tell him? "Adam," she said gently. But now he had fallen asleep. The veins in his temples were swollen, his nerve-hung face quivered. I'm driving him mad. I'm driving myself mad.

It had all come as a shock. The night Maria took Lili to Warsaw he came with a bottle of brandy and a pot of coffee. Emmi was already fast asleep. A lamp glowing on the night table plunged the room into a gentle half shadow. He had held her hand, a black, strange stare in his eyes. She appreciated his courtesy but wished he would leave her alone. She knew she'd burst out crying if he said a single word. But he said nothing. They slowly got drunk. It was dawn when he put her to bed and left. Then he was gone for two weeks touring the factories.

He came back on her name day. It was Ilona who found out about her name day and saved her from committing a gaffe. All her life she had observed her birthday and somehow had forgotten that celebrating her name day was part of her new religion. Ilona made all the arrangements and probably phoned Adam to invite him. She also decided that the party would be held in Adam's apartment and brought her younger sister to stay with Emmi. Elli got lots of flowers from the Treuhänder's office and a giant layer cake from Mr. Baryński. Natalia and her three satellites came with a huge tray of snacks; Georg provided drinks from the German officer's club. Lidia Halska, a sherry-eyed, dark blond divorcée whom Natalia introduced to Elli, came with her five-year-old boy whom they put to bed upstairs with Emmi. Ilona also invited Janusz Larski, a'young man Elli barely knew. Ilona had decided they needed more men. Larski was married but never went out with his wife. She always stayed home with their two small children and they used to laugh at him saying that he kept her locked at home out of jealousy. He made Elli nervous because he bit his fingernails with quick furtive bites, his squint eyes watchful.

Adam arrived at ten when the company was already in high spirits. He looked tired and tense. He congratulated Elli and immediately went over to Lidia to whom he was attentive the whole time. Only once he asked Elli in passing, "How have you been?"

"Fine," she said.

"Will you ever stop lying to me?" he asked quietly.

"I'm not lying." She wished he would leave her alone.

"OK. Have it your way." And he went back to Lidia.

Elli got drunk that night. The last thing she could remember was a black velvet cushion streaked with vomit. She awoke in Adam's robe, on his bed, with a cold compress on her head. The apartment was empty. For the next two days she tried hard to reconstruct what could have happened during those hours which were blank. Had she said anything? To whom did she talk? She faintly remembered Larski talking to her, then Adam who, it seemed to her, said something about Jews. Or did she? Ilona told her that oddly enough Adam was the only one who stayed completely sober till the last guest was gone. This was a clue. Elli was convinced now that he had stayed sober to get something out of her, and probably had, and would use it if only to make her life bitter.

Adam came two days later when Emmi was asleep and she was

stretched on the bed, reading. He sat beside her smoking, looking at her with that quizzical look that gave her creeps.

After a long uneasy silence she cracked. "Go ahead," she said. "What are you waiting for?"

He kept looking at her but said nothing.

"You've got me," she went on aggressively. "You did well though it cost you staying sober all night long."

"Wrong," he said.

"Anyway," she tossed away the blanket to get up, "I'm ready. Go ahead."

"You silly goose," he pushed her back. "Do you really think that I give a damn about sleeping with you? That I stayed sober to take you drunk to bed? Or perhaps to rape you? That I sneaked here at night to find you in bed? Oh, my God . . ." He threw the blanket over her face and slammed the door.

She avoided him for the next couple of weeks. She thought she would die if he ever mentioned this grotesque incident. If she could tell him how wrong he was. If she could tell him that it never occurred to her that he might like her, prefer her to Ilona, Lidia, or whoever it was. Women fell for his cynical, cool manner but not she. She was afraid of him.

At the beginning of February Mr. Quibus invited the whole staff to celebrate his wedding anniversary. Elli was sick at the thought Adam might get drunk and make a fool of her in front of the others. Squeezed in a corner, she heard Adam's voice behind her, "Remember what Anna Karenina said when she first met Vronsky?"

An omen? She turned to him. A glass in his hand, he swayed, looking at her intently. They stood staring at each other until Adam gulped down his drink, turned around, and walked away.

She was sitting idly in the armchair which replaced Lili's bed when he came next night. He knelt down beside her. "I need you, my little Nike," he said softly. "I need you."

She put her hand on his head and they remained motionless. She felt her fear, resistance, tension melting away. An unknown warmth enveloped her tightly. She did not dare to move lest the spell be broken. Her only thought was to have him near, to feel his body beside hers. At dawn Adam left her but came back the next night and every night after. Then one day he asked her to come to his room. She went. He laid her down comfortably on a big couch and sat beside her, looking at her, caressing her gently. They had a drink or two, smoked endlessly, and almost never talked. If only she could have told him everything, if she could give him a day-to-day account of her misery and fear. She would tell him about the Old Man, about Danny and David and Lili. About the days she spent before Abel found her; those days when all she wanted was to die, never to see again the hole in Danny's head, the cord around the Old Man's neck, the blood splashing from David's throat. She would tell him how her best friend, the gay and beautiful Stella just before she mounted the truck had strangled her own grandmother to keep her from falling into their hands alive. And why she had had to go back to the ghetto and what had happened there. She would tell him about Alfred and never again see at night the neatly wrapped candy boxes. She would tell him that every day here was agony, that she could stand it no longer, that she was frightened, lonely, helpless. He would understand. He would take her in his arms and make her forget the hell and the misery. He would save her from the darkness and the madness and the wrath of those left behind. He would tell her that she was a poor, hurt child and that his love was stronger than the harm that had been done to her. Every morning he would tell her that nothing bad would happen during the day, that she need not wait for the blow, for it would not come. At night they would be again together and nights would not be dark any longer. And then a day would come when he would take her far away and she would never be afraid again.

Of course she never told him anything. But it was she who made him lie beside her one night and kissed him passionately on the lips. Abruptly, as if angry, he pushed her away and stood for a long while looking at her stretched on the couch. Then he said slowly, "Elli, do you really want it?" It was then that it flashed through her mind that *he* might not want her if he knew. He might feel repulsion and loathe himself for being intimate with her and despise her for having cheated him into it. He didn't press her for an answer. He thought perhaps that she was embarrassed, not sure whether she really wanted him. Then she should have stopped it. Instead every night brought them closer until one day she came out with this "Everything but." She could not trust herself any longer, yet she did trust him. He looked puzzled but did not say a word.

The first glimpses of daylight were streaming into the room. It was time for her to go. She took his hand lying on her breast and kissed it lightly. He murmured sleepily, "I'm happy, I'm so happy with you, Elli."

When she looked back at the past two months she had an uneasy feeling of failure. She had failed the dead, betrayed the living. She was tormenting the man who loved her because she wanted to save her dignity, or what she thought was her dignity. She was capable neither of living or dying, of giving love or accepting it. She felt she had passed the limits of damnation. Yet there was life beyond these limits. Life was the black cold fear enclosing her as she fell asleep, still present in her bed like a faithful lover when she woke in the morning. Life was her yearning to feel Adam's body though a body was something one could chop in pieces, wrap neatly, and throw in the gutter. Life was to hold Adam's head in her hands and feel for the hole in

Danny's head and have her fingers, working on Alfred, kissed one by one by Adam. If he knew would he kiss them? She would end up with a glass of vodka which put her to sleep but the fear was still there. And the failure.

Then a night came when she found out that her dignity, this illusion for which she fought, simply did not exist. That night Adam told her that until he met her he had thought himself past love. "I'd long since written off love from my life," he was saying. "You came and a miracle happened." She felt his body clinging to hers and wanted to feel it forever. She held him tighter. "Elli," he said gently, "my love." He looked at her tortured face. "Elli, don't."

"Adam, Adam," she moaned.

"Elli, do you want to have a baby?" he whispered.

When she came to her senses she said slowly, "What did you say, Adam?"

He embraced her. "I asked if you wanted to have a baby."

Clumsily she shifted away from him and sat up in the bed. "Why should I have a baby, Adam?" She was really puzzled. "How?"

"Quite simply." He lit a cigarette.

She took it from him and turned on the night-table light. "Adam," she said, "you can't be serious."

"But I am." He took the cigarette from her.

"People don't have babies from what we are doing," she tried to smile.

"They do, Elli," he assured her.

"Adam, stop joking, please, it's a serious thing for me."

"I know," he said. She was watching him closely. "Don't look at me like that, Elli." He made a wry face. "I'm not joking. Maybe you are."

He couldn't be serious. He had promised her he wouldn't go beyond the limits she imposed and now was just making fun of her ignorance but it was hardly the time for it. Nor did he look very amused. "Adam, please," she touched lightly his chest, "let's be serious."

He sighed, "Oh, holy simplicity . . ." But then his eyes darkened, he looked at her quizzically, "Or is it a comedy? If it is, it's in a very poor taste."

"Adam," she said sharply, "how can you talk to me like that?"

"Very well, Elli." Now he sat up. "Either you pretend or you are the most ignorant woman I ever met in my life. How do you think children are made? Storks bring them or Santa Claus? No, it can't be ignorance. You are playing a dirty but very old trick. But I can't see what you would be after."

She got up, put on his robe and stood before him, the consequence incarnate of his logic. "Yes," she said. "You are right. I was just kidding." The months of torture, of self-denial only to make a fool of herself.

"Elli," she heard his soft voice. "Come to me, please." When she didn't move he came to her, freed her from the robe, and took her back. He turned off the light and drew her stiff body nearer.

"Elli, you wanted it, don't say you didn't. You wanted it as badly as I did. You didn't say it but your body did in a way that made words futile." He kissed her gently. "Why are you so frightened, dearest? You won't have this baby. You must trust me. We will have a child, we certainly will, later, not now." She lay silent as he went on. "I always wanted to have a child more than I can tell you. More than anything else in the world. My wife didn't want it. God, the nights I spent imploring her, begging for a child. We couldn't afford it yet, she said. Every time she said maybe next year. After three years she got pregnant. But she still wouldn't give in. We couldn't afford a trained nurse she explained to me. I told her that if she gave up her car we could afford the nurse. She refused. She loved her little red Fiat so much, she said. I drove her in this Fiat to the doctor who did the abortion. Remember, Elli," his voice grew hard, "remember, no matter how deep your love it can be killed. No one can hurt you more than the person you love."

"I will have a child with you, Adam," she said. "Not now. Later."

April 18, 1941

It's your birthday, Papa. You promised to come back.

April 20, 1941

When we first moved in here, I often met on our street a very attractive, well-dressed young woman with a boy of perhaps four. The boy drew my attention with his funny physique; a small edition of an athlete — very broad shoulders, narrow hips, muscular legs, a head covered with close-cropped golden curls. Today I saw her sitting against the wall, the skinny bald boy in her lap, begging.

April 22, 1941

Nelly's brother died of typhus.

June 10, 1941

Halina had typhus. She has lost all her hair and is completely bald. The doctor said it's unlikely that her hair will grow back. Her mother has promised her that after the war she'll get her a wig in Vienna so that nobody would ever know she has no hair. Halina didn't believe she'd be able to conceal it from her hus-

band and what if he found out. We kept discussing whether it would be better to tell him before the wedding or after or not at all, but reached no conclusion. Stella told her that she is only sixteen and has lots of time to worry about the husband and that baldness is not hereditary and Halina's children might have the bushiest hair in the world.

June 16, 1941

Lili stopped menstruating. Doctor Leder said it's undernourishment. I've got ugly ulcers. Same reason.

Life became much more simple. Now that the barrier was gone she responded to him without restraint. She discovered the taste of love. She liked it. More. She existed through it. Sometimes when they lay together, exhausted, still trembling, Adam would tease her, "Elli, whoever taught you the art of love was a master." And she would say, "Not one master, Adam, Old Masters, a whole gallery of them." She never knew what he really meant and didn't want to find out. Never again did she brood over the question of whether he would have wanted her if he knew. Not that she convinced herself he would. She just never thought about it. She felt that she was loved and this solved the problem. Yet there was a little spot in her brain always on guard, never entirely out, alert while the rest of the world ceased to exist. Even now when she was lying beside him, all his, the little spot remained hers.

"Adam," she whispered against his chest. "Adam, I'm so happy."

He kissed her wet forehead. "Say it again, Elli, say it again."

"Say what?" she laughed.

"Say Adam, Adam, Adam," he squeezed her arm a little too hard.

She propped her elbows on his chest, smiling, "You silly boy, I thought you wanted me to repeat I'm happy."

"No," he said. "I want you to repeat my name."

Her arm hurt. "Why, of course, Adam." Suddenly, without any reason, she felt entrapped.

"It makes me feel good when I hear it from you," she heard him saying.

"Yes, Adam," she said, and felt it coming.

"What if I had changed my first name too?" he went on. "I'd feel ridiculous and miserable if you whispered or cried or moaned Staś or Andrzej or whatever it might have been. How would I know it's me you call at night? Me and no one else when my name is all you can breathe?" So here it was. She knew one day he'd come out with it.

"You don't go advertising this holy truth, do you?" she asked, suddenly angry.

"What holy truth?"

"About your name." God, what a damn fool he is, she shrunk inside.

"Of course, I don't."

"So why tell me? How come Georg knows?" Before she had finished she wished she had never said it. She did not want to know why Georg knew, what he knew, and, above all, she did not want to know it herself.

"Georg doesn't know anything." Adam lit two cigarettes and stuck one in Elli's mouth. "And what's wrong with telling you? You won't betray me, will you, Elli?" He drew her closer.

"I don't know, Adam." She felt uneasy in his arms. "And I don't know how much Georg knows but he does know this fourth-grade education is a lie." She heard drumming in her head, *I want you to remember that nothing matters to them when they are drunk . . . no secret, no promise, no oath . . . they might mean no harm . . . and still betray you.* God, how could she ever think of telling him the truth. "Perhaps you confided to him when you were drunk?" She felt more and more unhappy. Instead of cutting off this conversation which never should have started each word made it worse.

"Perhaps," said Adam carelessly.

"Doesn't this bother you?"

"Thousands of things bother me and I can't help them, Elli," said Adam slowly. "My father in Dachau bothers me . . ."

"Your father . . ." Words failed her.

"My father was German, Elli." Now she knew that she could not have stopped him. He had to talk. "He stayed in Poland after the First World War, in Kraków. He was the dean of the faculty of mathematics at the Jagellonian University and published major works about quantum statistical correlations. Have you ever heard of Edmund Werner, Elli?"

"Good lord," she exclaimed, "my school textbook was written by him."

August 8, 1940

Bumped into Zosia in the street. A week before her whole family escaped from the ghetto in Łódź. She told me briefly about our classmates. Hanka Berger has TB; she was the best in our class, unusually bright, a good friend. I used to crib Latin translations from her. Judith, an expert in math (how many times did she save me), lost her parents, is herself dying of leukemia. Franka is working in a soup kitchen, supporting her parents, grandparents, and two old aunts. She was the best in physics. We nicknamed her Albertynka because of Einstein. Naomi is living on the Aryan side with a German officer. She was the beauty of our class. Not quite a year before each of us would have been expelled from school for merely showing up with a boy in the street. I remember the interrogation I was subjected to when Miss Marew met me with Lucjan. I had a hard time trying to convince her that he was my cousin. "You'd better be careful not to have too many cousins," she told me.

"No, Elli. It was written by Edgar Werner, my younger brother. We both started as my father's assistants. Edgar wanted to make money quickly and took to writing textbooks, almost entirely abandoning research. I stuck to my philosophical studies of the foundations of logic and mathematics. But that's beside the point. Anyhow, when the Germans came to Kraków they wanted us to resume the German citizenship at once. My father flatly refused. I fled. Edgar became a Reichsdeutsch." Adam got up, poured some alcohol in the glasses left on the table, and brought them to bed. "For a long time I had no documents. Adam Zbarski was my schoolmate. He was killed in Warsaw at the beginning of the war by a stray bullet. His mother gave me his documents." He was slowly sipping his drink. "Adam and I, the two Adams known as Siamese twins, we had been inseparable since early childhood. It all ended over the Jewish business."

"The Jewish business," said Elli.

"Yes. The day he learned I smashed windows in Jewish stores he spat in my face." She leaned on her elbow, reached for the glass on the bed table, and drained it at a draft. God, don't let him touch me. I'll scream. He was sitting on the bed, his face buried in his hands. "It was so long ago," he was saying. "The early thirties. The university had its traditions in national democracy and Jew-baiting. I had mine. The word *Jew* was taboo in our house. It was something you were not supposed to talk about. That was what we heard from our mother. She came from an aristocratic Christian family with archbishops, generals, countesses, et cetera. My father never cared one way or the other. All he really cared for were quantum correlations. I was very proud when the national fraternity invited me to join. I believed we should get rid of the Jews in the university, and in the economic and cultural life. They poisoned the newly reborn sovereign Polish Republic. They . . ."

"Adam," she half rose. "I don't care for politics in bed. Would you please stop."

He pushed her back. "No," he said. "I won't. It's not politics. You must know who makes you happy, whom you want to kiss you, whom . . ."

"I already know, Adam. I'm tired. I'd like to go now." She rose again and he shoved her back. "They offended our patriotic feelings . . ."

"And they crucified Christ. All right. And now let me go."

". . . by passing examinations with better marks, by graduating summa cum laude. Undernourished, tutoring at day, studying at night, they made it. Then they kept creeping into the very flesh of our country, surreptitiously, deceitfully, tricking, cheating, never really feeling Polish. All set to destroy the sacred body of our mother country, they sold it out piece by piece to the world Jewry. The only way to stop this conspiracy, to save my country, was to beat the Jew. That was my fraternity's religion. And mine."

Again he lit two cigarettes. Elli took one from his hand and crushed the part he had held in his lips. He could not see it anyway with his back to her.

"It was Bernard who dragged me out of it. The scar I have on my left arm is Bernard's knife. He later said that it would have been a pity if I couldn't go on with my work so he was careful not to cut my right hand. He was also studying mathematics. He knew my stuff." Adam laughed dryly. "His father was a rabbi. Bernard took me to him. He talked to me. Not about

Jews. About mankind and responsibility. I used to spend more and more time with him. After a hemorrhage he was paralyzed. Bernard was studying in Paris at that time and I moved into their house. If my mother had not been dead by then, this friendship would have killed her. The heir to countesses and bishops living in a rabbi's house. I lived there until the old man died." Adam lapsed into silence.

"So you are now, so to speak, a Jew-lover. A bosom friend, an old fatherly rabbi-teacher . . ." She saw his eyes flash with anger and quickly switched to a light, gay tone, "Oooops, pardon. I didn't want to hurt your feelings — this or the other way."

"I am not a Jew-lover." He literally shriveled with rage. "And you can't offend me this or the other way." He drew out the last words. "I am well aware of what I've done and even the old rabbi couldn't convince me they were 'youthful sins.' "

"And so you live a prey to haunting remorses and drown your sorrows in vodka," she chanted gaily.

"You know, Elli," Adam abruptly turned to her. "I didn't realize you are such a fool. You really didn't get much farther than Ilona."

"And now, will you please let me go!" She pulled away from him and jumped out of the bed.

"No, I will not let you go. Not until you know what I am drowning in vodka."

"I do not want to know. I don't care." She reached for her bra.

"You do, Elli, you do. I take back this Ilona stuff." He snatched the bra from her and flung it to the opposite corner of the room.

"I couldn't care less, Adam, whether you take it back or not. Ilona is perfectly all right, and your fraternity was perfectly all right, and I see no reason for being exposed to the history of your life. After all, I wanted to be your mistress, not your confessor. Those you can find in every church. You don't have to sleep with them!"

"Stop this nonsense, Elli. For heaven's sake, stop this nonsense. You didn't want to be my mistress. If you could hear how funny this word sounds when you say it." He took her in his arms. "Come, my sweet little mistress. Come to your jester."

She was exhausted. Fear, suspicion, disgust drained her of any other feeling. Why did he tell *her* about his "youthful sins?" About the Jewish friends? And his conversion? Did he tell it to every woman he slept with? Or did he tell it only to her? Did he suspect? Why did he confess about his name? To invite her confession? She lay stiff in his arms, her brain in tumult. He ran his fingers through her thick hair and lightly kissed her eyelids. "My dear little Nike," he murmured, "my love, my wife."

July 10, 1941

Mama came. She bribed the sentries to get in. She brought a bottle of red wine for the Old Man, candy and apples for Emmi. Mama looks so different. Young, beautiful, but entirely different. Aryan, I guess. Her face harder, she speaks in a different way; the delicate, elegant woman I knew has disappeared.

She asked us to try to find out about Papa through the Judenrat. She got a message that he did not manage to escape further into Russia. Mama would like him, and the rest of the family who also stayed there, to come and live with us. That's what they decided with Uncle Michael.

The German, Erna Weil, ceased to exist. Mama is now Polish, with a Polish Kennkarte, and a new name, Maria Chmielewska.

Mama asked about our lessons, our friends, but most of the time talked to the Old Man and Aunt Paula. The people on the Aryan side, she said, didn't imagine the extent of misery here. I do not believe it. She justifies them, because she lives in their world, not in ours. The change in her is not only an outward one. Not that I condemn her. It's just that she isn't the same anymore. Her self-confidence, the manner in which she holds her head or lights her cigarette, the note of mourning in her voice when she talks about us, and that of excitement when she speaks of herself, Michael, and the people living "there" — I didn't like all that.

What could I have told her? That what she had seen in the streets here isn't even a pale reflection of reality. That she'd never, never understand it! Should I have told her that I've got so used to starved corpses lying in the streets that I don't see them anymore? That I conceal the food I carry so as not to be robbed by somebody who is hungrier than we? Or perhaps that I'm sometimes so dizzy from hunger that I don't understand what I read? Or should I tell her about little Aron, the sole support of ten people, whom they made swallow the raw potatoes he was smuggling in only to smash his head against the wall later? What would she think of me if I told her I saw it with my own eyes, and slept at night, and went next day to classes, and discussed French literature?

She is a world apart now. There was nothing I could tell her, nor was there anything I wanted to tell her.

She left at four o'clock. None of us could walk to the gate with her. She is Aryan.

13

ADAM HAD NEVER TOLD HER where he spent the nights when he was not with her. In the morning his eyes were bloodshot and invariably he'd drink more during the day than usual. Once at the end of February she went downstairs to pick up Emmi with whom he often spent his spare time. She saw a knapsack on the kitchen table. Beside it lay two loaves of bread and some parcels wrapped in paper. This morning he had told her he wouldn't be home that night. At ten o'clock she heard the door of his apartment open and saw him quickly passing through the dark yard. Her heart sank. He had no night permit and wherever he was going it was a sticky business. He never said so but she knew he was connected with the underground.

There was nothing she could do about it. Could she ask him to stay away from it because of her? Their affair was a public secret. Adam knew she didn't care what "people might say," and he somehow liked to show off with her and Emmi. Himself an avowed atheist, he made a point of escorting them to church every Sunday. Anyway, she would be the first they would come after if he were caught. If he knew it would mean the end for her and the child would he stay away? From me, she thought pouring herself a drink, yes, but not from his work. Over and over again he came back to the old rabbi's teachings. He was clearly infatuated by them although he admitted himself that in this world the rabbi had never known, most were empty of meaning. Yet he stuck to them in a fanatic, obsessive way. He blamed himself for some obscure sins he was unable to define. All the same he insisted he was responsible or would be if he yielded to what he called "the Old Adam." Whether all this was connected with his German brother, the smashed Jewish windows, or some other frustrating experience she did not know. He accused himself of killing his child, of not having killed his brother, of not having hidden his father, but these he would say were lesser trespasses. He felt guilty for the fate which had befallen his country, for lack of communication among people, for the hatred they nursed. He was torn between an illusive omnipotence and virtual impotence, seeking for a confirmation that this phantom responsibility he assumed could transform his impuissance into power strong enough to improve all erring mankind. Half-drunk, he would drag out these arguments and deliberations for hours on end and she would never contradict, sensing something sick in him. Whatever his past, his sins, true or imaginary, only his work in the Resistance justified his present existence.

The next time he told her that he would not be at home at night she went downstairs as he was ready to leave. "Adam," she asked, "where are you going?" He put the knapsack on the floor and took her in his arms. "I'll be back, dearest," he said. "You want me to come up when I get back?"

Precisely, thought Elli, I want you to come and bring those who might follow you right to my room. But it didn't make much difference really. "Yes, of course, Adam," she pressed her lips to his, "but I must know where you are going."

"Elli," he held her at his arm's length and looked at her,

"that's something new. I'm not used to your asking questions."

"This is very important to me, Adam." Her eyes were averted. "Extremely important."

"I suppose so." He took the knapsack from the floor. "Otherwise you wouldn't ask. I have to feed some people. They are hungry." And he left.

She bumped into Mr. Quibus and almost threw her arms around him when, hearing the light knocking, she jumped out of the bed and opened the door. In a dark robe over his nightshirt, his upper denture missing, he excused himself for the intrusion. "I've got a call from the police," he said. "Do you know . . ."

"Yes, I know, Mr. Quibus," she interrupted him. She was so enormously exhausted, so utterly tired and she knew that this was not the end. This was the beginning.

"Was it you?" Mr. Quibus asked.

"Was it me?" she repeated mechanically, feeling drained out of life, all chilled inside.

"That's what I'm asking," said Mr. Quibus a little impatiently. "Did you leave the light?"

Light? What light? She had no idea what to say or even what she thought.

"The police called me because a night patrol found a light in the office. A violation of the blackout order," he said half mockingly. "They wanted me to tell them at once who left the light. Do you know . . ."

She heard herself from a far distance, "I don't know."

He stepped back. "I've also got a call from Director Labisch to join him in Krakau and I'm leaving on the six o'clock train. I wanted you to know they'll come in the morning to investigate. I'm sorry I disturbed you." He left her standing in the door and disappeared in the long corridor.

The man who asked briskly for Director Labisch was a civilian. He looked like a schoolteacher or a desk clerk. His navy blue-and-white striped suit hung loose on him and his fingers moved incessantly, pressing, breaking each other. The uniformed officer looked indifferently around and walked to the window. Elli explained that both the director and his deputy were in Kraków and would be back at night. "We had an inspection yesterday concerning the lights," she added.

"What lights?" asked the civilian.

"Oh, excuse me. I thought you came about the lights. There was a light left on in the office the other night and the police asked the director to report about it. But the inspectors have already talked with Mr. Urban," she explained stubbornly.

"We are from the Geheime Staatspolizei," said the man. The officer started to whistle "Lili Marlene."

"Yes?" said Elli.

"Who is in charge of the personal files?"

"I am."

The civilian went to the officer who was still whistling and whispered something to him. The other nodded.

"That's all we need." The civilian returned to her desk. He took a magnifying glass from his pocket and his busy fingers fumbled with the button of the leather case, opening and closing it with a metallic click-clack. "I don't like to intrude in the absence of your boss but the matter is pressing," he said. He took the glass out of the case, leaned over Elli's desk, and held it over a letter as if testing it. "You have a Jewish girl working on your staff," he said, his eyes focused on the letter. The officer finished "Lili Marlene" and changed the tune. He was whistling now the "Horst-Wessel Lied." He tapped out the melody on the windowpane. "You have a Jewish girl working here," the man repeated evenly.

"No," said Elli.

"I did not ask a question, miss. I made a statement." He did not raise his voice.

"It must be a misunderstanding," said Elli. "A mistake."

"I do not think so," the man said. "We have written information. From somebody who knows her. Our informers never lie and seldom make mistakes." He put the glass back in the case and looked at Elli. "She has a child with her. A girl."

The telephone on Elli's desk rang. She picked up the receiver, "Verwaltung der Klinkerwerke, guten Morgen."

"I love you," she heard Adam's voice. He was calling from Kolno.

"Yes," she said.

"Elli, can you hear me?"

"Yes."

"What's the matter? How are you?"

"Fine."

"You don't sound fine. Did something happen?"

"No, nothing."

"I said I love you."

"Adam." She wanted to say goodbye to him.

"Yes, dearest. You sound so strange. You have some people in the room, haven't you?"

"Adam."

"Elli, I'll be back as soon as I can. At five or at the latest at six. Don't be sad, please. Goodbye, dear. I love you." He hung up.

The officer abandoned his position at the window and came to her desk. She sat down. He got a box of cigarettes out of his pocket, carefully extracted one and put the rest on Elli's desk. "Warum sind Juno rund?" she read the inscription on the box. "Aus gutem Grund sind Juno rund."

July 5, 1940

Mama and Uncle Michael had a dangerous accident in Du-
bienka. A policeman turned them in. A Polish policeman. Un-
cle's friend, a miller, Mr. Olszewski (he knows who they really
are) helped them to flee, but it was too late. They got caught on
the way to the station. The German examining officer asked
Uncle Michael if he knew the policeman Lewandowski. Uncle
denied it. "So how can he know you are a Jew?" asked the officer.
God! Are the Germans naïve!

"Let us see the personal files of the employees," he said, politely
pushing the cigarettes toward her with an inviting gesture. She
took one, lit it, and walked to the stacks. She handed the officer
a fat file with an inscription *Personalakten.* Then she sat behind
her desk and deeply inhaled the Juno cigarette, a nice change
from the coarse tobacco she was used to. She looked quietly at
the officer skillfully fingering the files and did not budge when
he found what he was looking for. He said to the civilian,
"That's her baptismal certificate." The civilian cast one quick
glance at the paper. "Forged?" asked the officer. "Of course,"
the man replied. "By a complete idiot." He placed the magnifying glass back in his pocket, unused. Again he started to twist
his fingers. "Helena Rak," said the officer. "Where is she?" Elli
sat silent, her throat clogged. "She is a cook here," continued
the officer. "She must be in the kitchen. Will you please show us
to the kitchen, Fräulein?"

Helena Rak was peeling potatoes near the sink. Her little girl
was playing in the corner with a cup and two teaspoons. "Helena
Rak?" asked the officer in his subdued polite voice. She nodded.
"Komm mit," he said. She showed no surprise, no hesitation,
as though she was expecting them to come. She finished peeling
the potato she had in her hand, threw it into a half-filled pail,

took off her apron, folded it, and put it next to the pail. She tiptoed to the kitchen stove, carefully, noiselessly drew aside the boiling soup pot, took her coat from the hanger, and stood in the door ready to go. Not even once did she glance at the child who with a teaspoon in each fist sat in the corner, mute. The officer put on his gloves, smoothed the leather on each finger, slowly, meticulously. The civilian turned toward the staircase door. Helena Rak, now in evident haste, took two steps forward when the officer jumped at her, slapped her face with his gloved hand, and quietly said, "Das Kind." Helena Rak turned back and went to the child. She did not tiptoe any longer. She lifted the girl from the floor, put her on a kitchen stool, took the teaspoons out of the little hands and put them in a drawer. She laced the girl's shoes and, smiling warmly, said in a pleasantly modulated voice entirely unfamiliar to Elli, "Come my little darling, you'll go with your mama." The child lost its stony countenance and embraced her. "You'll not leave me here, Mama?" Tears were rolling down her cheeks. "No, my love, I won't leave you, ever." She took the girl in her arms and her head, for the first time since Elli met her, was lifted high. Her big black eyes were stern, knowing. She started first down the staircase.

Elli waited for Adam to come. She wanted him to take her in his arms so that she could breathe again. She wanted him to kiss her so that she'd forget, to tell her she was a miracle in his life, to make her believe in miracles. She wanted him to tell her he needed her, that he could not live without her. Otherwise, how could she live through this night and start another day. Eight o'clock passed, and nine. He came at eleven. Completely drunk.

The knapsack was ready on the table. "I can't take it like this," said Adam. "Don't we have some wrapping paper around?"

"I don't think so," answered Elli. "But I can get some from the office."

It was past the curfew, the yard was completely dark. As always when Adam was leaving for his mysterious knapsack expedition she was on the point of hysteria. She was sure he was feeding some partisans or perhaps refugees who refused the invitation to become German. He did not tell her and she never asked him again. Back home, she wrapped the bulky sack and tied it with string. If they got him it wouldn't make much difference whether this damn thing were wrapped or not.

They waited till ten o'clock smoking and talking about nothing. Then Adam left. Whenever she put in the knapsack the two loaves of black-market bread, a jar of lard, saccharine, ersatz coffee, potatoes, salt, she had a feeling of being an accomplice to Adam's doom. She resented these unknown people who jeopardized his life, hers, and Emmi's. Once she saw Adam squeezing a tiny doll into the knapsack. He thought she was in the kitchen and she never mentioned the doll to him. But then she knew there was a child there. Her indignation lessened but was back again when he next put the empty knapsack on the table. The hours when he was gone were endless. She would make numberless trips downstairs to see if he was back, she would try to read but most of the time all she felt was cold fear. He told her never to wait for him in his apartment. In case he got caught they shouldn't find her there. "Nothing would happen to you," he said, "you can say you came to see me about some office stuff, still it's better you stay upstairs." Though she knew she might not get out of it that easily, after the first hour had passed she'd start her trips downstairs. Adam had a dynamo pocket lamp which made a funny noise. When she heard the familiar sound on the staircase she knew it would be followed by the sound of the key in the lock and then a wave of strange warmth overwhelmed her. She would sit silently until she felt his arms around her and heard him whisper, "I'm back, my love, I'll always come back."

Emmi said half aloud, "I want a red hoop," and Elli looked at her watch. It was past two. Four hours since he left. At three he still wasn't back. At quarter to four she heard the squeaking of his lamp. Her body all gone limp, her mouth dry, she waited with closed eyes. She heard the key in the lock, the door of her room cracking. And then nothing. When she opened her eyes she saw Adam standing, his back against the door, his eyes fixed on her.

"They caught me," he said. "Thank God on the way home. I got rid of them for five hundred zloty." She looked at him, numb. "I've decided to tell you where they are, Elli. I might not come back one time. We can't let them starve."

"We?" said Elli.

"All right, have it your way," said Adam irritably. "*I* can't let them starve."

"Please, Adam, don't raise your voice. Emmi's sleeping." Elli trembled all over. He is mad, she thought. Why should I of all people risk my life and Emmi's for the sake of his pals! Perhaps they smashed the Jewish stores together? Fraternity ties, she suddenly remembered, were binding forever.

"Elli," he said in a subdued voice, "you must do it for me." He reached out toward her but she backed away. She stood now at Emmi's bed as if letting him know that her primary duty was to this child. "I know," he said. "You don't have to use such tricks. They have children there too." He waited for her to say something.

"I won't do it, Adam," she clenched her teeth. "I can't."

"If we did these days only what we could," he sounded sullen, "we'd be damned. All of us."

You fool, she thought, you conceited fool. You revel in these night trips. You need them to make sense of your frustrated life.

You like this role of a hero no matter how much it may cost you.

"Elli," his voice reached her, "these people . . . these people . . . they'd perish the moment I'm gone."

"You already said it, Adam." She tucked Emmi tighter. "I can't help it. I'd better go and make some coffee."

January 21, 1941

It was a crisp sunny day and I went for a walk with the Old Man. When we came home nobody was in. I made him some coffee, and then, I just couldn't help but tell him that I'm not convinced I should be proud of being Jewish. I told him I never really thought of myself being Jewish, and still was quite happy. I didn't mind children called me names; my father told me they were scum, and he believed his daughters above being bothered by them. That was the way I felt for a long time, I told the Old Man. Until later, at school, when I was eleven or twelve, my most beloved class teacher caught me cribbing. She said she couldn't punish me because I was Jewish, and it's only natural for me to cheat. Christian girls have a Christian ethic, that's why they don't do such things — but not me, she said. I couldn't get over it for a long time. I trusted her, I believed she was right. I told Papa about it; he said she was a fool. I argued that she was a docent at the university and he said wisdom doesn't come from education. But I didn't want to be a Jew any longer. I started to go to church, to read Eucharistic booklets that the other girls read. I believed I'd get this ethic somehow. Then, I saw the Christian girls cribbing. I was at a loss. I saw myself cheated by my teacher. I stopped going to church, never again looked at these booklets. Later I had classes in Jewish history. I liked it because I liked history not because I felt any ties with those people dispersed through the world two thousand years ago. *And I positively disliked their vengeful God, who kept thundering, punishing, and menacing them. Just as I feel no ties with those people here, the Hasids.* "Don't you think, Grandfather," I asked, "that I belong to Poland, to the Polish culture, tradition and future, more than to those people?"

The Old Man looked at me for a long time. Then he said, "You do and you do not, Elli. You do because you choose so, and you choose so because you've been brought up this way. You have been taught to love this country, its past, its writers, poets, national heroes. You were born here, you believe it's yours. The other world — that of the Jews — is alien to you, strange, frightening, because we didn't explain it to you before you were forcibly exposed to it. Nobody told you about your ties with this world, its past, its writers, poets, heroes. Remember what you read from Romain Rolland? Every time we are lulled by an illusionary truce we frantically cling to the idea of assimilation. We believe we can absorb a different culture and forget our own; we believe the people will entirely absorb us, regardless of our origins, religion, race, or whatever you call it, and let us belong. This, as we see once more, is not the case. All I can tell you now is that I hope you, and all my grandchildren, will learn a lesson from it which is not exactly what I'd like you to learn as I myself never was a very conscientious Jew. But there's not much choice left. Still, I don't suggest you feel a special allegiance to these orthodox Jews you see here; but I'd like you to understand that they are not just some bizarre exotic creatures, but men who, for right or wrong, saved a people from extinction. And yet I do not believe in living an isolated life, as they do. I believe we should seek for a status of equality among people we are living with, without ever forgetting who we are, without denying ourselves. Man must know who he is and where he comes from before he decides what he's going to do with his life — if he wants to live what I call a life. You see, you can't escape from yourself unless *you are nothing, a zero. When you try you are put back in your right place by others or, as some believe, by God. By the vengeful God, as you said." I asked him if he really believed in God. He said, "I believe in man."*

When she came back with the coffee he was sitting on her bed, greedily smoking. Without looking at her he said, "The last store in which I broke the windows was Yankel's. I saw him staring at me through this damned shining glass and ever since his eyes have been with me. I met him next years later in Kraków before I fled. I would have recognized those eyes in hell. He didn't wear the armband. He stared at me waiting for me to turn him in. Then I met him here before the liquidation of the ghetto. I saw him marching in a working squad. I spent days searching the ghetto to find him. I found him three days before the end. Georg told me about the destination of the trains. First Yankel wouldn't hear of hiding. He didn't trust me. I spent the last three nights working on him. Don't think I'd have convinced him but the news reached the ghetto too and he gave in. He said it really didn't matter whether I turned them in later or they were gassed immediately. I'd have slapped his face if not for those eyes staring at me from behind the shining window glass. He had his old father, his wife, and two kids with him. I talked Georg into lending me his car. I said I had made a girl pregnant and must drive her to a midwife in the country. I took them all to a place near the railway bridge and they live there in a burrow we dug together with Yankel." Adam dropped his head. "Ever since, I keep thinking that one night I'll come and not find them there . . . Or, they'll wait for me and I won't come. Elli," he whispered hoarsely. "Elli, would he think I let him down even if I died for him?"

"No, Adam," she said. "He will not. I'll go to him and tell him they crucified you."

At the end of April Adam told Elli that he'd take them to the country the next Sunday. The spring came late that year and it certainly was too cold for an outing but she knew how much Adam hated the four walls of the office where they spent at least twelve hours a day. Space made him feel free he said, and Emmi jumped at the idea of a whole day in the open. Georg promised to drive them to Zamość and then Adam planned a long walk in the woods. Sunday came full of sunshine. Emmi was up at six o'clock. Elli had a hangover and could hardly lift her head. When Adam rushed in at seven she was still in bed. "Adam," she couldn't open her eyes, "I think you should take Emmi and let me stay home. I'm not feeling well."

The first to protest was Emmi. She climbed on Elli, made herself comfortable right on her stomach, and begged Elli to go with them.

"But you'll be with Adam, dear," Elli said weakly. "I'm sick."

"Get up," said Adam irritably. "You have fifteen minutes to dress." At this she opened her eyes and looked at him amazed. "If Georg fed you poison," he went on in an agitated voice, "you'd eat it from his hand." Last night they had an argument at Georg's. It started as usual with Adam's remarks about her provocative behavior but the conclusion was that she'd sleep with anyone. She knew that Adam wouldn't have said it when sober but then she remembered her father saying that alcohol made people say what was really on their minds. She drank to forget Adam, her father, and the whole damn world. She forgot nothing and her head was heavy as lead. She drank two cups of coffee, dressed, and before they reached Zamość the scent of the fresh, cool air and the sunlight made her feel that something wonderful was going to happen. They wandered through the lofty trees stirring to life; Emmi, way ahead of them, was wild with joy. Elli touched the branches and fingered the emerging grasses, smelling them and letting the pale sun fall on her face. It was like a dream. Bushes waved in the gentle breeze, plants pushed the first green leaves through the earth, here and there buds opened and new flowers blossomed for the first time this spring. She was running, dizzy with the limitless open space, and Adam was chasing her until breathless she fell into his arms. Holding her hand, he led her across the meadows, back into the dense woods and she was filled with the scent, green and sharp, and was happy he had brought her here.

She felt the familiar surge of fear and her eyes became like an alerted animal's when they were stopped by a loud "halt." Two bayonets glistened from among the bushes. Adam said loudly "Balladyna." Two young men in battle dress emerged from the trees and saluted him. Their helmets were covered with leaves, uniforms spotted green and yellow. They were heavily armed. They carried machine guns, wore sidearms, and had hand grenades in their belts. The unshaven young faces were tanned and thin. Emmi was all eyes. She stood, her mouth wide with surprise, shaking Adam's hand. "Do they live in the woods?" she asked. "Like animals?" Adam laughed, "Not exactly, Emmi, but they do live here." He took Elli's arm and they followed the two men. Oh my God, thought Elli, I'll be damned, I should have never come here, I should never have spoken to this man, I'll rot and Emmi with me. Adam gave her a brief encouraging smile. "They are friends, Elli, don't worry." As if he knew what was eating her, the fool. Before she knew the location of this unit, before she met these people face-to-face, there still was a chance she wouldn't be accused of having contact with them. In a minute it would be too late. "I'd rather go home, Adam," she said. "Please, let's go home. I'm sick."

A look of dry stubbornness came over his long bony face. "I can't stand it any longer," he said. "Please, Elli, try to understand. It must be settled. It wrecks my nerves." He interrupted himself.

"But Adam," she was taken aback. "For heaven's sake what

are you talking about? What will these people, this 'walk' settle?"

He lifted his crease-surrounded eyes. "You'll find out," he said.

The man who greeted Adam with a cheerful "Good to see you, old boy," and kissed both of Elli's hands, was tall and straight as a pine. Well past fifty, he seemed to be bursting with life. In no time Emmi landed in his arms and there she was sitting on his broad shoulders, her hands on his shock of beautiful white hair. He excused himself for a moment and came back from the bushes followed by two soldiers. They addressed the man as "Mr. Colonel." Swiftly and noiselessly they set a table under a widespread tree, put meat, bread, and vodka on it, saluted, and went away. The Colonel with a pipe in the corner of his mouth was listening to Adam's prolonged speech which, Elli imagined, must have been a report. She couldn't see the point of bringing her here except that Adam wanted to dispel her doubts about his position in the Resistance which was the last thing she was anxious to know. *The less you know the better for you,* Uncle Michael had said, and sure as hell he was right. He always was. It was incomprehensible though that this Colonel, or whoever was in charge of this unit, agreed to bring her down here without any obvious reason. He should have advised Adam to choose a more appropriate place for a Sunday outing.

"I think it would be better to go over it before breakfast," she heard the Colonel saying and saw Adam nodding. "Agreed, young lady?" the Colonel turned to her.

"Why, of course," she said, not knowing what to say. He disappeared in the dense bushes with Emmi still on his shoulders. Adam walked over to her.

"Elli," he said very quietly and very slowly. "The Colonel is an army chaplain."

"Well," she said. "Is he going to say the Sunday Mass?"

"Not exactly." Adam was clearly embarrassed.

"A requiem?"

"No, Elli." Something in his voice hit her.

"So what?"

"He is going to marry us."

"To do what?" It was clearly the hangover. She couldn't even understand what he was talking about. She shouldn't drink so much. She made a gesture of defeat. "I'm sorry, Adam. I really don't feel well. Why don't we go home?"

"We will go home, dearest." His face was yellow, the jaw-bones nervously moving. "We will go home, husband and wife."

She saw a slim girl, in a long white dress with a rich lace veil sweeping the shining parquet, coming toward her. She was swinging gracefully to the sound of Mendelssohn's "Wedding March." Adam is going to marry her, she thought, the blur growing more and more dense. The girl passed her and she saw her again at the other side of the trees in a plain blue dress with Ian at her side, standing before an old bearded man in a wide-rimmed hat.

"Elli, don't stare at me like that," a voice reached her. "I meant nothing wrong. I wanted it to be a surprise. I thought a simple soldier wedding, with no bells, no veil was just what you'd like. I didn't want to hurt you, Elli." She could feel his breath on her face. "I need you and Emmi. I need you, I can't live without you, why don't you understand it . . . I know you'll go away one day . . . I can't bear this thought. You said I made you happy, *I*, do you hear, *I* made you happy. Say something, Elli. Don't look at me like that. If you really don't want it just say so."

She felt pain in her left hand which he held in his palms. "Why," she said in a stony voice. "*You* want it. That's enough. *You* made me happy. I pay cash."

•

That night she understood that sooner or later she would leave Adam.

He knew it first. I know you'll go away one day . . ., She never told him she would not only because she thought it absurd to think in terms of a future. You'll go away one day . . . Which day? Before they kill her or because of it. At no time before this grotesque wedding when he said she'd leave him, which he did whenever he got drunk, did she think she might ever want to live without him. His fits of jealousy, at first very romantic, tired her immensely, but she got used to them. He accused her of being afraid to tell him she loved him. She was. Afraid to tell him the whole truth, she would rather remain silent. Several times when she came to him later than usual she found him with a bottle of vodka. He would say he had thought she would never come back. Soon she found out that persuasion didn't get her far. He couldn't stand the tension, the peril, the haunting reminiscences, but there was more to it than that. It was something deep within him he feared, and he needed her to fight it or else it would totally destroy him. The point was — she could see it now — that he really did not believe he could fight it. He did not believe in himself any more than he believed in her. She mirrored rather than caused his anxieties.

She thought, I wish he'd hold me tight and tell me he trusts me, he believes in me, he knows I'll never let him down. She heard him groping after cigarettes on the bed table. He flashed the flame into her face.

"Elli," he cried.

"It's all right, Adam," she said. "Sleep."

April 12, 1942

The Old Man's eighty-third birthday. None of our friends forgot about him. Save that none of them resembled their old selves. Skinny, in rags, limping, but they came. Those who had not died in the meantime.

April 15, 1942

Mama has been arrested. A Polish policeman stopped her at the Central Station in Warsaw. He found in her bag a blank form of a Kennkarte. Suspecting her own documents were forged, he detained her. In this hopeless situation she bribed him with all the money she had. They were left penniless. We can't expect any help from them.

April 18, 1942.

Papa's birthday.

(FINAL ENTRY IN ELLI ROSTOW'S DIARY.)

The pale rays of the dawning day streamed through the black paper curtains when Maria suggested calling it a night. It was four o'clock, and she had to catch the eight o'clock train to Hrubieszów. Georg was sound asleep on the couch and the rest of the company protested vigorously. Natalia said that a couple of drinks would make them feel better than a couple of hours' sleep. "We will leave here at seven and I'll see you off to the station, Maria," she decided. Adam filled the glasses. His face was haggard, his eyes deep-sunk. Last night he had made his excursion to the bridge and slept very little, but it was more than fatigue. Was something wrong at the bridge?

On unsteady legs Elli walked over to him. "Adam, did you find them there?" she asked.

He shook his head. "No, I did not."

"Did they . . . did they go?" she asked foolishly.

"Of course, Elli. They went for a picnic. It's spring, isn't it? They took the paralyzed father, dressed up the youngsters, and gee-up! It's just that they forgot to take the knapsack with them. Want to see it? It's in the kitchen." He grasped her hand and held it in a iron grip. She stood until he let it fall to pour himself another drink.

Meantime Maria convinced Natalia that she had to get some sleep before the trip and motioned Elli to go upstairs. Elli told her softly that she'd rather stay with Adam, but Maria's eyes made it clear that she wanted her to go. "Natalia will keep him company," she said taking her handbag, "he won't be alone." If Maria knew what had happened she'd certainly let her stay but what was the use of telling her that Adam's redemption was making its way toward eternity?

Upstairs Elli started to make the bed for Maria. "I won't sleep," she heard her saying. "I must tell you something." Elli dropped the bedspread on the floor. Again, she thought. Who was it this time? Michael? Daniel? Emmi moved on her bed, she bent over the child but Emmi was sleeping soundly. "I didn't tell you before because we thought they'd leave us alone," Maria was saying quietly. "They came first before Lili . . ." Her voice broke. "Well, they came first last fall. A Polish policeman and another man. I wasn't home, I was in Warsaw. When they came Michael and Daniel had some customers. These men waited till they were gone and then merely asked Michael and Daniel to pull down their trousers. There was no way out. Michael gave them some money and they promised never to come back. They said it was all settled. They came back. Around Christmas. Said they needed some money for the holidays, food, drinks, toys for the kids and so on. Promised never to come back. They came last week. Their demands have grown gradually. They probably think we are making lots of money. The only money we have now is what we owe to Posch. Business is slack. Rita's landlord increased the rent. Last time I was at Abel's I left Rena just a little money to buy food for them. At least she admits that what Alfred got out of them is enough to cover the rent if the war lasted another twenty years. Anyway, we have no money. That's what Michael told them when they came last week. He also said, and I think it was the only thing he could do, it doesn't really matter whether we starve here or perish in a camp. He advised them to go ahead, to turn us in. They'll be commended for it and that should mean more to them than dirty Jewish money, he suggested. The men went away. God knows what they'll do. I felt I must tell you in case you don't hear from me anymore." Her eyes were dry, her mouth tight.

Elli blinked nervously. She didn't know what to say. She didn't want to know whether these men knew about her and Emmi.

"That's not all," Maria went on. "Posch told me yesterday that he has received three denunciations in the last two months. In one of them you were mentioned too. The charge that we are Jews he called 'eine lächerliche Lüge' and said how sad it was that our competition resorts to dirty lies which might cost lives were they true."

Drums were pounding in Elli's head, *We are surrounded by enemies . . . but I still can't see why you blame them . . . because I'm so afraid of them* . .

Maria didn't want Elli to see her off at the station. "They might as well get me there," she said.

14

Elli had heard the word "Kordian" mentioned by Adam many times before it hit her. Kordian, the romantic hero of Słowacki's drama, the unsuccessful assassinator of a tsar, vainly attempting to free Poland from the Russian yoke, was the lofty symbol of a fight against oppressors. When she first heard Adam murmuring this name in his sleep it struck her as a fitting code for a partisan operation. It also made her newly aware of the risk of falling asleep at his side. What if the roles changed? If she'd blab in sleep and he'd listen? Several weeks later, tossing in his bed, he repeated this name. In the middle of May at Georg's, out of the blue, Adam said it again. She gave him a dirty look, and he promptly added that Słowacki was his favorite poet. He could not take much vodka any longer. Three or four shots sufficed to blur his mind. Afraid he'd betray himself, Elli tried to stay near when he was drinking. Yet now and again he'd come home drunk, and until a day or two had passed without trouble she kept her fingers crossed. Two days after the incident at Georg's, Adam came home past midnight visibly upset. He said in a quick low voice, "Kordian failed. You must help us, Elli." Then the word hit her.

It was an operation, he explained, which took a long time and strenuous effort and was planned to be carried out by the Resistance net in Kraków. He was talking about English-parachuted weapons, building up the Resistance net in other parts of the country, training guerillas. When he came to the assassinations of top-ranking German officials Elli screamed, "Stop it! I don't want to hear about it! Leave me out of it! Do you understand? Leave me out of it!"

Adam's face showed disbelief, then rage.

She ignored it and, switching to a pleading voice of a helpless child, said, "Adam, try to understand. I'm not alone. I have Emmi. And please believe me I'm not the right type for conspiracy."

"Amen," he said. "Did you finish? Or do you want to go on?" His tired eyes gleamed spite but he gave her a charming smile and repeated, "Did you finish, darling?"

She looked at him, stunned, wondering what to expect next. Was he going to deny it? Was he going to say that she *was* the right type for conspiracy with the experience she already had? But he said, "I know you are not. But we need your help." He embraced her and went on, "I can't go to Kraków myself. Everybody there knows me. Not that I give a damn for my life but the point is to get to these people. Some of them can still be saved and the priceless arms they have, too. But we have to warn them somehow. I might be recognized on the train or in the street and never get to them. They'll be lost and so will the arms. On top of that the three boys we want to get to are living in the house where I lived all my life. With all the neighbors around it's hopeless for me to show up there. Can you understand that, Elli?" She could. But she was resolved to fight.

"I've already lost one job for leaving without permission," she said.

"Georg will get you a leave of absence."

"Does he know too?"

"Well, yes . . . no . . . you can trust him."

"How much does he know?"

"Nothing except that I asked him to go there before I asked you."

"He refused?"

"Yes."

"Why don't you send one of your boys?" The last words came out involuntarily with a sarcastic undertone.

"The station is heavily guarded. Some of our people have been arrested. There are hints that some of them, or at least one, broke down during the investigation."

She thought about Lili. "Still you don't mind my taking the chance?" The cold was coming out of her, she was badly hurt.

"I do mind, Elli, but I trust to God . . ."

"To whom?" she interrupted him.

"Sorry, a slip of the tongue. I'm sure nothing'll happen to you."

"How come you are so sure? Do I have a safe conduct from God?"

"Stop this nonsense," he cried. "There is no use beating about the bush. You refuse, do you?"

"Yes. I refuse."

"You did it once . . . with Yankel," he stressed every word.

"Do you have more Yankels around? More debts to pay?"

The muscles of his face tightened, his jaw grinding over the words. "It's a debt each of us owes to the country. Unless he is . . ." He stopped.

"Unless he is what? Why don't you say it?" She was very white, her forehead was covered with drops of perspiration. With closed eyes she was waiting for the blow. When she opened them again she saw him packing his briefcase. A shirt, socks, cigarettes, a bottle of vodka. He took his razor, flung it open, and fingered its shining edge. And then she said, "You win. I will go."

She left by the afternoon train. All she had to say to the

three men, after checking the password, was "Kordian died."
Then she could take the next train home. She went alone to the
station. They didn't tell Emmi she was leaving. Adam was to
take her downstairs later and explain that Elli went to Kolno
and would be back next day. When the train was approaching
Lublin the people in the compartment already knew that it would
be difficult to get out there. Word passed through the train
that the station was surrounded for a major roundup. As the
train slowed down the people threw out their bundles and one
by one jumped out. Only two old women stayed in the compartment. When Elli jumped down, the chimneys of Lublin were
already in sight. She did not know how to get to the town by
side roads. In a ditch sheltered by a spreading willow she waited
till dark. She reached the station by following the tracks. In
the bar she ordered hot sausages, a double vodka, and tea. The
next train to Kraków was at four in the morning. She fell asleep
on a bench and when she next looked at her watch it was two
o'clock. Stiff and chilled to the bone, she left the waiting room
and went to the platform. She stood staring at the train standing in front of her and she knew that she had lost her mind. It
did not surprise her. More than once she thought it was very
likely she was mad. In the dim light of the station lamps there
was a group of children facing her. They were nicely dressed,
in white, blue, red coats, smart bonnets and caps on the little
heads, holding each other's hands. The biggest was a girl perhaps nine years old in a navy blue coat with golden buttons. She
was holding the hands of a boy around five in spectacles and of a
girl the same age who was pressing a big doll to her face. The
children looked healthy, well nourished but there was something
dreadful in their silence. The platform was deserted save for a
worker checking the rails with a big hammer. When he approached the car in which the children were solemnly standing,
the biggest girl said, "Wasser bitte." Her little voice vibrated in

the nocturnal silence. The worker looked up at her, put down the hammer, and after a while was back with a bottle of water. The first shot hit him precisely in the small of his back. The second shot smashed the bottle which the girl was holding in her hand. Both were fired from behind Elli's back. As she turned, the German officer was carefully replacing the revolver in a leather case hanging at his belt.

She missed the four o'clock train. She was sitting on a bench in the waiting room until at some point she felt something cold on her lips. "Water," she heard a voice saying. "Drink it." The ugly, nauseous feeling came back. She pushed away the cool glass and the water splashed all over. "Wasser," she said. "Wasser bitte."

"You can't stay here," the low voice was saying. "They'll be back anytime. Why make it easy for them? They'll sweep you right out of here in the next transport. Come on, let's go." A firm hand grasped her under the arm and led her across the room behind the bar. Like a sleepwalker Elli followed.

"What's that? Again a guest?" This voice was gruff, unpleasant.

"Let her alone, Stefan, or I'll make your life bitter." The low voice was now shrill. "She's seen the wagon with the Dutch children. She must live in a cozy place with Mummy, Daddy, and a host of aunts. Not used to such shows." The young, red-haired woman flung the window wide open. "Come, sit down here, have some fresh air," she said and made Elli sit on a chair at the window. The man on a crutch critically scrutinized her and, limping, left the room.

"Coffee?" asked the woman.

Elli nodded.

"Where are you going?" The woman was pouring black coffee in two beer mugs.

"To Kraków." The coffee burned Elli's lips and insides.

"A cigarette?"

Not waiting for an answer, the woman stuck a homemade cigarette in Elli's mouth and lit it. "I saw you smoking last night," she explained. "I tend the bar here. He is my husband. You have missed your train, I guess. It's almost noon now. You'll have to wait for the three o'clock train. You can wait here."

"Thank you very much," Elli said. "You are very kind." The woman left her alone and came back to say it was safe to go now and that the train was due in fifteen minutes. She brought a dish of hot soup and forced a few spoonfuls down Elli. When she was in the train Elli realized that she might be coming too late.

She found the house with the help of the droshky driver who drove her from the station. The address which she had memorized escaped her and she explained to him that the house was on a small dead-end street not far from the Old Market Place. There were many small dead-end streets not far from the Old Market Place, the cabman said, but they'd certainly find the one she was looking for. She remembered then that the number of the house was nine, and at the driver's fourth attempt she recognized the mansion by its narrow windows and white columns supporting the arches. Adam had told her once that the windows of his room faced an old monastery and that the black flying robes of the monks gave him nightmares throughout his childhood. Two monks were just crossing the street and disappeared behind the heavy wooden gate of the chapel. Elli paid the driver and rang the bell.

A gray-haired woman opened the door. She gasped and stared at Elli in such horror that Elli would have run straightaway had not a man appeared in the hall in the same instant. The woman let her hands drop with a gesture of helplessness. The man shoved the door wide open and made an inviting nod. When Elli didn't respond, he took her hand, pulled her inside, and silently closed the door. The woman, her face buried in her hands, her breast heaving with checked sobs, vanished in the far end of the hall. The man was stout but still young, perhaps in his early thirties. His clean-shaven, homely face was expressionless.

"Please, come in," he said to Elli, opening a door.

She stood now in a room which fitted exactly Adam's description of his father's studio. Old, massive furniture, walls lined with bookshelves now almost empty, a fireplace just opposite a dark oaken door.

The man turned in the light and said, "Make yourself comfortable. You must be tired after such a long trip."

He motioned later to an armchair and, before she sat down, helped her out of the coat. She had an uneasy feeling that she had seen this face sometime, someplace. Even his voice sounded familiar to her.

"I have been waiting for you quite a while." He took a chair and sat down opposite her, his eyes fixed on her. "I had almost given up hope. It would have been a great disappointment."

She had the password on the tip of her tongue when the door opened slightly and the woman stuck in her face, red and swollen.

"Will you please leave us alone, Mrs. Jańczyk," said the man politely.

So this was the maid who took over the household after Adam's mother's death. Why was she so distressed? Elli decided to wait. The door closed and the man went on, "You did not disappoint us but I have to disappoint you. Your friends are no longer here."

"What friends?" she asked.

"Those," he answered amiably, "for whom you have brought the message."

She took the cigarette he offered her. "Yet I must disappoint you," she crossed her legs. "I do not know what you are talking about."

He got up, approached her, and lightly touched her foot with the tip of his shining brown shoe. "Don't," he said. "It betrays you." Surprised, she saw her right foot tapping upon the floor with quick nervous moves.

"I'll be delighted to explain," he went on, lighting her cigarette. "Three men have been waiting here for a message. All their contacts in Kraków were kaput. They have saved a part of the parachuted arms and have been expecting a liaison officer for days. But you came too late, miss. One of the people already confessed. It might be interesting for you to know where they have hidden the arms." He pushed the ashtray toward her. "Unfortunately you won't be able to transmit this useful information to your HQ. By way of performing the last rites. You see, they might well commit the same error again. But as I said you can't help it."

He got up, went over to the window, opened it, tapped the metal framework of the parapet. "These old houses," he said thoughtfully. "One would presume they'd hide their treasures in some decent secret vaults . . . We wasted lots of time digging in the basements, searching the attics, and here they were all the time lying within reach. How do you like that?" he turned to her.

"Smart boys," she said.

"In a way, yes," he agreed. "Let me see your documents." She handed him her Kennkarte, Arbeitsausweis, and travel permit. Sitting behind the desk, he studied them carefully making notes in a small notebook. Then he put them all in his breast pocket.

"Have you any written instructions?" he asked. "From the Armia Krajowa headquarters," he added by way of explanation.

"Neither written nor unwritten. I came to Kraków to see a doctor."

"Oh," he smiled. "That's how you got the travel permit from your office."

"Exactly," she confirmed.

"It's not forged, I can see this." He paused. "Did you expect to find a doctor in this house?"

"I've never been in Kraków before," she said. "I gave the address to the cabman and he brought me here. Either I was given a wrong address or the cabman misunderstood me."

"What was the address you were given?"

"Długa Street, seventeen." She knew that such a street existed.

"I won't even bother to check it. I'm sure a doctor is living at this address. I don't underestimate your bosses. I'll only have your director called in the morning to request of him more vigilance when signing documents." He sounded embarrassed when he said, "Now I must search you. Will you please take off your dress."

"What do you expect to find under my dress?" she asked angrily.

"Perhaps arms, perhaps orders, who knows?" When she didn't move he took a revolver out of his hip pocket. It was a small revolver with a mother-of-pearl handle. "I'm sorry," he said, "but you seem not to understand my words. Although my Polish is no worse than yours." She unzipped her skirt and flung her blouse on the chair. With skillful fingers he felt the shoulder straps, the pants around her waist, the garters and all the hems. Then he passed her the skirt and the blouse and said, "They'll search you more thoroughly later. I just wanted to avoid any surprise. And now let's go."

They walked three or four blocks, completely dark and deserted, when he said, "It's still a long way. I should have had my car sent. You must be tired."

"Never mind me," said Elli. "I enjoy walking. I like fresh air."

"You would rather walk with your boyfriend, wouldn't you." He sounded most courteous. "Why not pretend for a while that I'm your boyfriend?" He slipped his arm through hers. It started to rain. The wind rose. "You might catch cold in the rain," he said with deep concern. "I wouldn't like you to misunderstand me," the note of embarrassment was back in his voice, "but perhaps you feel like having a drink?"

"A gorgeous idea!" exclaimed Elli. "And I'm starved to death."

"I live not far from here," he hesitated, "in a small house with a little garden. I love flowers, gardening is my hobby. And we'll find something to eat, too. So," he halted, "if it's all right with you . . ."

"Perfectly all right," smiled Elli.

A leather-framed photograph was the first thing that caught her eye when he turned on the lights. It stood in the soft shadow of the desk lamp next to a cigarette box and a silver lighter. She turned and saw the man standing with his feet apart, looking at her.

"You recognized him, didn't you, Miss Rostow?" he grinned at her. "My father thought very highly of yours. Perhaps you also know that I had the pleasure of driving your mother to the station in Łódź several years ago. Let me see," he said pensively, "this must have been in the winter of nineteen forty."

Of course she recognized Egon Gründig. "You are Kurt, aren't you?" Her voice was sober.

"Yes. And I didn't change my name either," he said. "Not that I object to your doing so. I can well understand it. I just wonder if I would have recognized you if not for this name in your papers. It somehow stuck to me from the old days. Eleonora is not a very common name here and it's the name of my mother."

"Oh, is that so?" marveled Elli. "And how is your dear mother?"

"She is fine, thank you," Kurt bowed. "My parents live now in Vienna."

"That's just wonderful, isn't it?" Elli took a cigarette from the box. He jumped to light it. "You promised me a drink, Kurt." She stretched herself on a sofa covered with a Turkish spread, kicked off her shoes, and put a small leather cushion under her head. Kurt was busy at the bar built in the library and brought her a drink, cigarettes, and matches.

"I'm glad you've made yourself comfortable," he put a light woolen blanket over her legs. "I'll go now and fix a snack."

From the kitchen he called to ask whether she'd like scrambled eggs or an omelette. She called back that scrambled eggs would be fine. It crossed her mind that he was stuffing her as the witch had stuffed Hansel to make him more tasty.

The square table in the small dining room was nicely set, a small bunch of violets at her place. There was bread and butter, thinly sliced smoked ham, salmon, salad, and a cheese plate. He served the scrambled eggs from the frying pan so they would not grow cold, he said smiling, and the vodka in an ice bowl so it would not grow warm. He lit two tall candles, turned off the lights, and held the chair for her.

Following Adam's instructions, she started her meal with a spoonful of butter in order not to get drunk though for a moment she considered whether, after all, it wouldn't be better to get drunk.

Never was a host more charming, thoughtful, protective. He wanted to know whether the ham was too salty, whether she preferred her salad with French or Italian dressing, if the candlelight bothered her eyes, or perhaps depressed her? He passed the cheese plate to her explaining the nuances of each kind, fearing some might be too pungent for her. He deliberated at length choosing wines, asking for her advice and preference.

When they finished he got up, walked over to her, and pressed her hand to his lips. "So, that's the small girl — Elli, they called you at home, didn't they? — all of a sudden turned into an attractive woman, a splendid companion with a taste for good drinks and on the top of it playing Mata Hari. Come," he drew aside her chair, "let's sit where it's more comfortable." Holding her tightly, he led her back to his studio and settled her on the sofa.

She lay down. "May I have some cognac, please?" she asked.

He brought a bottle of Napoleon from the bar. "The coffee will be ready in a while," he said, sitting down beside her. His face lost its smiling countenance. It was serious, almost sad. He kissed her lightly on the cheek then on the lips. A church clock struck twelve.

"Midnight," said Elli.

"You are not in a hurry, are you?" He flung his coat on the armchair and lay down beside her. Her eyes were focused on this carelessly hanging coat containing her documents. Even if she drank him under the table, even if she got her documents and escaped, he would find her. He unbuttoned her blouse and gently caressed her breasts. Then he turned off the lamp behind the sofa. Except for a streak of light under the kitchen door the room was dark. She felt him pressing closer and closer to her and was just about to ask him if he was a necrophile when he said, "I'll save you, my poor little girl, I'll save you." As she lay silent he went on, "You mustn't fall into their hands. They'll tear you apart before they let you die." He was holding his hand on her heart as if to feel its beating, then pushed away her hair from her forehead and put his cheek on it. "No, no," he whispered. "They won't get you, don't be afraid." He buried his mouth in her hair breathing heavily. "You must trust me."

He was now on top of her and immediately she knew his problem. "Just as she trusted me." His voice was hardly audible. "She was so beautiful, so incredibly beautiful. Skin like white marble, long black hair. She had nothing else to cover this wonderful naked body of hers but that hair. She jumped out of a train." He struggled with his shirt and put Elli's hand on his nipple. "There she was lying in the dirt, all pure and chaste, her eyes begging for help, her hands passionate, her body ready to receive me." He groaned. "And I caressed and fondled her until she fell asleep, relieved and hopeful. I promised her that I'd save her." He grew silent and then said in a clear voice, "She will never know pain again, she will never know love. She belongs to me. Forever. I saved her, she is mine." He gave a short laugh.

Elli could feel on her the heavy quality of his flesh, trembling now and twitching. "Your skin is so delicate, so smooth," he murmured, "your body so young and warm. I won't let them harm you. Sleep, my love, sleep, you are saved." The voice slowly died out; his body shaken by quick spasmodic convulsions grew finally inert. The gasping heavy breath turned into loud snoring. With one hand gently rubbing his nipple Elli moved the other below toward the sharp edge cutting into her flesh. She felt the trigger and pressed the revolver precisely to the nipple between her two fingers. He must have felt the sudden coldness of the muzzle for he quivered but then lay silent again.

She crawled from under the heavy body, stretched her cramped limbs, and turned the lights on. He was lying flat on his face and she thought it would take quite a long time until the blood soaked through the soft cushions. Even if it did, the fluffy carpet would absorb it. She poured herself a glass of brandy and gulped it down. *One doesn't drink cognac like that,* she heard. *You must learn how to do it properly, my dear, otherwise you'll never be a lady.* She blushed. Fi donc! Incorrigible! Incorrigible! You'll never be a real lady. She went to the bathroom, stripped herself naked and took a shower. Steaming hot and very cold and again hot and cold until she felt fresh and lively. On a crystal shelf above the wash basin she found Kölnisch Wasser No. 4711 and rubbed her body from top to toe. She took a big bath towel from the cupboard, tucked it around her, and returned to the studio. Cuddled into the armchair and drinking the coffee which was still hot, she meditated when would it be safest for her to leave this place. Anyway she had to wait till the end of the curfew which gave her almost four hours to sleep. She went to the bedroom, set the alarm clock for six, and slept soundly on the wide comfortable bed until it rang. Then she dressed very carefully and without haste, made up her face and did her hair. She brought the small bunch of violets from the dining room and fastened it in her hair. Before she left she took her documents and the small notebook from his coat. When she was closing the door the telephone on his desk started to ring.

She spent the spare time in the public garden, sitting under a tree. There she tore his notebook page by page, dug a hole in the earth, put the small pieces of paper into it and covered it with leaves. She arranged the leaves with much care and looked very pleased at her work.

Funny! Why didn't she think seriously of becoming a gardener? She loved flowers, she could do quite a job. Lili's suggestion, after all, wasn't so bad. Or perhaps she should study to become a landscape architect? Requires knowledge of mathematics. But who knows? As a matter of fact if she really set her mind to something there was a chance she could achieve it. She got up, deciding to take a walk. The garden was in full bloom, wonderfully colorful, still deserted. She found a white daisy and replaced the withered violets with it. From the gate she saw the steeple of the Church of Our Lady. Okay, let's go pay God a visit. Let Him now take care of her. She hadn't bothered Him recently, had she? He could not deny she took good care of herself. Yet she had two more hours to kill. Let Him worry about it. It was a fair deal, wasn't it? Or was it too much to ask Him? Let's see. She skipped down the street, smiled brightly to a streetcar driver, to a milkman, to a dog. For a moment she stopped before a white poster still wet with fresh paint. It said that three men whose names were listed below, arrested on May 19, 1944, on Karmelicka Street number nine, found guilty of conspiring against the Third Reich, were hanged last night. Kordian died, she remembered, when Chopin's "Funeral March" greeted her at the church entrance. Died and will never rise again, she smiled softly.

15

THE ATMOSPHERE in the office was heavy and unpleasant. Director Labisch definitely put an end to manipulating the colored pins on the map behind Elli's desk. For a long time he had been continuously moving them westward a little bit every day or two until one day he came in the morning and went straight to his office neglecting the long established ritual. The big green spot on the map, pricked all over, must still have exasperated him, for one day the map disappeared altogether. The telephone rang incessantly. Berlin, Bratislava, Vienna, Kraków, Warsaw. Both directors held innumerable conferences in and outside Chełm and gave contradicting orders to the staff. Elli was constantly smiling, carefully made up, always with a flower in her hair. The gloomy faces of her superiors did not bother her in the least. Neither did Adam's bitter remarks. At first with disbelief, then with suspicion he met her requests to go to parties, to restaurants, to bars. She became a demon for work. Director Labisch no longer mourned the loss of his German secretary. He even said that it was a pity for Elli to stay in Poland. After their final victory there was not much of a future for her, he told her, as Poles were destined by the Führer only to fertilize the German soil. She must have German ancestors, he suggested,

even if she was not aware of it, and thus he offered to arrange
for her to go to Germany where she would get proper education
and training. She jumped at this glorious prospect and made
clear how much she appreciated his generosity. Then she had
a wild row with Adam who said she was definitely crazy. Somehow, amidst the forthcoming events Labisch never repeated his
offer.

As the days passed the chaos in the office grew. One day they
were told to pack up all the files, the next to unpack them. One
night Labisch called them to the office and ordered them to fold
up the posters "Pass auf! Der Feind hört mit!" and others as
"Die Räder rollen für den Sieg!" only to request the next morning that they be put back on the walls. On Tuesday they were
given travel permits to Katowice where the office was to be
moved, on Wednesday they were asked to give them back. Elli
was tremendously amused, Adam grew more restless, Georg more
silent. One day he didn't show up in the office. A few days later
Labisch told them that Georg had been killed in a car accident.
His automobile had rolled off a steep embankment of the
shoulderless road not quite a hundred miles from the German
border.

"This certainly calls for a celebration," cried Elli, and Adam
looked at her stupefied. "For a funeral repast," she corrected
herself, and absolutely insisted they have some friends in that
night for a drink. Adam gave in, clearly disgusted.

He gasped in horror when she came downstairs later that night
all dressed up with heavy makeup. "Where do you think you
have come? To a brothel?" Adam hated it when she used cos-
metics. "Where did you get this dreadful dress? You might as
well have come stark naked." True, the carrot-colored dress was
low cut and strapless, but Elli thought it was great and had bor-
rowed it from Ilona's sister especially for that night. "I thought
Georg meant something to you," said Adam sulkily. "He was a
good friend, after all. Go and change, please."

"Mourning does not become me," grinned Elli. "I need a hairpin. Would you please bring me one from the bedroom. I always seem to lose them in your bed."

He turned his back and went to the kitchen. She found the hairpin herself and fastened a white carnation behind her ear.

The guests arrived shortly before the curfew. Nobody could leave till it was over so these parties dragged on until the small hours of the dawn. Ilona came escorted by two men, one middle-aged, baldish with a fresh scar across his forehead, the other young athletic with a curly blond head and a square freckled face. She introduced them by first names only, the bald was Roman, the blond Gustaw. Lidia came with her little son whom she put to bed in Adam's bedroom. Janusz Larski, contrary to his habit, brought his wife.

After an awkward minute of silence when all sat with glasses in their hands while Adam told them about Georg's death the tension broke. Soon they were trying to outdo each other listing friends killed, murdered, arrested, until somebody remarked that after all Georg was just another German bastard.

Elli burst out laughing, "He was not really German. He was Polish. He just underwent a transformation."

Adam said in a hard, angry voice, "It's the war. People do different things to save their lives. We have no right to judge them."

Gustaw got up, "They do, indeed. Different things. But I wouldn't say we have no right to judge them. There are rules even in this game. There is a limit beyond which man turns to beast. If a dirty swine who was born Polish claims German ancestry to avoid the lot of his people, it certainly is not something I'd justify. If a Jew agrees to his wife's being killed to save his own skin, it certainly is not something I'd justify."

Lidia Halska rose. She suddenly looked fragile and vulnerable. "It's unfair to say this in one breath. You can't compare Poles who turned German to avoid our lot with Jews whose only choice is death. Besides, I don't believe this Jew turned in his wife to save his life."

Gustaw smiled faintly. "You've got it all wrong, madam," he said. "I didn't say he turned her in. There was a girl who wanted him to marry her and all the man did was give his silent agreement to have his wife killed."

Lidia rose again but he went on, "I assure you I know these people. This couple was in hiding in my father's barn. This girl is my sister."

"You should blame your sister rather than this man," Lidia burst out. "What do you know about him? How do you know he doesn't loathe every moment of this life?" She was getting the words out with visible effort. "How do you know that the mere idea of touching your sister does not repel him?" She interrupted herself, her eyes reddened with checked tears.

"I do know it in a quite simple way," said Gustaw quietly. "My sister is four months pregnant. Exactly to the day of the other woman's death. And if you think, madam," he bowed toward her, "that I enjoy the idea of raising a generation of kikes in my family, let me tell you I do not."

Elli cried at the top of her voice, "Speaking of children three cheers for Mrs. Larska! At last she decided to leave them home and come out of her hiding." Turning to Larski's wife, she went on, "How nice you could come today. Every time we invited Janusz he'd say you must stay home with the children. How are they? Did you get somebody to stay with them?"

"I . . . I . . . I have no children," stammered the girl, a very young pretty creature with reddish hair and green almond-shaped eyes.

"But you have," insisted Elli, "a baby girl and a boy."

"No, no," the girl bit her lips nervously. "She had them, not me. I am his wife. We are married."

At this Ilona stepped in. "Leave her alone, Elli," she said. "It's not her fault. He didn't even tell her before they were married."

She took Elli aside and, already a little hazy, explained in a hushed voice that the girl Larski formerly lived with was never wed to him. She was Jewish. He was hiding her and then they had these children so he let her stay. A month ago the Germans came, took her with the children, and he married this girl.

"Oh, how wonderful!" exclaimed Elli. "How smart! Adam!" she shouted to the other end of the room. "Adam, did you hear this fantastic news? Janusz Larski got bored with his girl friend and handed her over to the Germans. Together with his children! Isn't that smart! Look here!" She pointed toward the crying girl. "This is his new wife, a real one, not a fake, I swear, just look at her, isn't she beautiful! Three cheers for the new Mrs. Larska." She raised her glass.

A stony silence fell in the room. Larski half rose and sat down. Adam stood motionless, an empty glass in his hand.

A loud sobbing interrupted the silence. The green-eyed girl looked wildly around. "I did not know," she cried hysterically. "He never told me before."

Adam put his glass on the table and with his hands in his pockets went over to Larski. "Tell me, Janusz," he said in a strained voice, "did you turn this girl in?"

Larski slowly got up. "Don't meddle in my affairs, you bloody fool," he shouted.

Adam grabbed Larski by the lapels and screamed into his face, "Tell me if it's true you son of a bitch!"

"Of course, it's a dirty . . ." Before Larski finished the sentence Adam landed on the floor against the wall. Gustaw's backhand was firm and skillful. Roman helped Larski back to a chair.

"I don't see what's the big problem," said Gustaw phlegmatically. "One Jewish slut more or less doesn't make that much difference." He straightened his tie.

"It certainly does not," Elli laughed shrilly. "Let's all have a drink and forget it." She filled the glasses. "To the well-being of the newlyweds," she cried through Mozart's Concerto no. 21 somebody switched on. "And damn all Jewish sluts!"

Lidia rose, pale and shaking. "I'd appreciate not discussing this problem in my presence," she said. "I am Jewish myself."

They came to take her next night when she was feeding her little son supper. Ilona knew all the details. They agreed to wait until the boy had finished. Lidia poured a glass of milk, drank half of it herself, and made the boy drink the rest. She asked him to hurry so as not to keep the gentlemen waiting. She remained sitting stiffly, the boy cuddled in her lap. The police were furious for letting themselves be tricked by this polite, innocent-looking woman.

A week later Director Labisch took Elli to Warsaw. She was relieved to get away from Adam even for a day or two. Adam's attempts to get out of her what had "befallen" her remained futile. He was obviously suspicious about her high spirits and she did not know why. He told her that her radiant humor and showy je m'en fiche were beneath her dignity.

"But I have no dignity," laughed Elli. "Why should I? I have delicate, smooth skin, a body so young and warm — that's what you've told me — won't that do for you?" She'd embrace him passionately and he'd tell her that she was all he had in life, but she was getting tired and bored. Why should she pretend she was cracking up, while actually this new sensation, this new and hitherto unknown world offered her security and happiness. Out of some perfidious, perverted reasons he wanted her to be depressed and frightened as she probably was or had seemed to be at some remote time. He lived in a nightmarish, neurotic world, surrounded by corpses and cripples, consumed by fear and evil, watching only for an opportunity to drag her in. She would not let him do it to her. Sometimes the familiar ugliness would creep into her at night or catch her in broad daylight without any reason at all. She'd freeze for a second but immediately the subdued, soothing voice, "Sleep, you are saved," would shake her out of it. Once these words came to her from the lips of the crucified Christ when she attended the Sunday Mass with Adam and Emmi. Thereupon she would often run to church, pray fervently, with a new exciting deep faith in the Son of God who suffered for her in order to save her now. This revelation lit her eyes with a strange light, her face with a sweet smile, strange to the uninitiates, as Adam was. Of course, she could not tell Adam anything about it. He would never understand.

The trip was pleasant and she had fun. Labisch kept her busy only the first day, then he let her take a day off and stay in Warsaw. He also told her that the Chełm office would not be removed to Katowice for the time being as the Russian army was halted by the heroic German soldiers. He accepted her warm congratulations. She called the apartment on Marszałkowska Street where Maria rented a room. Maria herself answered the phone and told her in a shaky voice to come over at once.

"What has happened?" Maria greeted her downstairs, pale and upset.

Elli was amused. "Why, nothing. I just came to Warsaw."

"Jesus Christ, I thought you had to escape or something," Maria embraced her.

"Why should I have to escape?" laughed Elli. "My boss had a meeting here and he brought me along."

"Thank God," said Maria, opening the door to her room. A man was sitting in an armchair puffing a pipe. Elli had met him often in the other world. Only his hair had turned gray in the meantime and his face had more creases. "You know Filip," said Maria, a little embarrassed. "You haven't seen him for all these years. I guess he's changed."

"We all do," Filip kissed Elli's hand. "A POW camp can hardly be considered a spa. See, Elli, last time I saw you I kissed you on both cheeks, I wouldn't risk it today."

"Better not," grinned Elli. "I have a very jealous husband."

"Boyfriend," corrected Maria, and Elli let it pass.

Filip invited them to a fancy restaurant for dinner. The waiter addressed him in a stage whisper "Mr. Major," and Elli sensed a new conspiracy against her. But the dinner passed quietly and they went back home. Filip gave Maria a drink and asked if Elli would have one. They had already had several at dinner, he excused himself, and she was still so young. Elli had one, then another. She told them funny stories about Emmi, the office, the parties she attended with Adam. Every time her shrill laughter resounded in the room she saw Maria looking at her uneasily. Again! Again somebody expecting her to cry. A mad world. Mad people. Sitting and looking at her as if she were a harlot, as if it were a crime to laugh and be happy.

They spent the next day together, Elli growing more and more suspicious that Maria like Adam wanted to drag her into the darkness she herself lived in. Maria told her a long story of how she had been arrested last month. She did it deliberately, of course, to frighten Elli. But neither the circumstances of the arrest nor the details of the forty-eight hours' investigation interested Elli. She found the verdict of the Gestapo man witty and intelligent. He told Maria that what finally convinced him the denunciation was false was her countenance. "Nicht die Gesichtszüge sondern der Gesichtsausdruck" is what counts he said. "Do you know what they considered most incriminating?" Now Maria, thank God, laughed too. "They found in my wallet this slip of paper you once put in with the quotation from Remarque's book, 'We had begun to love life and the world and we had to shoot it to pieces.' Do you remember, Elli?"

Elli did not remember.

*

The man on Adam's bed was snoring loudly. The haggard, several-days' unshaven face quivered in his sleep. Elli had come late the night before from Warsaw and had not seen Adam during the day because he was in Kolno. Now she had come here expecting him to be back. She felt a little guilty and came to tell him how much she missed him in Warsaw. Going downstairs, she imagined him lying on his bed, smoking, waiting for her. She saw herself safe in his arms, feeling the warmth of his body. Instead she found this dirty stranger. She stood at the bed looking at him angrily until he opened his eyes. For a moment they were absent then filled with wild horror. He rose, looked toward the window then toward the door. Then he said in German, "Who are you?"

Elli retorted coldly, "Who are *you?*" She wanted to tell him to go away immediately and never to show up again but he was quicker.

"Don't turn me in," he gasped heavily. "Have mercy."

She heard a little voice, "Yidn hot rakhmones," and asked surprised, "Have what?"

"Have mercy on me, madam," the man moaned, "they'd kill me."

"Why should I have mercy?" She sat on the windowsill and dangled her legs. "Why shouldn't they kill you?"

Terror distorted the man's face. His eyes bulged, he was shaking all over. Elli started to whistle "Lili Marlene."

"You aren't German, are you?" His teeth were chattering.

"What if I am?" she grinned.

"I'd be lost," he whispered.

"I guess, I'd survive it," she laughed and changed the tune to the "Horst-Wessel Lied."

At this Adam entered the room, kissed Elli, and walked over to the man. "Did you have a good rest?" he asked in German. The man, wordless, pointed toward Elli. "You frightened him,

Elli." Adam put his arm around her neck. "I forgot to tell him you have the keys to the apartment." He turned to the man, "I'll bring you something to eat. And don't worry, we'll work something out."

In the kitchen Adam told her that his man was a deserter and had escaped from a train going to the Russian front.

"Escaped from a train," repeated Elli slowly. "Jumped out of a train."

Adam looked at her, "What, darling? What did you say?"

"Nothing," she said.

He would have to keep the man, Adam went on, until his con-tact would take him over. "Now will you make him something to eat, dear?" he smiled to her.

"No," she said. "I will not."

"What's the matter, Elli?" Adam was surprised. "Did I do something wrong?"

"Nothing is the matter, Adam," she stood in the door. "And you did nothing wrong."

Adam came after midnight. She dismissed his apologies with a vague smile, "It really doesn't mean a thing to me. I should have got used to my own private Christ." She embraced him.

"That's exactly what I don't want you to think," he was sup-pressing annoyance, "that I'm playing the role of a redeemer. This man needs help."

"We all do," she said kindly.

"Well, yes, Elli," he patted her hand. "Yes and no. Sometimes I wonder if you need it. You are so strong, so independent."

She sat cool, rigid, looking at herself from a distance, at her old self which had lived for years in sleep and in wakefulness locked in a nightmare. Even now she could feel the old, dull, heavy pain and she could scream at him with indignation but instead she gave a high burst of laughter. "Sure I am, Adam, strong and independent and thirsty. Let's have a drink."

He filled the glasses and lay down beside her. "That's not as simple as that," he said. "I know it is not. But I know too there is something inside you I cannot reach, I am not able to understand. Last night I was lying awake and I was seeing this girl as I met her in the office: arrogant, a little wild and yet timid and helpless. Sometimes her eyes seemed to cry for help only to turn mocking when she was offered it. I saw her in the streets, in the church, in the meadows, tenderly cuddling the child, ostentatiously drinking vodka; sad and gay, serious and amused, tempting and passionate, cold and distant, contemptuous and prideful in moments of anger, ardent and lustful when making love; kind and affectionate, gentle and submissive, provocative and vulgar. A strange creature full of contradictions but alive and human, real and mine." He was talking to himself and she was stunned by the meaninglessness of his words. "The dearest, closest human being whom I need to be able to live. And though she was far away I felt her near me and I told her about my love and desire and yearning, about my fear and anxiety, hope, pain and anguish." If he would now take me in his arms, she prayed, if he would make me talk, if he would part for a moment with that little sore soul of his, with that I, I, I, me, my, mine . . . But he was lying motionless, his eyes closed until she heard him breathing evenly. Then she found herself standing at the window, drinking. She was a little shocked but not enough to stop.

The deserter drifted away two days later. On the third he was replaced in Adam's locked bedroom by a man with a bad wound in his abdomen. The surgery was performed at night by a partisan physician. The doctor gagged the wounded man and ordered Adam to bind his legs and hands. Elli sterilized the instruments, mopped the patient's head, made coffee for the doctor. Several days later the man was taken away and thereafter Elli told Adam that she was leaving with Emmi. First he looked at her half angry, half disbelieving and then said in that long forgotten mocking voice, "My little Nike got scared, eh? Running away? Do you think I'll let you go just like that? Do you think I don't know why you want to go? Why you want to leave me? Why you refuse to help us? Well, let me tell you I do know. Now listen and get this straight: either you'll stay or I'll make you stay." The eyes of the stranger were full of spite.

She said in a detached, clinical voice, "I do not know what you know and I don't care a damn. I'm going to leave Chełm by the first train tomorrow morning."

In the afternoon he came to apologize. He said he had lost his temper but he loved her and implored her to stay with him. He'd never again bring any people home. He'd never again ask her for help. She listened politely but said nothing. It was a bright, sunny day and they went with Emmi for a walk. She wondered whether he purposely chose the road leading to an old windmill paved with tombstones from the Jewish cemetery. The menorahs and Hebrew letters on the stones were only a little blurred. Not many people strolled here.

She went to him at night to tell him that she had decided to stay. The apartment was empty. She made herself a drink and stretched out on the couch. The voices which awoke her were German and loud. Three men in uniforms preceded by Adam entered the room. "I'm sorry, Elli," he stammered drunkenly. "They are friends. They just want to have a drink with us."

In the kitchen, when she was taking out the glasses, bells in her head were ringing, and each bell rang with a different familiar voice she had not heard for months, for years. She was completely, pleasantly relaxed. Then Adam came in, his face dead white, and took her in his arms. The officer who followed him was friendly. "Sind sie fertig, Fräulein?" he asked.

She choked laughing at the sound of the broken glass overlapping the bells. The blood dripping from her cut wrist made an ugly spot on her fresh, white summer dress. "Yes," she said. "I am ready. But let me bring the child."

"Why?" said the officer. "This is not a Kindergarten."

Also Available from Pandora Press

Desert of the Heart *Jane Rule*	£3.95	☐
Memory Board *Jane Rule*	£3.95	☐
Charleyhorse *Cecil Dawkins*	£3.95	☐
This Place *Andrea Freud Loewenstein*	£4.95	☐
Seven Miles from Sydney *Lesley Thomson*	£3.95	☐
Oranges are not the only Fruit *Jeanette Winterson*	£4.50	☐
Passion Fruit Ed. *Jeanette Winterson*	£4.50	☐
A State of Fear *Menan Du Plessis*	£3.95	☐
A Woman called En *Tomie Ohara*	£3.95	☐
Utrillo's Mother *Sarah Baylis*	£9.95	☐
Bear *Marian Engel*	£4.50	☐
The Biggest Modern Woman of the World *Susan Swan*	£5.95	☐
Jesus and Fat Tuesday *Colleen McElroy*	£4.95	☐
Kindergarten *Elzbieta Ettinger*	£4.95	☐
Storia 1 Ed. *Kate Figes*	£5.95	☐

All these books are available at your local bookshop, or can be ordered direct by post. Just tick the titles you want fill in the form below.

Name ....

Address ....

....

....

Write to Unwin Hyman Cash Sales, PO Box 11, Falmouth, Cornwall TR10 9ED

Please enclose remittance to the value of the cover price plus:

UK: 60p for the first book plus 25p for the second book, thereafter 15p for each additional book ordered to a maximum postage charge of £1.90

BFPO and EIRE: 60p for the first book plus 25p for the second book and 15p for the next 7 books and thereafter 9p per book

OVERSEAS INCLUDING EIRE: £1.25 for the first book plus 75p for the second book and 28p for each additional book.

Pandora Press reserve the right to show new retail prices on covers, which may differ from those previously advertised in the text and elsewhere. Postage rates are also subject to revision.